The Breakdown of Public Security

The Case of Ireland 1916-1921
and Palestine 1936-1939

"WHERE'S THE (IRISH) POLICE?"

CHIEF CONSTABLE. – *"H'm! – Shooting Landlords! – Wrecking Private Property! – Burning Stores! – Seizing Arms! – Breaking Heads! – Murder and Intimidation! – 'Pon my word, if they go much further I must really –*
DO SOMETHING!!!"

The continuance of bloodshed and disturbance almost without check in Ireland, while the Irish Land Bill was being debated, as well as the reticence of Mr. Gladstone regarding coercive measures caused angry uneasiness in England. – *Punch,* March 1870.

The Breakdown of Public Security

The Case of Ireland 1916-1921
and Palestine 1936-1939

Tom Bowden

With a Foreword by
Gabriel A. Almond

SAGE Studies in 20th Century History *Volume 8*

 SAGE Publications · London and Beverly Hills

For information address

SAGE Publications Ltd.
28 Banner Street
London EC1

SAGE Publications Inc.
275 South Beverly Drive
Beverly Hills, California 90212

International Standard Book Number
0 8039 9865 1 Cloth
0 8039 9866 X Paper

Library of Congress Catalog Card Number
76-56682

First Printing

Printed and Bound in Great Britain by
Biddles Ltd., Guildford, Surrey.

CONTENTS

For Patsy

TOM BOWDEN is Senior Lecturer in Politics, Manchester Polytechnic. He is the author of *Revolt to Revolution, Community and Change, Army in the Service of the State,* and the forthcoming Penguin, *Beyond the Limits of the Law,* a study of the police in crisis politics. He has also been a contributor to *Police Forces in History* (SAGE, 1975) and *Dynamics of Public Policy* (SAGE, 1976).

FOREWORD

Tom Bowden's book is an important contribution to our understanding of the conditions leading to the breakdown of public order, the collapse and transformation of regimes. Political science has been remiss in its treatment of this aspect of politics, particularly in an age in which what Bowden calls 'politics in extremis' − terrorism, guerrilla warfare, revolution and wars of national liberation − has become commonplace. Studies of regime crises and of breakdown illuminate the bases of stability and legitimacy in ways that studies of normal politics never can.

The literature which does deal with organized political violence and revolution consists, on the one hand, of studies of individual rebellions or revolutionary movements, and, on the other, of sweeping general sociological or social-psychological theories of collective violence and revolution represented in the work of such writers as Crane Brinton, Chalmers Johnson, Harry Eckstein, Ted Gurr, and Charles Tilly. Bowden's study of the Irish crisis of 1916-1921 and the Palestinian crisis of 1936-1939 represents a significant methodological step forward from these approaches. He draws intelligently from sociological, psychological, and political theories in his construction of his case study framework, but his primary method is that of the historical clinician whose use of theories and hypotheses is disciplined by what he actually encounters in his individual cases.

Thus, while it is evident that Bowden has benefited from Ted Gurr's elegant processual theory of collective political violence, in Bowden's hands the crucial balances of regime versus dissident institutional support and coercive control are

ix

converted into explicit structural and cultural properties measurable and comparable in concrete cases. His enumeration of the seven structural elements necessary for a full-scale people's revolutionary war, and his use of this schema in comparing the Irish and Palestinian rebellions, brings us closer to a research programme which can illuminate conditions associated with regime survival and breakdown. Thus the successful Irish revolution was implemented by a movement which developed an effective headquarters-regional structure and division of labor, an effective intelligence organization, specialized systems of recruitment and training, communications and propaganda, an effective fighting arm, and a political department to operate in the international arena. The Palestinian rebellion never got beyond the development of dispersed fighting, propaganda and intelligence units.

One may describe Bowden's contribution as a structural-strategic theory of regime breakdown, for he not only stresses the crucial importance of differentiated organization on both the regime and dissident sides; he also stresses the importance of strategy and tactics, in particular the relative balance and interaction of regime and anti-regime terror. In his disciplined comparison of the Irish and Palestinian cases he demonstrates the crucial importance of this balance of dissident-regime terror. In the Irish case systematic, 'targetted' terror disorganized and disintegrated the civil and police authorities, and converted Irish disaffection into popular support of the revolutionaries. In the Palestinian case the balance was at first in favour of the dissident Arab groups, but gradually turned into a systematic and effective counter-terror when the British military were brought into the picture.

What makes Bowden's contribution 'better theory' is that

it assigns a more appropriate weight to political organization and the goals and means of political elites and counter-elites, in the interpretation of regime breakdown and revolution. The degree and kind of discontent, dissatisfaction, and resentment (Gurr's 'Relative Deprivation') in a society constitute the constraints and opportunities affecting the elite and counter-elite struggle for control, but the crucial variables are the creative ones of human choices of goals and their implementation.

Gabriel A. Almond
Stanford University, 1977

PREFACE

The goals of this book are threefold. First, it seeks to describe, in the light of new materials now available to researchers, the violent events occurring in Ireland in 1916-21 and Palestine in 1936-39. In this sense it is an historical analysis examining in detail the origins and causes of two attempts to overthrow colonial government. Second, and crucially, it seeks to isolate and then analyse both the factors creating the breakdown of public security in Ireland and Palestine and the patterns resulting from it. In this sense the book is wider-ranging and is concerned with political analysis, focusing as it does upon two political systems and possible substitute institutions, in the form of guerrilla undergrounds, operating under severe stress. Third, the study attempts to demonstrate the centrality of efficient police units, and particularly their intelligence services, to the short-term resolution of conflict and the preservation of civil government. In this sense it is concerned with the theory and problems of policing.

The study is then eclectic spanning political analysis, sociology, history, military history and policing theory. Yet the framework within which the problems of declining security and escalating violence are assessed is most definitely that of the political historian.

Each of the case studies is of course historically unique.

Yet despite this there do emerge from both cases situational constants which enable one to suggest some firm conclusions about the origins and pattern of the decline of public security. The rationale behind this study is perhaps best expressed by the Chinese military theorist Sun Tzu, who was of the opinion that 'war is a matter of vital importance to the state; the province of life or death; the road to survival or ruin. It is mandatory that it be thoroughly studied.' (Sun Tzu, *The Art of War* (Oxford, University Press, 1963, p. 3). An understanding of internal war is doubly important for both government and the governed. It is hoped that this study will help a little towards that end.

T.B.
1977

INTRODUCTION

The motive behind this study is to look into the chaotic world of targeted political violence and internal war and by so doing to examine the interaction of the revolutionary terrorist and the political police in the British colonial context in an attempt to determine cause, sequence and effect of the breakdown of public security and the end of governability.

The cases of Ireland, 1916-21, and Palestine, 1936-39, were chosen because both were extreme crisis situations where revolutionary groups sought, by attacking the police of the respective colonial governments, to win independence by demonstrating the incompetence of the incumbents. The Irish underground achieved that goal in 1921. The Palestinian Arabs came close to breaking the Mandate government between 1936 and 1939. The two cases were also chosen because it soon transpired, after a general reading of resistance struggles in the British colonies during the twentieth century, that many of the personnel who left Ireland in 1921 arrived in Haifa to police Palestine a few months later. Such a coincidence made a comparative assessment all the more interesting and valid — especially since those who transferred to Palestine appeared not to have retained any of the politico-military lessons taught by the course of the Irish War of Independence.

This is then a study that moves in the arena of the morbid, often criminal, violent and chaotic world of sub rosa politics. Specifically it is concerned with assassination as a weapon of revolutionary war, reprisal and the centrality of efficient police intelligence operations to the preservation of public order in crisis. Historians and political scientists tend to concentrate on analysis of the stable, system-maintaining variables of political life. They ask why men give their allegiance to political systems. Less frequently they analyse why, at certain times, and for considerable periods, men withdraw that allegiance. Even less do we seem to study in any systematic fashion why men accept, condone or take part in organized terror, violence and bloodshed against a system to which, at one time, they may have freely given allegiance. Political man is analysed, in the main, at his behavioural best, civilized to varying degrees by the restraints of the lobby, the forum of Parliament, in his group activities constrained by the framework of constitutions or, more often, by the accepted rules of the political game. Only rarely do we get a glimpse into the underworld of political life where subversion, propaganda, political assassination and intelligence operations are the norm and civilized politics the aberrant. It is hoped that this book provides one of those rare views.

The aim of the study is then to attempt to understand how and when a political system becomes disequilibrated by focusing upon the condition of public security, the maintenance of which is a prerequisite of a stable system. By so focusing on the police as the public security units serving, as it were, 'in the front line' in both Ireland and Palestine, it became increasingly apparent that the intelligence function of the public security units was perhaps the critical element in the short-term maintenance of internal order and control.

The history of Ireland throughout the nineteenth century clearly demonstrated that efficient police services, in the shape of the Dublin Metropolitan Police (DMP) and the Royal Irish Constabulary (RIC) Special Branches, were quite capable of controlling or diverting putative rebellion. This style of preventative policing was at the centre of the maintenance of British control in Ireland. However, at some point in the 1880s, during the Land League agitations in particular, it became apparent that the RIC had begun to go into decline. Political expediency and financial stringency were both applied to public security work. The outcome was that rebels and subversives prospered while the police, demoralized, could only watch. Eventually the rebels attacked and broke the public security units in Ireland after first nullifying their vitally important intelligence sections. With their defeat, not only public security, but civil government went into abeyance.

A very similar process occurred in Palestine – the major difference perhaps being that the Mandate government had never been able to establish the degree of control over its people and territory achieved by the Dublin Castle government in Ireland during the nineteenth century.

Hence, in both Ireland and Palestine, political expediency and financial stringency supplemented by revolutionary terrorism succeeded in debilitating and then breaking both the condition of public security and the police forces themselves.

SOME PROBLEMS OF THE ANALYSIS

The Form of Struggle

It is important to indicate at this stage that the study is problem-orientated. Particularly, it treats two styles of internal war, a rebellion in Palestine and a people's revolutionary war in Ireland. Internal war in general is regarded here as neither an exotic nor an aberrant method of political argument but rather as a radical outcome of the failure to resolve internal conflict. Eckstein in a seminal study of internal war saw it as belonging,

> to the realm not only of social force but also to *political competition* since their object is to obtain political outputs advantageous to the groups that urge them — favourable policies, offices or general control of the political structure of society.[1]

People's revolutionary war, as this study reveals, is perhaps the most sophisticated mode of internal war. Rebellion, such as that which occurred in Palestine, is, however, a less sophisticated form of internal struggle.

With regard to people's revolutionary war there is something of a definitional problem. No two studies seem to have applied the same methodology or produced comparable definitions. Here the approach is to subsume 'people's revolutionary war', 'revolutionary terrorism' and 'rebellion' in the overall umbrella category of 'internal war' while providing in the body of the work explicit inventories of the characteristics of both rebellion and people's revolutionary war as they occurred in Palestine and Ireland.[2] Both the struggles examined in this book were 'people's wars' since they involved popular aspirations and widespread participation. Hence a particularly satisfactory definition of people's war for our purposes is that of Pustay, who defined it as,

> that composite conflict phenomenon which can be defined as a cellular development of resistance against an incumbent political regime which expands from the initial stage of subversion – infiltration – through the stage of overt resistance by small armed bands and insurrection to final fruition in civil war.[3]

It is the developmental emphasis inherent in this definition that has particular utility for this study, since in both Ireland and Palestine opposition to the colonial governments mutated from simple peasant rebellion towards sophisticated people's revolutionary war. In Ireland peasant rebellion had been the prevailing mode of political protest down to the 1880s. However, by 1919 a sophisticated revolutionary war was being fought – Chapter 3 of this study attempts to trace the forces inducing this change in the mode of struggle. In Palestine the mutation away from primitive banditry towards a more sophisticated form of internal war took place during the first two years of the Arab Rebellion, between 1936 and 1938. In Ireland the process was less instantaneous, beginning in the 1880s and reaching fruition by 1920 under the guerrilla leader Michael Collins.

The essence of internal war is that it seeks to work through the people, to mobilize them behind the opposition cause. The Irish case in particular reveals a struggle for the differential mobilization of the people – a struggle eventually won by the Irish because they had conducted it with an acute awareness of the need to exploit all possible aspects of the struggle, not only the military but the political, economic psychological and propaganda arenas. Palestine, as we shall see, saw no such concerted plan of campaign. Nevertheless the rebellion there performed a similar function to the revolutionary war in Ireland. The function was similar, since, as Kornhauser has noted,

Rebellions are ways of making demands on authority, whether for the change of specific acts or rulers or of structures of authority. They are alternatives to established ways of making demands on authority in an orderly manner. . . . Rebellions therefore signify failures, small or large in the political system. Nevertheless, rebellions may be a way of performing political functions in the absence of political structures capable of accommodating political demands. Rebellions also may help to create more effective political arrangements.[4]

The crucial difference between the two internal struggles was the relatively primitive stage of politico-military development at which the Palestinian rebellion stood.

Approaches to Political Violence and the Stimuli to Revolt

Amitai Etzioni has noted that,

we tend to think of group violence as a major aberration in a democratic society, as a sickness that comes only in extraordinary times. A deeper reading of the past belies this notion . . . group violence has accompanied periods of serious social stress from Homer to this morning's newspaper . . . . Violence has been used by groups seeking power, by groups holding on to power and by groups in the process of losing power. Violence has been pursued in the defence of order by the satisfied, in the name of justice by the oppressed and in fear of displacement by the threatened.[5]

Somewhat in the same vein, political violence is conceived throughout this work as a continuum in political life, present in most systems, endemic in others. Nature, it seems, has endowed man with the capacity for violence. As the case studies demonstrate, whether or not man exercises that capacity is dependent upon the interaction of social, economic, political and behavioural factors as well as contingency.[6] There is of course a wide variety of approaches to political violence. No attempt will be made to cite them here but rather to draw on those theorists particularly relevant to this study. Fanon is especially helpful, since he viewed political violence as a cultural product capable of being fostered or inhibited.[7] In the body of this work there is much evidence to suggest that there emerged both in Ireland and Palestine sub-cultures of political violence.[8] In Ireland, as we shall see, this sub-culture took the form of a mystic, nationalistic, sacrificial spiritualism. In Palestine it took a more overtly religious form in the shape of a *jihad* and tribal blood feuds.

Fanon is especially helpful also in his treatment of the peasantry and their political potential. He perceived the peasantry as being capable of making the transformation from 'spectator to major revolutionary actor'[9] on the leading strings of the revolutionary party. Interestingly, in both Ireland and Palestine one can clearly see the peasantry becoming first politicized and then mobilized behind a cause espousing systematic political violence. In Palestine, however, the mobilization was less systematic, the party less cohesive and the peasant rebellion, when set against the rising in Ireland, little more than an extension of the traditional peasant *Jacquerie.* Irish revolutionary protest evolved beyond its original peasant base. The rick-burning of the peasant was replaced by the tactical assassinations from an urban guerrilla cadre provided by Sinn Fein and the Irish Volunteers.

What is thus crucial in the internal war situation is, as Fanon observed, the transition from passive spectator to revolutionary actor. It is the expansion of, or increase in, the number of people prepared to use violence as a political weapon that can move a political system from a position of unstable equilibrium into disequilibrium. Such increased participation is often, as Huntington has identified, the product of the rapid expansion of political consciousness, which results in 'the rapid mobilisation of new groups into politics at a speed which makes it impossible for existing political institutions to assimulate them'.[10] Linked with this phenomenon in both Palestine and Ireland was the existence of inflexible, unyielding political institutions seemingly unwilling to work with or recognize the forces of protest. Again as Huntington observes, 'Ascending or aspiring groups and rigid inflexible institutions are the stuff of which revolutions are made.'[11] In Ireland and Palestine a clear spiralling of conflict occurred as a response to this perceived frustration – an occurrance that would appear to be confirmed from other comparative assessments of civil disobedience conducted by T. R. Gurr[12] and others.[13]

What then could have effectively met this escalating frustration – this aggression and the resultant political violence directed towards overthrowing the incumbent regimes in Palestine and Ireland? This work is based upon the premise, drawn from the case materials, that for the short-term resolution of conflict in Ireland in 1916-21 and in Palestine in 1936-39 it was the police, but above all their intelligence sectors or Special Branches that held the ring between the maintenance of the existing political system and varying degrees of system change ranging from riot to revolutionary overthrow. Of course, there are other important variables to weigh in such complex situations as those prevailing in

Ireland and Palestine. For example, the condition of the rebel movement was crucial to the condition of public security. Yet here again efficient intelligence operations can prevent the development of an infrastructure of alternative underground government either by selective arrests and constant harassment or by discreet, selective assassinations. Similarly, such movements can and have been diverted from their path by infiltration. Should opposition forces be allowed to coalesce, accumulate support, organize cellular structures and finally mobilize the native population through an amalgam of terror, persuasion, example and propaganda — as they were in Ireland and Palestine because of inadequate intelligence, inefficient policing, non-application of the law and political expediency — then public security will decay.

Similarly, in both cases there were sets of crisis-inducing contingent events. In Palestine critical factors affecting the political environment and antagonizing Palestinian Arabs particularly were the scale of Jewish immigration, legal and illegal; the Arab freedom struggles in Egypt and Syria; the condition and activities of the Muslims under the British Raj in India; and the overt support which Palestinians received from the Hitler-Mussolini axis. In Ireland contingent factors affecting the overall political environment were multiple. For example, the Bachelor's Walk incident of 1914 with police firing into a crowd bearing illegally imported arms to Dublin; the Curragh Mutiny; the bombastic, threatening behaviour of the Carsonite Ulster Protestant Volunteers; the death of Thomas Ashe, a prominent Republican, while being forcibly fed; the enforcement of a conscription campaign in Ireland for a war in Europe to guarantee the independence of small nations and, above all, the execution of the leaders of the failed Easter Rising of 1916 acted as severe aggravation in an already unstable situation and mobilized supportive opinion

behind those determined to break the Dublin Castle government.

Exacerbating these frustration-compounding events was
the tension produced in Ireland and Palestine by barriers to
the effective expression of discontent. Again, Etzioni has
noted that,

> History is full of violent disasters that occurred because channels for
> peaceful presentation of grievances were blocked and because
> governments did not or could not act to correct the underlying
> injustices or to control disorder; history also contains examples of
> disasters that were averted by governments which kept the channels
> of protest open and applied a judicious combination of reform and
> control.[14]

Palestine and Ireland both had administrative systems which
were little more than tempered despotism. The Palestinian
Arabs lacked any formal channels of representation through
which to express their opinions to the Mandate government.
What representation there was took the form of an élite
Effendi class who had little nor nothing in common with the
discontented *fellahin.* As a result, as in Ireland, dissent went
underground where it could be neither moderated nor controlled. In Ireland frustration was particularly compounded
by the virtual suspension of emigration. The figures in Table
1[15] indicate the dramatic curtailment of the exodus of
discontented persons. Given that most emigrants were single
young men or young families, the effect of restrictions can
only have multiplied the alienated and able-bodied who were
capable, physically, of combating the government of the day.
Policemen were not even allowed to resign from the force. At
the same time the expressive modes of discontent such as
nationalist cultural-political associations were harrassed, and
all meetings proscribed.

TABLE 1

Emigration Statistics, Ireland 1907-1918

Year	Emigrants
1907	39,082
1908	23,295
1909	28,676
1910	32,457
1911	30,573
1912	29,344
1913	30,967
1914	20,314
1915	10,659
1916	7,302
1917	2,129
1918	983

By these broad fronts revolutionary stimuli were provided. In both Ireland and Palestine a political and/or guerrilla leader or party canalized the dissent, giving it a focus. In Ireland the revolutionary leader and party were represented in the person of one man — Michael Collins, an Irish Lenin. Collins in effect controlled the Irish underground. Through the clandestine Irish Republican Brotherhood (IRB) he succeeded in reinvigorating Irish revolutionary thinking. He also developed a strategy of guerrilla warfare with selective assassination as its leading tactical edge and then turned both of these on the British in Ireland. Similarly he helped create a united policy merging all the fragmented opposition organizations with Sinn Fein after the *Ard-Fheis* of 1917.[16]

In Palestine the challenge to the administration was less cohesive or controlled. As we shall see, in Palestine dissent took the form of a spontaneous peasant rebellion which became increasingly politicized. However, its leadership was fragmented. There were several contending guerrilla leaders and feuding political families. The Mufti of Jerusalem, Haj Amin, while presenting himself as the overall leader of the rebellion, was little more than an opportunist. No single revolutionary party emerged, though previously antagonistic parties formed a brittle united front in 1935. Still, internecine struggles soon returned to bedevil the rebellion.

However, in both cases political violence quite clearly became more organized, more systematic. In Ireland and Palestine the downturn in the condition of public security became most noticeable only when there was a move by the opposition away from random, spontaneous, violent events, often the product of individual frustration, towards systematic violent events planned in advance as part of an overall political strategy and enforced by committed, like-minded men. In both Ireland and Palestine, at the centre of the escalation of violence and its increased impact was the development of tactical assassination. The British experience alone in Ireland, Palestine, Cyprus, Malaya, South Yemen and now in Northern Ireland testifies to the effectiveness of systematic tactical assassination used as a political weapon by indigenous peoples against foreign rule. It is a weapon capable first of intimidating both people and government and then terminating the condition of a secure public. Killing became a mode of political procedure, a class of professional assassins emerged, and spontaneity was ended. It is upon the interaction of this group of men — the attackers — with the political police — the defenders — that the condition of public security and the coninuance of governability turned, since, as Trotsky noted,

Intimidation is a powerful weapon of policy, both internationally and internally. War, like revolution, is founded upon intimidation. A victorious war, generally speaking, destroys only an insignificant part of the conquered areas, intimidating the remainder and breaking their will. The revolution works in the same way: it kills individuals and intimidates thousands.[17]

Ireland and Palestine both saw the application of the tactics of targeted and random terror. Indiscriminate, random terror particularly weakened the condition of public security since no one was safe. Targeted terror broke the resolve of the police forces. The two acting in concert ended governability. This study seeks then to trace the interaction of the terrorist and the political police in order to determine the reasons for the breakdown of public security in Ireland in 1916-21 and Palestine in 1936-39.

NOTES

1. H. Eckstein (ed.), *Internal War* (New York, 1963), 12.
2. See Chapters 3, 4 and 6 of this work.
3. J. Pustay, *Counterinsurgency Warfare* (New York, 1965), 5.
4. William Kornhauser, 'Rebellion and Political Development' in Eckstein, op. cit., 142.
5. Amitai Etzioni, *Demonstration Democracy* (New York, 1970), 79-80.
6. T. R. Gurr observes 'Man's resort to violence is unreasoning but does not occur without reason. . . . All of us have the capacity for violence and there are circumstances in which almost all of us would

use it.' 'Violence in Politics: Some Conclusion on the Use of Force in Society', *Princeton Alumni Weekly*, (March 1970) 7.

7. For a discussion of this particular aspect of Fanon's theory, see P. Worsley, Frantz Fanon and the Lumpenproletariat', *Socialist Register* (1972) 193-230.

8. A sub-culture is here taken to be quite simply a normative system of some group or groups smaller than the whole of society.

9. Worsley, op. cit., 202.

10. S. P. Huntington, *Political Order and Changing Societies* (New Haven, 1968), 266.

11. ibid., 274-75.

12. T. R. Gurr, 'A Causal Model of Civil Strife: A Comparative Analysis Using New Indices', *American Political Science Review* (December 1908), 1104.

13. Particularly I. K. and R. L. Feierabend, 'Aggressive Behaviour within Politics 1948-1962: A Cross National Study' in J. C. Davies, *When Men Revolt and Why. A reader in Political Violence and Revolution* (New York, 1971), 229-49.

14. Etzioni, op. cit., 91.

15. See the Command Papers nos. Cd 8230 (1915); Cd 8520 (1916), Cd 9013 (1917) and Cmd 77 (1918).

16. See Michael Collins, *The Path to Freedom* (Dublin, 1922), 62. The Ard-Fheis is the Annual Convention of Sinn Fein.

17. Leon Trotsky, *Terrorism and Communism* (Ann Arbor, Michigan, 1961), 58-59.

I

IRELAND

1

THE DEFENDERS:
The Royal Irish Constabulary
and Dublin Castle

I want a public man to come forward and say what the Irish Question is. One says it is physical, another spiritual. Now it is the absence of aristocracy, now the absence of railways. It is the Pope one day and potatoes the next. A dense population in extreme distress inhabit an island where there is an established Church which is not their Church, and a territorial aristocracy, the richest of whom live in a far capital. Thus they have a starving population, an absentee aristocracy, an alien Church, and in addition the weakest Executive in the World. . . . Now what would honourable gentlemen say if they were reading of a country in that position? They would say at once, 'the remedy is revolution'. But the Irish could not have a revolution, and why? Because Ireland is connected with another and more powerful country. Then what is the consequence? The connection with England prevented a revolution and a revolution was the only remedy. England is obviously in the odious position of being the cause of all the misery of Ireland. What then is the duty of an English Minister? To effect by his policy all those changes which a revolution would do by force. That is the Irish Question in its integuity.

Benjamin Disraeli, House of Commons, 16 February 1844

17

In both Palestine and Ireland the police were reflective of the general condition of their respective governments. Indeed, in both Palestine and Ireland the police operated as the chief executive and retributive instruments of their administrations. Thus by analysing the police in detail, and particularly declining public security, one is at the same time saying much more about the nature of government and about the condition of governability. Of all the variables involved in the breakdown of public security in Ireland and Palestine, none was thus more seminal than the police forces serving as the principle agencies of government in society.

However, it should be made clear at the outset that the RIC was a para-military police force — a very different creature from the native English police force. It was a political police force whose structure and role echoed the counter-revolutionary traditions of the continental *gendarmeries* sired by anxious enlightened despots. In Machiavellian terms, it was very much a 'police of the Prince', that is, one conceived as having multiple duties in and over society. Nevertheless its prime task was to locate, isolate and then defuse the whole spectrum of political discontent running from localized sporadic dissidence through to widespread revolutionary subversion.

Historically it is possible to detect two broad styles of policing,[1] one based in common law the other stemming from the Roman law tradition. English policing, where the policeman serves as little more than a professional citizen, exemplifies the common law style of law enforcement. In countries that adhere to this style there has tended to be a narrower conception of the functions of government and certainly a less intrusive police apparatus. The Roman law tradition historically has led to a far more 'positive' state apparatus. Government and its agencies are at one and the same time fare more pervasive and paternalistic. Policing thus reaches down into the interstices of society. Crucially, the 'police of the Prince', in the Roman law tradition, exists to monitor the condition of society and the body politic. The police of the continental despots, and European police forces since that time, have all operated within this tradition. It is a tradition that perhaps reached its acme under the care of Napoleon's master policeman, Fouché, the Duke of Otranto. Strangely, the RIC, created in what was then 'English' Ireland, can also be placed in this European, Roman law-style of policing.

It is then something of an anomaly that England, the initiator of the common law mode of policing, should in almost all of her colonies have adopted the European mode. However, it was a style of policing not easily established in Ireland. A history of policing in Ireland is interesting not least because it reveals fragments of the long debate over the style of police England was prepared to accept. Ireland indeed became something of a testing ground for police reforms and innovations later applied in England as well as throughout the Empire — Palestine included. Certainly the RIC were a para-military force. Throughout the life of the RIC the distinction was clear-cut that, while in England the common law mode of policing gave more freedom to the individual and placed men in public offices not beyond application of sanctions of law, in Ireland there existed a curious tempered despotism. There the police could, if necessary, adopt the 'military way' and repress dissent out of hand. Yet in spite of this licence, perhaps the fundamental weakness of the police in both Palestine and Ireland was that, while conceived, trained, structured, equipped and recruited as a para-military gendarmerie, the forces were never consistently allowed to act in that capacity. Despite their para-military training, conception and appearance, their role was never tightly defined — were they a civil police force with military training and equipment, or a military force with civilian responsibilities? The dilemma was that they were a police force fashioned along the lines of the Roman law police of the Prince, administered by a common law country. The result in both Palestine and Ireland was a most inadequate and confusing halfway house.

THE ROYAL IRISH CONSTABULARY –
THE DEVELOPMENT OF A
NATIONAL POLICE FORCE

The Royal Irish Constabulary, or Irish Constabulary, since it was not awarded the Royal title until 1867, was a force born out of crisis. As a unitary structure it emerged out of a mélange of regulations and reforms whose sole intent was to keep fractious Ireland quiet. It existed, indeed was created, to suppress subversion and guarantee law and order. Policing in Ireland was thus from the beginning more a military than a civil exercise.

An Act of 1787, introduced 'for the better execution of the law and the preservation of peace within the counties at large',[2] can be taken as a convenient starting point of policing in Ireland. The Act empowered the Lord Lieutenant of Ireland to appoint a chief constable to each of the baronial administrative districts into which Ireland was at that time divided. Though the Act was poorly enforced, it did at least enable the creation of a skeletal baronial constabulary where grand juries appointed sixteen sub-constables to each local district. The only proviso was that all those appointed should be Protestants.[3] This system continued as the only form of policing, other than the militia and the army garrison, until 1792, when a further Act for 'regulating the office of constable and for better enforcing the process of criminal law in certain parts of the Kingdom' was passed.[4] The latter in effect gave additional powers to the grand juries. Owing to the sporadic and far from thoroughgoing nature of public order legislation, and the generally loose application of a more thorough response to disturbance, the Peace Preservation Act of 1814,[5] policing in Ireland was to remain, until the establishment of the Irish Constabulary in 1836, very much an affair of unstructured responses to local disturbances. There was a tendency to leave public security in the hands of the local gentry and magistracy. The Baronial Constabulary in particular, operating as little more than a quasi-feudal rentinue, did little more than reflect, extend and uphold their interests.

Thus in quiet times both local government and security were built around the crenellations of the baronial halls. Indeed, the landed lords can be typified as the colonnades and the magistrates the mortar in the interstices of a somewhat shoddily built edifice of local government. However, when the rebels – the 'midnight legislators' – became heated and active, the continued English presence came to rest heavily upon the military garrison. Surprisingly perhaps, the latter was less overtly partisan than the police-magistracy unit. Resident magistrates, dependent upon the local lord, possessed little probity or judicial independence. Similarly, over time their taste for vigorous law enforcement had become jaded since often they were the most available targets for the galaxy of bandits and freedom fighters operating in rural Ireland. Remote from the people, effete, partisan and thus unpopular, the baronial mode of policing not only proved to be inadequate for the maintenance of security in times of crisis, but on many occasions itself provoked or exacerbated local disturbances. It was out of both the inadequacy of that force and the consequent disturbed state of Ireland that police reform came, in the shape of the Peace Preservation Force (PPF) established in 1814.

Created during a period of political alarm in both England and Ireland, the PPF was to prove a mobile, hard-hitting armed police force. It was the forerunner of the RIC. The nature of the PPF can best be understood by reflecting upon the overall political environment and the mood of the times in which it was created. The French Revolution and subsequent revolutionary war had traumatized the English aristocracy and many politicians. Similarly, a European war had just ended. There were repeated warnings from English politicians, based upon the information of an army of spies, that Wolfe Tone's legacy was about to be fulfilled and a rising, financed by the French, was to take place in Ireland. No less a political personage than Peel had stated in the House that 'combinations certainly had been formed, the object of which was to call on a foreign power'.[6] To meet the troubles in Ireland, both real and imagined, a Bill for the creation of a police force, the duplicate of Fouché's much feared and maligned police of Paris, passed through the House of Commons with little more than a whimper of protest — certainly without any recorded opposition. Thus what would have been condemned as tyrannical for England was applauded as potentially remedial in Ireland.[7]

The PPF, like the later RIC, was thus in effect a gendarmerie recruited mainly from the Army. Overall civil control of the force was guaranteed by making the stipendiary magistrate of the locality a paid, full-time police official appointed by, and responsible to, the Irish administration in Dublin Castle. The PPF soon developed into an effective, if small, anti-terrorist unit. By 1833, some three years before it was absorbed into the RIC, it was operating in nine counties. However, it could not police the whole of Ireland, many parts of which continued to be intensely, if episodically, disturbed.

With the exception of the Constables (Ireland) Bill of 1822 no further serious attempts to restructure the police of Ireland occurred until 1832. Again, in 1832, crisis provoked a studied response, though what eventually became known as Goulborn's Act of 1832[8] was based upon a thoroughgoing policing blueprint formulated by Peel between 1815-1818 and left in abeyance.[9] An armed police operating in tandem with the existant PPF thus became both a less expensive and a less effective prosecutor of rebellion. One member of the British House of Commons was so moved by the spectre of an armed, professional police in what he regarded as British territory that he remarked,

the new system which the Rt. Hon. Gentleman [Goulborn] proposed to introduce, appeared to be a system of military police, or at least he did not know where to place the distinction between it and the police of France.[10]

The Act of 1822, when implemented, proved to be a significant departure from the baronial pattern of policing if only because it was more systematic and the force itself more extensive. The PPF continued to function alongside the new, local force, and thus Peel's aim to achieve 'that which had never yet been effectively done, namely to enforce the common law of England in Ireland'[11] came closer to realization. The force created in 1822, coupled with the PPF, proved to be the bases out of which the Irish Constabulary (IC) was created in 1836. Like the later IC, the force of 1822 was a county force supervised by senior constabulary officers in each of the four provinces of Ireland.[12] The inspectors possessed a measure of autonomy since they could formulate the rules and requirements of their region. However, such rules could be implemented only with the approval of the Lord Lieutenant. Police inspectors received the then princely sum of £500 p.a.,[13] on which, in penurious rural Ireland, they were literally able to live like lords. Each of the county areas was also divided into districts under the command of a chief constable earning no more than £100 p.a. with the additional bonus of a police house. The basic qualifications for entry into the force, other than a good physique, were an ability to read and write. Yet because of the scales of pay the force attracted a high calibre of recruit and was a distinct improvement upon any other force then existent. This pattern of policing continued to operate until the major reorganization of 1835-36.

Rationalization was the overriding goal of the 1835 Act. Viscount Morpeth, who introduced the Bill into the House in 1835, stated that he wished to repeal the laws 'by which the Constabulary and police establishment in Ireland were at present formed and regulated . . . in order that a sufficient force should be established under one improved and uniform system'.[14] Peel was himself so convinced of the necessity of police reform, and hence the un-amended passage of the 1835 Bill, that he urged MPs to see it as

> not a party question. It was one which arose from a desire to improve the condition of the country; for before they could give up the operation of such extraordinary measures as the Peace Preservation Act, or the Insurrection Act, they must have an improved police and habituate the people of Ireland to that which was the greatest of all national blessings — an equal, unvarying and impartial administration of justice.[15]

The 1835 Act dispensed with the four regional inspectors, establishing in their stead an inspector general, responsible to the Lord Lieutenant, as commander of the force, with two deputy inspectors serving under him.[16] However, the 1835 Act did see the end of Peel's concept of civil policing in Ireland, for it created a centalized, colonial gendarmerie, a 'police of the Prince'. In time the IC became the strong right arm of the English presence, earning not only its 'Royal' title but the epithet 'prime oppressor' during the rising of 1867 which it mercilessly crushed.

Thus it was the wish to keep Ireland quiet, for both strategic military considerations and the moderating effect a quiet Ireland had upon English domestic politics, coupled with the neuroses of landlord and politician alike, who pressured successive British governments and Irish administrations into believing that, secreted in the damp mists of every bog and by the peaty fire in every cottage, was an Irish Catholic subversive, or worse a French agent, which determined that the IC could in no way emulate the London Metropolitans, who had succeeded in quelling that disturbed and irreverent city by winning the sympathy, respect and allegiance of the people.[17] Housed in barracks, trained and at times behaving like an army of occupation, the IC, and later the RIC, could not effect such a liaison. As a Sinn Fein pamphlet observed,

There is in Ireland no police force for the maintenance of the peace such as exists in other countries. The Irish Police, so-called, are the more stationary parts of the army of occupation; they live in barracks and are armed with rifles and revolvers; they are directly under the control of the English Government and no policeman is ever located in his native district lest he should be on friendly terms with the people.[18]

It is hardly surprising then that since the institutionalization of the IC, there was an evident benign enmity between the police and the people. The Bill of 1836, commonly referred to as that which created the Irish Constabulary, was in effect little more than an amendment of the 1835 Act.[19] Largely the work of Thomas Drummond, under-secretary for Ireland, it was again based upon a framework that was essentially Peel's. Taken together, the legislation of 1835 and 1836 established a unified and, down to 1880, a highly efficient police force.

Once established, the IC expanded rapidly. Most of rural Ireland was brought under its drilled jurisdiction. In 1836 the rural police numbered 7,319 officers and men.[20] By 1840 this figure had risen to 8,590[21] reaching 12,758 in 1850[22] — a total that was exceeded only at the height of the War of Independence in 1919-21 when the RIC, augmented by Black and Tan and Auxiliary Police recruits, stood at around 13,000 men.[23]

Thus the makeup, organization and role of the RIC that served in Ireland down to 1921 was a product of those political attitudes responding to the episodic crises occurring throughout the early nineteenth century. Structure, methods, training, tactics and duties were to change little throughout the eighty-five years of its existence — one prime reason, perhaps, for its eventual demise.

THE STRUCTURE OF THE RIC

The RIC, despite being subjected to minor periodic changes in its complement, recruitment patterns and of course its personnel, changed very little during its existence in terms of its organizational structure. Such inertia was in fact one of its principle weaknesses. Police forces are notoriously conservative, unchanging administrative structures. The RIC was incredibly so. For eighty-five years it remained in a condition of suspended animation. The lesson that was never learned was that a force that had been superbly efficient in the 1860s was not necessarily still efficient by 1916 or 1920. Rather was the opposite the case: the techniques and skills that the RIC had applied with considerable success in the 1860s had become anachronistic by the 1880s and utterly outmoded by 1920. Whereas, as we shall see in later chapters, the Irish underground progressed in motivation, organization and technique, the RIC marked time and then regressed, harassed as it was by the constraints of political expediency and financial stringency, both of which were consonant with the reduced role the Irish administration was forced to play at the beginning of the twentieth century. An editorial in the *Constabulary Gazette* of 1918 captured the mood when it referred to the force as 'a wooden velocipede – a marvellous invention fifty years ago'.[24] Similarly, an earlier editorial of 1916 had suggested that 'the RIC may be likened unto a noble mansion of the early Victorian era, still occupied but showing visible signs of decay'.[25]

The constables themselves were housed in 1,397 barracks and huts throughout Ireland,[26] many of them isolated in distant and desolate niches of population – a state of affairs that made it difficult to deploy reinforcements in the event of an emergency. The distribution of the barracks, and the fact that the force was barracked, isolated them further from the Irish people. Similarly, the movement of police units about the country on horseback, bristling with arms, cannot have failed to induce terror rather than confidence into Irish hearts. Basic training was structured around a somewhat diluted version of the military manual with an excessive amount of drill and rote learning. Weapons instruction, at first adequate, later declined to become thoroughly inadequate. Such techniques of training, marching orders, drill and line tactics in no way enabled the force to be ready for the species of war it was later called upon to fight – an urban and rural guerrilla war based on selective assassination and avoiding the deployment of forces in fixed positions.

Yet, paradoxically, despite its quasi-military appearance and training and its inception as 'a police of the Prince' to cauterize 'subversion', the RIC was daily called upon to act out a distinctly more civil function. Here indeed was the force's perennial dilemma – the lack of clear definition of both role and duties. Birrell, Chief Secretary of Ireland at the time of the Easter Rising, had referred to the RIC as 'an amphibious force . . . some people say they are much better soldiers than policemen. People who do not like them say they are much better policemen than they are soldiers'.[27] Indeed, between 1912 and 1915 there was an earnest if inconclusive debate over the precise status of the RIC. Dublin Castle, that is the civil administration, held to the belief that 'military service is quite distinct from constabulary service. We think it is quite clear that the RIC are not a military force.'[28] The British War Office however preferred to see them as a part of the armed forces of Ireland. Similarly, a memo to the Lord Lieutenant in 1895 on the condition of the RIC advised far too optimistically that,

> Little more can be done as regards the training of the RIC as policemen, but without impairing their value as police, much might be done to increase their value and efficiency as a semi-military body, or, possible contingencies, a purely military body.[29]

The dilemma of what was to be their precise role was never satisfactorily resolved — so little so that as late as 1919 one anxious RIC constable 'asked the Constabulary Gazette's legal column for advice on how to act if an armed band attacked one's barracks. Should one use the baton first and then, if forced by circumstances to fire, should the Riot Act not be read first'.[30]

However, if the role of the force was uncertain, at least the distribution of the force was straightforward. The county was the basic unit of the force. In their turn the counties were divided into districts and sub-districts. The county inspector had his headquarters in the county town and, depending upon the size of the county, had between three and eight district inspectors under him.[31] The headquarters of the district inspectors were located in the most important town of the district. Each district was further divided into sub-districts, again varying in number from seven to twelve depending upon the size of the district. A sergeant or acting sergeant served in each sub-district with some three of four constables under him. This system of force distribution, with many separate units, led to an unusually high number of officers, particularly sergeants, a state of affairs that was compounded by the force rule that each squad of constables must be under the guidance of an officer.[32] The RIC was in fact an over-bureaucratized, unwieldy administrative apparatus. The *Constabulary Gazette* noted in 1918 that the fundamental ethic of the force was to 'use two men for one man's work and underpay both'.[33]

Administratively the force was divided into four separately constituted sections — Free Quota, Extra, Reserve and Revenue. However, the division was somewhat academic since the four units were recruited, disciplined, regulated and governed as one. The Free Quota element, financed out of the Parliamentary Vote, that is English taxes, was the backbone of the force.[34] Its strength, initially fixed in 1848, gave a Free Quota complement of 35 country inspectors, 260 sub-inspectors (later district inspectors), 350 head constables and 10,006 sergeants and constables.[35] These figures changed little from 1848 to 1921 and represented the statutory maxima (see Table 2). The actual number of serving officers at any one time was however dependent both upon the state of Ireland and upon the condition of the Force,[36] rather than upon abstract organizational quotas. The Lord Lieutenant determined the size of the force within the constraints of political and policing contingencies, though it is true that the actual membership of the force was normally kept below the statutory maximum[37] for financial reasons.

The Extra Force of some 733 officers and men was concentrated in Belfast with an additional 40 men in Londonderry. Belfast was in fact treated as a separate unit and not policed by the RIC proper until 1865.[38] A commissioner of police and town inspector were in charge of the force, which was organized into the divisions A, B, C, D, E and F rather like both Dublin and London Metropolitans. The Extra Force commissioner was directly responsible to the inspector general of the RIC.

This unit of the force was not without problems. It became an accepted practice that unreliable constables were transferred from the south to the north, and to Belfast in particular, when the south was disturbed.[39] Such a policy unfortunately had the effect of establishing a coterie of disaffected constables within a force which, because of the almost daily stresses it faced, was by no means a sanctuary for the faint-hearted. Thus the Extra Force operated as a reservoir of reinforcements for those sections of the RIC that were at any one time under pressure. Given the endemically

TABLE 2

Operational Strength of the RIC, 1849-1919

1849	12,422	1873	11,401	1898	10,921
1850	12,507	1874	11,209	1899	10,923
1851	12,293	1875	11,059	1900	10,920
1852	12,213	1876	10,935	1901	10,972
1853	12,165	1877	10,877	1902	10,925
1854	11,835	1878	10,842	1903	10,512
1855	11,849	1879	10,926	1904	10,055
1856	11,765	1880	11,140	1905	9,708
1857	11,875	1881	11,591	1906	9,084
1858	11,774	1882	12,592	1907	10,112
1859	12,116	1883	14,559	1908	10,479
1860	12,216	1884	13,542	1909	10,473
1861	12,225	1885	12,849	1910	10,449
1862	12,133	1886	12,394	1911	10,373
1863	12,019	1887	12,482	1912	10,412
1864	11,654	1888	12,493	1913	10,259
1865	11,485	1889	12,486	1914	10,181
1866	11,399	1890	12,455	1915	9,668
1867	11,334	1891	12,294	1916	9,456
1868	12,083	1892	12,052	1917	9,452
1869	12,525	1893	11,939	1918	9,275
1870	12,593	1894	11,891	1919	7,609*
1871	12,288	1895	11.730	Totals exclusive of	
1872	12,010	1896	11,612	officers	
		1897	11,006		

*In the official records the 1919 figure was not totalled although the returns appeared to be complete. The figure of 7,609 was calculated by the author from the returns available. No other record of the strength of the force in 1919 appears to exist since the British Government ceased to publish them after 1916.

Source: HO 184, RIC Records Vols 35 and 36, Public Record Office, London.

disturbed state of Ireland, the strength of the Extra Force was always kept high.[40] Two cases may suffice as examples. On 31 December 1914, although 329 sergeants and constables were authorized to be employed in 'proclaimed', that is disturbed, areas, only 261 saw service.[41] Similarly, in 1917 the Extra Force, although it had fallen in strength to 265, saw only 110 men of that potential force used in the inflamed counties of Clare and the East and West Ridings of Galway. Perhaps some of the reluctance to employ the full complement of the Extra Force stemmed from the fact that half the cost of the Extra Force serving in any locality had to be borne by the disturbed district. This was in itself intended as a punitive measure,[42] but the Irish administration found it so difficult to collect the fines that it was reluctant to incur extra costs by using more than minimum force. The outcome of this incredibly parsimonious and myopic policy was that disorders tended not to be quickly cauterized, caused greater damage and higher costs than might have initially been the case, and usually terminated with military intervention — a development that neither enhanced police morale nor mollified Irish animosity towards the British presence.

A Reserve Force established in 1839 was an additional supplement to the Extra Force. It too was available for duty in any part of Ireland where both Quota and Extra forces were under pressure. Its strength was originally fixed at two district inspectors, four head constables and 200 sergeants and men.[43] As with the rest of the force its complement was subject to periodic fluctuations. The final unit, the Revenue Force, functioned only briefly and ceased to be recruited as a special segment of the RIC in 1896.[44]

THE CONDITIONS OF SERVICE IN
THE ROYAL IRISH CONSTABULARY

When it was first established in 1836, the RIC attracted men from a variety of occupations and background but especially, as the data in Table 3[45] reveals, it recruited the sons of farmers. The force appears to have had a preference for dutiful, malleable material of good yeoman stock. The ethic behind such recruitment policy was the same as that expressed by Sir Edward Henry, Commissioner of the London Metropolitan Police, who stressed that, 'we like to take them right from the plough . . . they are slow but steady; you can mould them into any shape you please'.[46]

TABLE 3

Figures Indicating the Background of RIC Officers on Recruitment:
A Comparative Analysis of the Years 1901 and 1913

1901		1913	
Farmers' sons	325	Farmers' sons	338
Labourers	28	Labourers	63
Shop assistants	33	Shop assistants	38
Clerks	15	Clerks	8
Teachers	7	Teachers	4
Carpenters	6	Carpenters	4
Postmen	4	Postmen	6
Gardeners	3	Gardeners	9
Groomsmen	2	Groomsmen	4
Herdsmen	5	Ex-soldiers	8
Musicians	5	Blacksmiths	5
Various professions	42	Various professions	47
No trade or calling	63	No trade or calling	67
Total	536	Total	598

Yet, despite the intent of creating dutiful policemen, even
the most cursory examination of the *Constabulary Gazette*
from 1908 onwards, or a reading of the evidence presented to
various Committees of Inquiry into the RIC, reveals that by
the twentieth century the morale of the RIC left much to be
desired. The basic grievance was the poor conditions of
service that applied throughout the force but especially the
inadequate pay, which had remained static for a number of
years.

Candidates for admission into the force had to be at least
5ft. 9in. in height, no less than thirty-nine inches around the
chest and between the ages of nineteen and twenty-seven.[47]
The age limit for 'cadets', who were regarded as officer
material, was twenty-six. After a short period of training they
were appointed to serve as district inspectors. Such tele-
scoped promotion and élitism caused great resentment within
the force. Indeed, the random and tardy nature of promotion
procedure was one of the most consistent grouses of the RIC
officer. In the normal course of events men had to serve at
least ten and very often fourteen to twenty years before
reaching the rank of sergeant. Constables could, at least on
paper, be promoted to sergeant after seven years by means of
an annual examination in 'literary and professional subjects'
conducted by the Civil Service Commission.[48] Yet in practice the promotion system was seriously flawed. It was certainly far more convoluted and involved than the regulations
seemed to indicate. A constable could in fact be promoted to
sergeant in three ways: first, from the 'ordinary list', that is
the ranks; second, from the assistant clerks' list; and third, by
the yearly competition. From the rank of sergeant he could
be promoted to head constable by four distinct methods:
first as a result of seniority; second via service as chief
inspector's clerk; third by competition among sergeants; and

fourth, as a result of special promotion granted by the Inspector General in reward for exceptional service. In practice, however, sergeants were usually promoted by seniority, the average sergeant having served sixteen years in the rank before rising to head constable. However, one's religion and membership of Freemasonry appear to have affected one's chances of promotion. An ex-RIC officer noted:

> Illiteracy and stupidity are no bar [to promotion] if the character of the Protestant is even fairly good and we have known Protestants having bad records, who, after a period of freedom from complaint were promoted to all grades, even the rank of District Inspector. Not only have the Protestants the sympathy and support of the great majority of the officers, but they have behind them the Protestant and Freemason influence of the country. A County Inspector will not neglect the request of the Parson or treat lightly the whisperings of the Mason with whom he dines and sups at the local lodge or club. . . . The position of the Protestants in the Constabulary is never in doubt. But if Protestantism is a good recommendation for the Irish policeman, Freemasonry is better still.[49]

As has been noted, the force was housed in barracks or huts. For the most part they were not purpose-built but rather were hired houses held on a yearly tenancy or under a lease for twenty-one years with a provision for surrender of the lease at seven or four years.[50] The Irish administration, ever with an eye for economy, an eye especially keen where the police were concerned, also utilized old military barracks or disused Bridewells maintained by the Board of Works.[51] Much of the accommodation was shabby, none more so than the Central RIC barracks at Phoenix Park, Dublin, where three baths were made to meet the needs of 500 men.[52] When suggestions were made to relieve the fetid conditions a lengthy parliamentary debate ensued in England over the addition of a further six baths.

Constables also had to request permission to marry — and then could do so only after ten years' service and when the bride had been approved by the commanding officer. Similarly, constables were not allowed to serve in the district in which they had been born or recruited; they had no recognized off-duty period, day of rest or annual leave; they were confined to barracks at night; and they could not vote. Discipline was extremely authoritarian and police service came to resemble, in due course, more of a sacrifice than a rewarding occupation. These conditions were only exacerbated by the increasingly inadequate pay. What improvements were granted failed to keep pace either with the rising prices or with the wages of fellow workers who had effectively organized into trade unions — the police were not allowed to unionize. Thus the RIC had to run fast to stay financially in the same place. Frustration and stagnation within the force increased further, when in 1915, as a result of the Police (Emergency Provisions) Act, all resignation and retirements were stopped for the duration of the war. Promotion thus came to a full stop. Since emigration from Ireland was also stopped, frustration in the country, as well as in the force, became bottlenecked. With the escalating internal political crisis there seemed little or no future in police service. Antagonism, then boycott and violence, began to be directed against members or potential recruits. Policing in Ireland by 1917 had ceased to be a rewarding, a respectable or a safe pursuit.

THE ADMINISTRATION, THE POLICE
AND THE BEGINNING OF THE DECLINE
OF PUBLIC SECURITY

It is a central premise of this work that one vital aspect of a government's responsibility with regard to the maintenance of public security — its intelligence system — holds the key to the tactics of the government in a crisis situation. In the short term a sophisticated intelligence system can help to accomplish either the containment or defeat of an anti-system threat. Without detailed information as to the organization, personnel and strategies of a militant subversive group or groups, the incumbents have to act 'blind'. Lacking insight into the path events are taking, without a measure of empathy with the rebels, government becomes reactive rather than preventive. By infiltration and the use of informers it is possible to know where, how, when and by what means the insurgents are acting. Moreover, where this technique is perfected, it is possible not only to slow the pace of the insurgent movement but to divert it from its path by controlling it. Throughout Irish history the British had demonstrated considerable skill at infiltration and intelligence operations. It was perhaps a reflection of the general malaise affecting this Dublin Castle administration that this expertise should be replaced, during the first two decades of the twentieth century, by ineptitude. It was not until the summer and autumn of 1920, halfway through the War of Independence, that the British government made serious and systematic efforts to shore up the ailing Irish administration. Only then, as we shall see, were intelligence operations restructured and British intelligence given every encouragement, financial and political, to reassert itself.

Naturally, like the police force, the RIC intelligence system was very much a creature of crisis. It had come into being as a product of the various rebellious upsurges in nineteenth-century Ireland. The system turned upon Dublin Castle. The intelligence system, or at least the collection, sifting and collation of political intelligence, was extremely rigid and centralized. In every police station of Ireland the station sergeant was required to submit information to his district inspector, who, if he thought the material worthwhile, would forward it to the county inspector. The latter, in turn, forwarded yet another precis to force HQ and the 'Crime, Special Branch' in Dublin. Throughout most of the period under discussion, the 'Crime, Special Branch' section of the RIC had remained an incredibly small establishment, consisting of just a chief inspector and a district inspector who had been specially selected for duty. The two officers took it in turns to visit all parts of the country to discuss Special Branch affairs with local officers and men. In time all the important intelligence gleanings were gathered into a monthly report, forwarded to the Under-Secretary and eventually to the Chief Secretary and Lord Lieutenant. This system remained the same from the 1860s down to 1920. Thus, like both the overall police structure and the administration, the Special Branch too lapsed into suspended animation and decline. Indeed, it is impossible to view the decline of these segments of the Castle administration in isolation; rather was the inadequate condition of the public security structures reflective of the overall malaise in, and retreat of, the Dublin Castle administration from the 1880s onwards. As the leading executive instrument of Dublin Castle, the RIC was thus a cameo of the administration. Naturally the policy of the RIC was also the product of the general policy orientation of the Irish office and the home government in England. That policy, certainly from the turn of the century if not from 1880, was one of disengagement. Yet the disengagement was covert, characterized by one author as 'concealed abdication'.[53] Sir Neville Chamberlain, Inspector General of the RIC, giving evidence before the Royal Commission inquiring into the Easter Rising, was of the opinion that 'unquestionably the policy of non-intervention, which was practised, tended to discourage activity on the part of the police and inclined them to turn a blind eye on what was going on'.[54] Thus the overall policy for Ireland was reflected, at one remove, in the policy and actions, or rather the enforced inaction, of the police and police intelligence.

This withdrawal and lack of administrative vigour was singularly unfortunately timed. It coincided with a battle for the political will of the Irish people which had increasingly been at the crux of Irish affairs since the 1880s. Britain had at first held the initiative. The majority of Irishmen remained faithful to the 'colonial' administration down to 1916. However, that initiative had begun to be eroded long before 1916. There appear to have been several factors to which this development can be attributed. First, Irish support for the British presence was lost because of the completely inadequate way in which Ireland was being governed. Second, allegiance began to change because of the contemporaneous growth of a separatist cultural-spiritual-subversive movement throughout the country. Later chapters will focus upon both the genesis and nature of that movement in both its military and spiritual forms.

It was the condition of the administration though that triggered so much of the malaise in Ireland at this time. The administration lacked vigour and was devoid of real authority. By 1914, with the Home Rule Bill on the Statute Book, the Irish administration had become a 'lame duck' —

this despite the fact that application of the Bill was deferred
until after the end of the First World War. Similarly, one of
the few measures to be rigorously enforced was a policy of
stringent economy in all departments of the Irish Office.[55]
Commencing in the 1890s, the financial retrenchment[56] was
compounded by the survival of laissez-faire concepts of
governance – in essence, that time would heal Ireland.
Governing Ireland became a mere holding operation. The
rationale of policy and action, or rather the lack of both, was
to avoid inflaming Ireland's brewing discontent.

At the nub of the desire to avoid political crises was the
ability of the dying Irish Parliamentary Party to still cause
anxiety to the government of the day in the lobbies of the
House of Commons. Its potential opposition was sufficient to
induce the discontinuation of the 1881 Peace Preservation
Act (Arms Act) when it was the one real litigious power that
the Castle administration possessed for controlling the use
and importation of arms. The Act of 1881 had been passed at
the height of a rash of agrarian disorders. Amended and
continued for one year by the Act of 1886, it was later
extended for a further five years by the Criminal Law Procedure (Ireland) Act of 1887. Section 8(a) of that Act
determined that the measure should be continued from year
to year under inclusion in the Schedule of the Annual Ex-
piring Laws Continuance Act. In 1906 a major debate ensued
over the issue of whether or not to retain the Act. The
Resident Magistrates and police administrators advised reten-
tion of the Act. The British government however was aware
that the Act had been debated each year since 1900 –
members of the then-serving 1906 Cabinet had voted against
it. In 1900 five members of the 1906 Cabinet had voted
against it at the third reading; in 1902 three members; in
1904 one member voted against its omission from the

Schedule; in 1905 an additional two members voted against
its omission. Clearly, there was a division of opinion within
the Cabinet. Thus the law was allowed to expire quietly
because,

> the Irish Nationalists will vote its exclusion and a debate will arise
> which may occupy some little time and excite some feeling. Refer-
> ence will be made to votes given by the members of the Government
> to it.[57]

In short, it was expedient to do nothing. This piece of
politicking resulted in an influx of arms into Ireland. The
Irish Catholic newspaper somewhat unpatriotically reported
in 1909 that 'it is nothing short of an astounding evil to
repeal the Peace Preservation Act. For months past arms have
been pouring into the provincial districts'.[58] The only
remaining power to control that importation was an ancient
and inadequate Riot Act of the Irish Parliament[59] and a Gun
Licence Act of 1870 which could only be enforced by the
Customs and Excise Department.[60]

Not one, but successive British administrations refused to
take a stand over Irish issues. What few teeth the police still
possessed were effectively drawn by political expediency.
Colonel Edgeworth Johnstone of the RIC reported,

> I have this force under my command with an Assistant Commis-
> sioner to assist me and I have a freehand as regards discipline —
> practically a freehand as regards discipline so far as ordinary
> breaches of the law are concerned, but in cases where there is any
> political tinge of any kind, everything has to be referred to the
> Under Secretary. . . . Anything that would involve, for instance, the
> arrest of any of those Sinn Feiners, or anything of that sort, I mean
> — in a case of that kind I daren't move on my own initiative.[61]

Ireland was to be kept quiet almost at any cost. The law, if thoroughly enforced, would be provocative. The expedient solution was simple − the law not enforced. Sir Neville Macready, later to have command of the security forces in Ireland, wrote of the effect of such a policy upon the RIC that,

> This once magnificent body of men had undoubtedly deteriorated into what was almost a state of supine lethargy, and had lost even the semblance of energy or initiative when a crisis demanded vigorous and resolute action. The immediate reason was not far to seek. If an officer of whatever rank took it upon himself to enforce the law, especially during the faction fights which are the popular pastime of the Irish, this action would as often as not be disavowed by the authorities at Dublin, on complaint being made to them by the Irish politicians by whose favour the Government held office. This is no idle assertion on my part.[62]

The RIC was cut back because of grumblings in the British press and constituencies about its cost. A letter to the Lord Lieutenant of Ireland in 1895 stated that 'the question of maintaining so large and expensive a force as the RIC is one that has frequently engaged public attention'.[63]

The treatment afforded the police, and particularly the Special Branch of the RIC, is in itself indicative of the loss of political will and lack of determination to hold on to Ireland felt by both the British people and their government. Special Branch activities were reduced even after the lesson provided by the 1916 Easter Rising that an Irish government could not ignore the warnings of its police intelligence apparatus without encountering serious consequences. As late as 1919 the extra allowance to the RIC Special Branch was cut altogether. Ormonde Winter, later to command a rejuvenated British intelligence apparatus in Ireland in 1920, stated that it was 'the parsimony of Birrell', Chief Secretary of Ireland 29 January 1907 to 11 August 1916,[64] that,

> had resulted in the decline of the Secret Service Organisation; and the Police Commission of 1919, by the abolition of the extra allowance to the Crimes Special Branch of the RIC [which] went far to limit the zeal of those man.[65]

Prior to 1920 only one significant attempt to reform the vital intelligence apparatus was made. H. E. Duke, the Chief Secretary to replace Birrell, tried to systematize the disparate intelligence groups. In a memo submitted to the Cabinet[66] he stated that,

> the General Officer Commanding in Chief and the two Chiefs of Police argue, and the heads of the Administration concur in the view that there is urgent necessity for better organisation, and some development of the branch of police investigation which deals with criminal conspiracies and other classes of organised crime and especially with the plotting of revolutionary movements and disorder akin thereto. . . . I am satisfied that the present organisation of C.I.D. in Ireland is entirely inadequate. . . . Scotland Yard, M.I.5 the censorship and C.I.D. of the Irish police forces require to be associated for the purpose of intelligence mutual action.[67]

Included in the memorandum from the Chief Secretary was a detailed description of the existing hotch-potch of intelligence groups he was hoping to centralize. Prepared by the Inspector General of the RIC, the report is worth quoting at length. It provides an excellent picture of the intelligence groups operating in Ireland prior to the reorganization of 1920. The report stated that:

a) The Chief Commissioner of the [Dublin] Metropolitan Police has
under him a special service division (known as the G Division)
dealing with the investigation of crime. A number of selected men
from this division are employed on work connected with political
crime and intelligence.

b) The Inspector General of the RIC has under him a Crimes Branch
and a Special Crimes Branch. The former, which is staffed with
civilians, deals with ordinary crime as distinguished from political
crime, and is to a great extent merely a record office. The actual
police work connected with these ordinary crimes is as a rule
dealt with by the local Police. The dividing line between political
crime and ordinary crime in Ireland is often a very narrow one.
The 'Special Crimes Branch', which deals with political crime, is
in charge of a County Inspector and he has under him a District
Inspector and a few sergeants and constables. There are however
in each county certain sergeants and constables whose duty it is
to keep in touch with political matters throughout the county.
These constabulary although belonging to the 'Crimes Special
Branch' make their reports through the County Inspector. The
County Inspectors are, in addition, permitted to apply to the
Inspector General for small sums of money to be expended in
secret service when suitable occasions occur.

c) The G.O.C. in Chief has under him a Special Intelligence Branch
which to a large extent deals with political matters. There has
been placed at his disposal a County Inspector (Major Ivor Price)
and two constabulary officials from the 'Crime Special Branch'.
The information gained by this Branch is chiefly obtained from
the police, supplemented by information from military censors
and military intelligence departments of the War Office. I understand that four or five military intelligence officers have now
been appointed for work in the county districts.

d) Admiralty Intelligence. This is under the charge of Mr. Harrell,
Assistant Commissioner of the D.M.P. It only employs a small
personnel and need not be considered in any scheme of
amalgamation, although it would doubtless benefit from an improvement of the existing system.[68]

The Chief Secretary urged co-ordination and centalization in Dublin which he saw as the brain of any seditious movement. His recommendations were not acted upon. The opportunity to regain some lost initiative passed. Duke himself left office on 11 May 1918. His concern for rearranging intelligence was not sustained by his successor.

This overlapping and duplication of the intelligence services was severely to hamper British efforts to counter the growing threat posed by the Irish underground. However, the muddle in the intelligence sphere was symptomatic of the general condition of the Irish administration. It was not merely the detection of offenders, political and otherwise, that became inadequate: prosecution of all crimes lapsed. In part this was a product of the overall administrative incapacity. That incapacity was exacerbated when the Irish underground, the Volunteers or IRA, began to terrorize jurors and magistrates. Difficulty was found in enforcing the law over minor matters. Again the decline in prosecutions coincided significantly with the retrenchment of the administration generally and political and economic strictures imposed upon the police in particular. The condition of a secure public and vigorous prosecution of the law seemed to be passing into abeyance – especially on the streets of Dublin and Belfast.

The Chief Secretary, Augustine Birrell, more than anyone other public person, must shoulder the brunt of the responsibility for the decline in the condition of both the security services and public security. He was Chief Secretary for Ireland during the critical eight-year period 1907-16. Undoubtedly Birrell achieved much in the realms of education and land reform. Indeed, at first he was most enthusiastic about his new job and followed the activities of the Irish underground with interest. He also supported the police in vigorous prosecution of offenders. However, he wearied of his job, especially after his wife's death. By 1915, he could write 'I am only waiting for an opportunity to bid the world of politics goodnight — but the opportunity never comes.'[69] At a vital time in Irish affairs Birrell demonstrably lacked both the will and conviction to fight the increasingly violent and organized opposition. Despite the innumerable police reports dispatched to him stating that something was brewing in and around Dublin, Birrell could calmly write 'Ireland is always quiet and peaceful. It is in England all the fuss is made.'[70] Thus, while Birrell was surprised by the Easter Rising the police were not. Small wonder then that the Royal Commission of Inquiry into the 1916 revolt should report that,

> The main cause of the rebellion appears to be that lawlessness was allowed to grow up unchecked and that Ireland for several years had been administered on the principle that it was safer and more expedient to leave law in abeyance if collision with any faction of the Irish people could thereby be avoided.[71]

By a variety of techniques of civil disobedience running through a spectrum from strikes, boycotts, demonstrations, marches and riots to rebellion and finally to the organization of the infra-structure of alternative government, the formal rules and political will of the regime in Ireland were tested, found wanting and then broke. Neither the regime's legitimacy, for it had little, nor its authority, which it had effectively lost by 1919, nor its instruments of force, the police, fast becoming effete, were able to contain or control the level of anti-systemic conflict. Even prior to the 1916 Rising, which effectively demonstrated the myopia of the Irish administration's leading personnel and the lack of preparedness on the part of its security units, both police and Dublin

Castle had shown their attitudinal and organizational in-adequacies. The tasks that were eventually faced by the administration and security forces proved to be beyond their capacity for effective response — a result of years of malad-ministration. Increasingly, as we shall see in subsequent chapters, the Irish administration yielded its authority and even responsibilities for law enforcement to the Volunteers or IRA. It was the combination of decline on the part of the British and the emergence of not only a vibrant Irish national consciousness but the evolution of the tactics, will and instru-ments of an armed alternative government, that stimulated the revolutionary War of Independence in 1919-21 and ultimately broke not only security but the British presence in Ireland . To a consideration of the emergence of that alter-native underground government, the opposition, the narrative now turns.

NOTES

1. See B. Chapman, *The Police State,* (London, 1970).
2. 27 GEO 3 cap 40.
3. H. L. Adam, *The Police Encyclopaedia,* 8 vols (London, 1912) 158.
4. 32 GEO 3 cap 16.
5. 54 GEO 3 cap 131.
6. *Hansard,* 28 (23 June 1814) 163.
7. ibid. for the debates.
8. *Hansard,* 7 (7 June 1822) 22: Constables (Ireland) Bill.
9. Peel's plan consisted of creating a force based upon the counties with detachments commanded by chief constables. The local

magistrates were to direct the operation of the force. However, the Irish government and not the magistrates would select the chief constables and the force as well as being able to dismiss and discipline them. See 'Peel to Wellesley', 12 April 1882, Wellesley Papers, British Museum Add MS. 37299.

10. *Hansard,* 7, op. cit.: Sir Henry Parnell in the House of Commons. The Bill provoked opposition elsewhere — a correspondent in the Annual Register of 1822 saw the PPF as 'a species of *gens d'armerie,* hitherto unknown to the laws or practices of a British Government'.

11. Peel in the House — *Hansard,* op. cit. (22 April 1822) 1553.

12. 3 GEO 103 (5 August 1822).

13. ibid.

14. *Hansard,* 31 (18 February 1836) 553.

15. ibid., 6, (7 June 1882) 861.

16. The first inspector general was Colonel Shaw Kennedy who had supervised the return of the British Army of Occupation from France and who had experience of police work in London. ibid. 540.

17. Note F. C. Mather, *Public Order in the Age of the Chartists* (Manchester, 1959) 108, where he refers to 'the approval of the community which is so essential for the proper functioning of the constabulary'.

18. Sinn Fein pamphlet, series No. 12: *The Case of Ireland* 3.

19. The Bill was introduced into the House of Commons on 10 August 1835. *Hansard,* 30 (10 August 1835) 1189.

20. 'Amount of force employed in each County or City in Ireland' January 1840, H.O. 1840 (290) XLVIII, 159.

21. ibid.

22. ibid and H. C. 1850 (431) January ci 287.

23. HO 154. Returns of RIC personnel 1841-1919 and HO 184 *Auxiliary Journals,* LII(1) and LIII(2).

24. *Constabulary Gazette* XLI(2) (10 August 1918).

25. ibid. XXXIX(7) (4 September 1916).

26. Irish Police Forces Commission of Inquiry, Cd 7637 (1914), Appendix 15, 346.

27. Royal Commission on Rebellion in Ireland, Cd 8279 (1916), Minutes of Evidence and Appendix.

28. CO 904/174/2 Part I Military Status of the Police 1912-1915.

29. CO 904/174/1. 20 October 1895 Harrell to Lord Lieutenant.

30. Quoted in R. Hawkins, 'Dublin Castle and the RIC 1916-1922 in T. D. Williams (ed.) *The Irish Struggle* (London 1968). See also the *Constabulary Gazette* XL(47) (21 June 1919).

31. CO 904/174/1. RIC mobilization.

32. Cd 7421, 33. The barracks also contained a cell consisting of a 'small stone-paved room, unheated by any means, without windows other than scattered ventilators, open at all seasons, and provided only with a wooden couch without mattress or covering'. *Hansard* 21 (16 February 1911) 1214.

33. *Constabulary Gazette* XLI(2) (10 August 1918).

34. Cd 7421 'Irish Police Forces', 25.

35. ibid. part 2 95 (i).

36. The allocation of constables was made to meet annual requirements and was subject to revision at any time under the Constabulary and Police (Ireland) Act of 1914, by order of the Lord Lieutenant. For further details and allotment of officers, see the 'Report of the Proceedings of the Irish Convention', Cd 9019 (1918) Schedule A — 'Memorandum on the Question of Police Administration Under the Irish Government', 121.

37. See Table 2.

38. Cd 7421, 22. With regard to these administrative divisions it is interesting to note Sir Neville Chamberlain's remark as inspector general of the RIC in 1916 that 'It seems to me there is not much meaning in these terms though they are still perpetuated. The force is one force for all intents and purposes.' Cd 8279, 192.

39. CO 906/27: Notes on Police Forces. A report on the Special Constabulary in Norther Ireland by General Ricardo.

40. Cd 7421, 26.

41. ibid.

42. ibid.

43. ibid.

44. ibid., 98(4), 26. The Revenue Force was originally constituted to suppress illicit liquor distillation.

45. *Irish Police Forces.* Report of the Committee of Inquiry, 1914. Cd 7637, 182.

46. Quoted in R. Fosdick, *European Police Systems* (New Jersey, 1969), 201.

47. CO 904/174/1, op. cit.

48. ibid.

49. *Promotion in the RIC* by 'One Who Knows' (Dublin, 1906), 8.

50. Cd 7637.

51. Cd 9019, Irish Convention, 122.

52. *Hansard* 193 (25 July 1908), 2089.

53. Hawkins, op. cit., 169.

54. Cd 8279 (25 May 1916), 48.

55. CO 904/172/2: Establishment and Salaries of Chief Secretaries Office.

56. CO/174/1, op. cit.

57. For this whole issue see the Bryce Papers MS. 11,009(3), National Library, Dublin.

58. *Hansard* 1 (23 February 1909), 596.

59. 27 GEO cap 15.

60. CBS (Crime Branch Special), ex-Green File 28 (April 1913), State Papers Office, Dublin Castle.

61. Cd 8279 (1916), 51.

62. Sir Neville Macready, *Annals of an Active Life,* Vol. I (London, 1924), 179.

63. CO 904/174/1 (20 October 1895).

64. MS. 8166 List of Chief Secretaries (Ireland 1797-1921) National Library, Dublin.

65. Sir Ormonde Winter, *Winter's Tale* (London, 1955), 290.

66. CAB 37/154/1, 7-8.

67. ibid.

68. ibid.

69. Letter to T. P. Le Fanu, 21 February 1915, MS. 8.3 (3) Birrell Papers, Liverpool University Library.

70. ibid. MS. 8.2 (3), 1915.

71. Cd 8279, 12.

2

THE EVOLUTION OF OPPOSITION:
The Inspiration, Organization and Tactics
of the Irish Underground

The Irish race is preeminently intuitive, that is to say, it feels its
conclusions rather than thinks them and often proceeds direct from
feeling to action, which subsequent events fully justify, though
reasoned calculation would have condemned. Its genius in this
respect rests on a radical difference of psychology, a sealed book to
John Bull, and to all peoples devoid of the education of untamed
suffering necessary to read it . . . .

Sinn Fein and the Gaelic League . . . in isolating the national
spirit from foreign influence and reviving the national past, not only
enhance the consciousness of each individual, but bring to bear a
great combining force to weld individuals together. . . . For good or
ill, not intellect but emotion is the element of agreement and
combination among men, whether their combination is that of
wolves who hunt their prey, or of bees who make their honey in
common.

Two great emotional forces make for the unity of Ireland, her
nationality and her religion. . . . Sinn Fein seeks to restore the soul.

J. R. White, The Significance of Sinn Fein
— Psychological, Political and Economic
(Martin Lester, Dublin 1918), pp. 5-9.

In the previous chapter some aspects of the decline of governability and, consequently, the onset of the breakdown of public security in Ireland were discussed. That decline, was, however, exacerbated by the development of a revived, vibrant, violent Irish political culture taking the form of an almost messianic nationalism. In time this resurgent nationalism led to the creation, throughout the local communities of Ireland, of viable alternative social, judicial and governmental structures and to the emergence of a cohesive, politico-military structure in the shape of the Irish Volunteers or Irish Republican Army.[1] Together these social, psychological, political, administrative and military factors, coalescing in 1919 and 1920, went to make up the constituent parts of a sophisticated Irish underground which first filled the increasing void left by the declining Dublin Castle administration and finally supplanted it. It is upon the emergence of this alternative government and belief system – the motivation and organization of the opposition to the British in Ireland – that this chapter concentrates.

THE EVOLUTION OF REVOLUTIONARY
STRATEGY

Ireland was dogged by a tradition of equivocal policy on the part of English politicians, composed of a mixture of conciliation and coercion – neither course being resolutely pursued. There developed, in response, a matching duality of Irish protest. Historically, Irish resistance to British rule was made up of unequal parts of constitutional agitation and revolutionary violence. Down to the opening years of the twentieth century and the eclipse of the constitutionalist Irish Parliamentary Party as a force in Ireland's affairs, both at home and in Westminster, the imbalance marginally favoured constitutionalism. Yet, slowly, Irish sedition passed through a series of tactical evolutions. Constitutionalism was rejected. A growing awareness manifested itself that 'England would never concede self-government to the force of argument only to the argument of force'.[2] The crucial transitional stage in tactics came during the 1880s and 1890s when not only was a new resolute notion of Irish independence incubating, but the constitutional solution was passing with the character assassination of Charles Stuart Parnell. While as late as 1914 there was a remote chance that home rule would be granted by the British, the posture of Carsonite Ulster indicated that at some stage a measure of violence would be necessary to enforce independence.

Superficially, the Land League agitation of 1879-82 excepted, the period 1870-90 was unusually quiet. In a country noted for political effervescence the calm was unsteadying. It was also misleading. Yet there were changes taking place in Ireland which were cerebral and hence not immediately visible. Importantly, this period saw the end of agrarian-centred protest as the dominant style of Irish political disturbance. A more sophisticated notion of revolutionary republicanism was replacing outmoded rick-burning. In time a European mode of protest, selective political assassination, was to be adopted and justified as legitimate. If one wishes to understand the events, the scale of violence and the nature of the political conduct during the War of Independence 1919-21 and its climax in November 1920 with 'Bloody Sunday', the earlier metamorphoses of Irish resistance must be grasped.

At the nub of both Anglo-Irish and Irish civil disobedience

was an extremely hazy dichotomy between moral and physical force. The Irish political activists frequently hopped from one camp to the other with alacrity at the behest of event, circumstance or mere whim. Yet the gun was never long absent from Irish politics. Similarly, the Irish displayed a relish for clandestine political activity. And there persisted, like some military albatross, the tactical dinosaur of the 'once and for all' periodic insurrection. It was not until the total *military* failure of 1916 that this particular bogey was buried. After 1916, under the influence of Michael Collins and Tom Barry, attrition rather than cataclysm became the tactical expedient. It is especially instructive here to detail, succinctly, the major examples of Irish political disobedience that impinge upon our story – that is, those that help explain the evolution of revolutionary strategy and help locate the roots of the tactics and structures employed by the Volunteers or IRA during the War of Independence 1916-21.

The Secret Societies

The secret societies were Ireland's primitive rebels. They were agrarian both in goals and membership. One of the earliest such societies recorded in Ireland is the Defenders, connected with the insurrection of 1641. In Ireland at that time Roman Catholicism had been proscribed – worship at that particular altar had thus to be performed in secret. An alliance – a periodic one in Irish history – grew up between rebel and priest, since both were branded outlaws. Thus, while priest and congregation celebrated Mass in some remote glen, the Defenders held the mountain passes and tracks. Irish priests therefore came to be held responsible for the disturbed state of the countryside, were proclaimed guilty of rebellion *en masse* and sentenced to death. As an extra inducement to those who pursued the priest, the £5 reward given for a wolf's head was also offered for his.

The secret societies were agrarian both in their goals and in their membership. Directed against the landlord and the tithe and towards the relief of their own abject poverty, theirs was the restricted aim of alleviating local grievances. They were the archetypal primitive rebels – conservative, reactionary, seeking piecemeal change and lacking an ideology. A tendency to schism, product of their localism, was their greatest weakness. Indeed, it was not until the birth of the United Irishmen under Wolfe Tone's leadership in 1798 that the divided clandestine segments of Irish resistance, for a time at least, took on a measure of unity embracing Tone's ideal of a Brotherhood of Irishmen. Tone himself recognized the weakness of schism when he wrote,

> Our provinces are ignorant of each other, uncemented, like the image which Nebuchadnezzar saw, with a head of fine gold, legs of iron and feet of clay, parts that do not cleave together – we must unite them – that is our end.[3]

Indeed, it was Tone's United Irishmen who were the first Irish rebels in the modern period to create serious and widespread alarm in both the Irish and Westminster administrations.

The United Irishmen

Tone wrote,

> the establishment of a republic was not the immediate object of my speculations. My object was to secure the independence of my

country under any form of government, to which I was led by a
hatred of England so deeply rooted in my nature that it was rather
an instinct than a principle.[4]

Fear of revolt by the United Irishmen was exacerbated
when in 1793, with England at war with the new French
Republic, Tone declared his allegiance with France. Despite
Tone's capture, deportation and the political suppression of
the movement, it revived in 1795. By this time it was more
efficiently organized, the Supreme Executive containing men
like Thomas Emmet and Edward Fitzgerald, a former British
Army officer who formulated the military planning. Success
seemed possible when in 1796 a force of 15,000 Frenchmen
sailed for Ireland. However, the invasion fleet was shattered
and prevented from landing by storms. In 1797 the British
government moved against the rebels, who despite this set-
back and without French assistance rose in 1798. The revolt
was speedily and viciously suppressed by General Lake. With
its leadership imprisoned, and the movement shot through
with police agents and informers, the rising collapsed into
ignominious defeat. Tone, again captured, and sentenced to
be hanged, drawn and quartered, cheated the hangman by
committing suicide in his prison cell. Despite his aim of
liberating Ireland from external dominance by England, the
inconsistency of attaching that cause to the French *petard*
seems to have escaped Tone.

Robert Emmet and the Plan of 1803

Emmet's was the epitomy of the bungled revolt. It began
ostensibly in the early morning of Saturday, 23 July 1803.
Widespread support seemed guaranteed, yet no more than

eighty men eventually took to the Dublin streets. It is particularly rewarding to follow its course through Emmet's own account since this draws out the make-believe world in which Irish revolutionaries lived at that time. Planning, it seems, was a tiresome burden. Action was everything. Emmet wrote,

> The whole of the plan was given up by me for want of means, except the Castle [which he intended to capture] and lines of defence; for I expected 300 Wexford, 400 Kildare and 200 Wicklow men, all of whom had fought before [with Tone in 1798] to begin the surprises at this side of the water and by the preparation for defence so as to give time for the whole to assemble. The County of Dublin was also to act at the instant it began; the number of Dublin people acquainted with it I understood to be three or four thousand. I estimated 2,000 to assemble at Costigans Mills – the grand place of assembly. The evening before the Wicklow men failed through their officer. The Kildare men, who were to act particularly with me, came in and at five o'clock were off again . . . . on a report from two of their officers that Dublin would not act. In Dublin itself, it was given out by some treacherous or cowardly person, that it was postponed till Wednesday. The time of assembly was from six till nine and at nine instead of 2,000 there were eighty men assembled. When we came to the marked houses, we were diminished to eighteen or twenty.[5]

The preparations for arming the revolt went even more awry. There were scarcely any blunderbusses; the man who was to turn the fuses and rammers forget them; jointed pikes were lost by an explosion in Patrick Street, Dublin; the slow matches for the 'grenades' could not be found; cramp-irons could not be collected in time from the smiths; and the scaling ladders necessary for the attack on the Castle were not finished.[6] As Emmet concluded, 'There was failure in all

— plan, preparation and men.'[7] The insurrection scarcely reached the proportions of a street riot.

O'Connell and the Constitutionalism of the Catholic Association

Perhaps it was the abject failure of these two armed insurrections that caused Irishmen to transfer their political activism and enthusiasm for independence to the moderate, constitutionally orientated Catholic Association of O'Connell. Established in 1823, the most significant contribution of the association to the cause of Irish independence was the measure of Irish Catholic unity that it created.[8] The Catholic Bishop of Limerick, Dr Jebb, suggested that the Association had created 'What we of this generation have never before witnessed, a complete union of the Roman Catholic body . . . . In truth an Irish revolution has in great measure been effected.'[9]

Yet the association's impact did not go deep into the Irish political psyche. The Revolt of 1848 reverted to the established military pattern of disorganized all-out abortive insurrection. Planned by social romantics at the height of Ireland's worst famine, it stood scant chance of success. The Royal Irish Constabulary had infiltrated what organization there was; the leadership was uninspiring and planning minimal. Paradoxically though it was out of the military disasters of 1848 — and out of the severe famine in particular — that the most significant of Ireland's revolutionary societies, the Fenians or Irish Republican Brotherhood, emerged.

The Fenians

The Fenians were dedicated physical force men. Not for them the well worn moderate clichés of a constitutional search for independence. Military action and targeted political violence were their chosen modes of political action. They developed to a high point the philosophy that independence could be won only by force of arms. By so doing they achieved the vital, initial revolutionary reorientation, from a dedication to the redress of narrow local grievances to the total commitment to a more abstract and intangible ideal — Ireland for the Irish. Fenianism, however, not only added a new dimension to Irish revolutionary thought, but succeeded in preserving whatever was of merit in the Irish revolutionary or military past. Thus Fenianism was also at the heart of the survival of the useful parts of the Irish revolutionary tradition. It became the convenant of political violence from one generation to another. It was 'the channel through which the revolutionary tradition was transmitted . . . it links the United Irishmen of 1798 and the Young Irelanders of 1848 with Pearse, Clarke and Connolly'.[10] And, one might add, with the military genius of the 1916-21 independence struggle, Michael Collins.

Yet historians have attributed too great an importance to the Fenians as the sole base from which the 1916 and 1919-21 struggles were launched. There is ample evidence that the really significant development of tactics and the stimuli for a protracted people's revolutionary war, with systematic terror at its centre, took place outside the framework of Fenianism. The revolutionary groups already examined, including the Fenians, may have provided some of the theoretical preconditions for a tactical change of emphasis. However, they had a less important part in establish-

ing systematic terror as the tactical vanguard of the revolutionary war. From whichever standpoint the Irish independence struggle is examined, its successful, if partial, completion in 1921 was brought about by the impact of terror.
Ireland's independence, the total breakdown of public
security and the collapse of the RIC were accomplished not
by the constitutionalist, the Fenian insurrectionist or petty
dynamitard, but by the professional assassin for whom one
group, the Irish Nationalist Invincibles, prepared the ground.

The Irish Nationalist Invincibles

Easter 1916, and also the risings of 1798, 1848 and 1867, all
revealed an *idée fixe* at work in Irish revolutionary thought.
As we have seen, the goal was 'once-and-for-all' success; an
all-out engagement, committing forces totally in a static
battle for a well defended position. Little tactical or strategic
thinking was done by those in the revolutionary mainstream.
No practical initiatives were taken to develop the techniques
of protracted war. The Invincibles, a radical offshoot of
Fenianism, took the first practical steps towards a tactical
reorientation. It was their example or demonstration of the
military utility of systematic targeted assassination that was
later taken up by the guerrilla leader, Michael Collins.

The Invincibles were responsible for the assassination of
the Chief Secretary, Lord Frederick Cavendish, and his
Under-Secretary, Thomas Burke, in Phoenix Park, Dublin, on
6 May 1882. The act was a crucial tactical change. Its
conscious goal was the same as that behind Collins's advocacy
of selective assassination, namely, the wish to provoke a war
with England, in Ireland, so as to transfer the struggle for Irish
independence to the international arena.[11] Assassination, for

the Invincibles as for Collins, was to form the core of a war of attrition. Here then was a positive alternative to the military restrictions imposed by a belief in the need to wait for the right time. Through their tactics the Invincibles sought to determine the timing and scale of the conflict, an example on which Collins later improved. P. J. P. Tynan, a leading member of the Invincibles,[1][2] summarized the group's philosophy and drew a connection between the events of 1882 and the development of later tactics when he wrote,

> The enemy has trampled on his own constitution and torn into shreds the last strip of mock legality under which Ireland was supposed to be governed. A species of guerrilla was determined upon (it was the future making its appearance on the scene) to meet the relentless attacks of the invader . . . . the chiefs of Ireland's ravagers, the men from whose bureaux sped the orders of bloodshed and destruction . . . were termed by the enemy the 'Chief Secretary' and 'Under Secretary of State'. It was resolved by the earliest council held by the Executive of the Invincibles that these ferocious offices should be kept vacant by the continual 'suppression' of their holders. This order was not levelled at any particular or special occupant of these bloodstained posts of the foe, but against all and every succeeding foreign invader who came to occupy these 'suppressed' bureaux; and it was decided that as soon as a newcomer planted his foot on Irish soil, invested by the illegal alien administration with the authority of either these offices to perpetuate Britain's role of spoilation, they should at once be 'suppressed' in mercy to the Irish Nation, and further that every satrap of Britain carrying on and conducting her way of extermination in our part of the island should be summarily 'removed' from the scene of devastation.[13]

Coupled with this reorientation of strategy and tactical thinking was a change in the location of revolutionary protest. Previously the emphasis had been rural, but from 1880 onwards it was to become increasingly urban-centred. Dublin, Cork and Belfast became the foci of revolutionary military activity.[14] This change also brought about an alteration in the class composition of the militantly active. From the 1880s onwards there was a rapid decline in the conservative, middle-class leadership of Irish politics. It was a change parallelled by the equally speedy emergence of far more radical, separatist, lower-middle-class leaders epitomized by Padraig Pearse.[15] Strangely, there was little popular social radicalism other than that stimulated by the activities of James Connolly and Jim Larkin in Dublin. Theocratic Ireland was altogether too stultifying for that particular brand of radicalism to survive. Even so, the contribution of Larkin and Connolly to the military component of the later revolutionary war was significant. Connolly could write with some justification that, prior to his politico-military activities, the Fenian tradition of an exclusive coterie of zealots had dominated the mainstream of Irish revolutionary thinking.

> The thought of revolution was the exclusive possession of the few remnants of secret societies of a past generation [he wrote], and was never mentioned by them except with heads closely together and eyes fearfully glancing round; the socialists broke through this ridiculous secrecy and in hundreds of speeches in the most public places of the metropolis [Dublin] as well as in scores of thousands of pieces of literature scattered throughout the country, announced their purpose to muster all the forces of labour for a revolutionary reconstruction.[16]

Michael Collins was the inheritor of Connolly's lessons as well as of all the stimuli thrown up by the pantheon of Irish revolutionaries. Following Connolly's revolutionary framework, Collins sought to increase the participation of Irish men and women in the cause of independence. Collins, however, prepared the ground more thoroughly, though his task was made easier by the simultaneous cultural-spiritual revival and the impact of the 1916 'martyrdoms'. Collins began to prepare the Irish people for a war of independence through extensive propaganda. At the same time he developed his personal military vanguard by selecting a small strike force of assassins. The breakthrough that Collins achieved in the theory and practice of revolutionary war was not so much that he perceived the lessons of Irish revolutionary history — the need to eradicate informers and spies; the necessity of nullifying the police Special Branch while at the same time developing one's own intelligence network; and the political possibilities inherent in the military tactic of targeted assassination; rather, his politico-military genius was that he provided the correctives. Under his leadership spies, informers, and the police Special Branch were nullified. A class of professional killers came into being and intimidated almost every officer of the British administration in Ireland — an administration that was failing in quiet times, as we have seen, but which under strain broke down altogether. Assassination, in conjunction with both rural and urban guerrilla warfare, became the distinctive politico-military style of the Irish underground from 1919 to 1921. Michael Collins, it seems, had grasped the principle behind the Russian revolutionary dictum that,

> The terrorist cannot overthrow the government, cannot drive it from St. Petersburg and Russia, but having compelled it for so many years to do nothing but struggle with them, by forcing it to do so still for years and years, they will render its position untenable.[17]

In addition, the terror established by Collins had a direct set of practical effects. Primarily it was a weapon of intimidation directed against all officers of the administration and also against reluctant patriots. Crucially it also acted as an internal coercive sanction and removed the traitors, spies, informers and blackmailers who had bedevilled previous Irish insurrections. Thus the terror apparatus helped maintain solidarity behind Sinn Fein, as well as act as the swift arm of retributive revolutionary justice. Finally, through the vitally important and often neglected revolutionary medium of rumour,[18] the terror and the Irish cause reached a mass audience, not only in England and Ireland but internationally, through the medium of the press.

The terror was therefore vital to the success of the Irish underground, maintaining the Irish political will while at the same time destroying that of the British.

These were some of the mutations through which Irish revolutionary thinking and military tactics evolved prior to 1919. In essence it was a progression from rural protest to people's revolutionary war. At the nub of the progression was not only the development of the structures of underground government and the creation of a viable alternative government; not only the theoretical and tactical developments, but crucially the growth of a sacrificial religious nationalism and a political sub-culture of violence. It is to these latter developments in particular that we now turn.

RELIGIOUS NATIONALISM AND THE SUB-CULTURE OF VIOLENCE: THE UNION OF THE ROSARY AND THE GUN

> If . . . a revolution is to eventuate, a dynamic of a genuinely spiritual and religious kind is absolutely necessary . . . without a super-rational 'theological' dynamic, no great revolution is possible.[19]

Rooted in the changes occurring within the Irish political culture after 1880, the events of the period 1916-21 seem to validate Connolly's judgement that 'no nation can be enslaved if its people think death less hateful than bondage'.[20] An almost deceased and redundant Gaelic culture was successfully revived and proselytized throughout Ireland from the 1880s onwards. By 1919 it had become a prime mover in the creation of a dynamic and regenerated Irish Republican political will. An ethos had emerged to bind together the disparate forces for independence. It was an ethos steeped in militant Catholicism. Through its links with the revolutionary cause, the patriotic clergy and certain religious institutions sanctified the sacrifice of a life in the national cause and absolved the political assassin from sin. However, the Catholic Church of Ireland resisted throughout any alliance with the terrorists. Yet as we shall see, sectors of the Catholic priesthood and religious orders did espouse the Republican cause.

By 1920, backed by a popular movement for independence, political violence had become very much an integral part of the Irish way of life. Such violence had begun, as it certainly did in Palestine and seems to have done in many other insurgent situations, as an erratic, ragged, random set of acts destined to have little effect and then to disappear. Yet,

given an initial impetus, in Ireland the violence became increasingly organized, and grew in scale and effect, and the
perpetrators of that violence gradually edged their cause
towards legitimacy. The British administration in Ireland first
failed to sustain compliance from the minority of revolutionary activists and then from the mass of the Irish people.
By 1919 at the latest, the British administration in Ireland
was regarded as being no longer worthy of obedience. In the
place of allegiance to that administration there emerged a
faith in Catholic Republican nationalism. Alternative allegiance was given to the emerging institutions of a Republican
people's army and government. By 1920 the majority of Irish
men had transferred their allegiance to the Republican cause.
Dublin Castle and the British presence came to be regarded as
totally alien.

What was it that provoked such a transference of allegiance? What inspired the Republican revolutionary fighters?
It seems possible to suggest that there were at least three
principle stimuli: first, the influence of the cultural renaissance transmitted by the participation of many Irish people
in the covertly political cells and meetings of language and
literary associations; second, the influence of radical Republican clergymen in the localities; third, the violent sanctions
imposed by a ruthlessly efficient, politico-military underground aided by its superbly prepared propaganda. Together
these psychological, behavioural and structural stimuli provided the necessary element of facilitation for political disobedience.[21] If by these means they were not persuaded and
organized into tacit support for Republicanism, coercion
would be applied to native Irish men, women and children. In
Collins's eyes the end justified the means.

THE CULTURAL REGENERATION

By the 1840s, the Gaeltacht, that is the area in Ireland in which the Gaelic tongue was almost exclusively used, had dwindled. A Gaelic culture became the preserve of a minority of scholars. The depressed condition of the peasantry, the English presence and emigration all militated against the preservation of 'Irishness'. It was only when the severely depressed economic circumstances of Ireland had begun to ease, in the 1880s, that the nationalistic cultural societies began to prosper. Education rather than simple physical survival became a key issue in Irish politics. The Gaelic League (GL) came into existence on 31 July 1893 and the Gaelic Athletic Association (GAA) on 1 November 1884. These two groups can be taken as representative of the nature of the cultural renaissance since they were its vanguard. They had been presaged throughout the nineteenth century by cluster of cultural-linguistic societies such as the Gaelic Society, the Iberno-Celtic Society, the Celtic Society, the Irish Archaeological Society and the Ossianic Society.[22] The vital difference between these earlier groups and the GAA and GL was the emphasis that the latter placed upon separatism. Thomas Davis, one of the men of the abortive 1848 episode, identified the revolutionary potential inherent in a Gaelic revival when he wrote that,

> A nationality founded in the hearts and intelligence of the people would bid defiance to the arms of the foe and the guile of the traitor. The first step to nationality is the open and deliberate recognition of it by the people themselves. Once the Irish people declare the disconnection of themselves, their feelings and interests from the men, feelings and interests of England they are on the march for freedom.[23]

The Gaelic League was one of the most powerful movers of
the spiritual regeneration. Michael Collins, the guerrilla
leader, wrote,

> Irish history will recognise in the birth of the GL in 1893 the most
> important event of the 19th century. I may go further and say, not
> only the 19th century but in the whole history of our nation. It
> checked the peaceful penetration and once and for all turned the
> minds of the Irish people back to their own country. It did more
> than any other movement to restore the national pride, honour and
> self-respect. Through the medium of the language it linked the
> people with the past and led them to look at a future which would
> be a noble continuation of it.[24]

Collins perhaps gave undue emphasis to the League. There
was not one supremely important group but rather a coalescence of like-minded activists at some point after the
1916 Rising. The Catholic Church, the GL, the quasi-
monastic teaching order, the Christian Brothers, Collins himself, Padraig Pearse and earlier advocates of revolution such as
Thomas Mitchell, Tone, Emmet and the disciplining terror of
the IRA each played a part. The literary and romantic revival
of Synge, Yeats and others was an added embellishment.

But to return to the cultural revival. Both the GL and the
GAA had by the twentieth century become thoroughly
politicized. Despite the plea of the founder, Dr Hyde, in
1914 to members of the GL that,

> If you really desire to be true to the great and hopeful, and I will
> say, the fruitful ideas on which the GL was originally founded then I
> will ask you to keep politics and all contentious matter out of your
> branches during the coming winter.[25]

the League became a captive of Sinn Fein and the IRA

leadership. The *Freeman's Journal* duly recorded that,

> The Gaelic League has now, in effect, become the property of Sinn Fein. Its *Feiseanna* have been formed into Sinn Fein propaganda figure for their own political purposes . . . . Irish plays second fiddle to politics.[26]

Even so, the GL began to provide a meaningful alternative to the alien 'West Britonism' imposed by the Castle administration. It both educated and disciplined those who joined its ranks. Pearse, recognizing this, wrote in 1913 that,

> Our Gaelic League time was to be our tutelage; we had first to learn to know Ireland, to read the lineaments of her face, to understand the accents of her voice; to repossess ourselves, disinherited as we were, of her spirit and mind, re-enter into our mystical birthright. For this we went to school in the Gaelic League,. . . but we do not propose to remain schoolboys forever.[27]

An important adjunct to the GL was the GAA. Its message was directed particularly towards Ireland's young men. Importantly, it offered an alternative to English athletics and games traditionally sponsored by the police and military. An important point of contact and potential fraternity with the administration was thus lost. When, in like fashion to the GL, the GAA became politicized by the ideas of Sinn Fein and the Irish Republican Brotherhood cadre, it ostracized any Irishman playing other than GAA or 'Irish' games. Separatism, militancy and patriotism came to dominate the GAA. Great numbers of young men throughout Ireland took to the discipline and community offered by the GAA. Not since the early, heady days of O'Connell's Catholic Association had Irishmen been involved to such an extent in a political movement. Such involvement appears to have helped establish both individual and collective self-respect. Michael Collins in fact stressed that 'The Gaelic revival and the learning of our national tongue were teaching a new national self-respect.'[28]

The GL, or, as was often the case, the GAA and GL in tandem, became local sources of recruitment for the nationalist cause. One authority on the period notes that,

> Each GAA club became a social focus for the youth of an area . . . the movement spread with astonishing rapidity from parish to parish, the length and breadth of Ireland. It has been described as the first modern example of a national democratic movement, supervised by local and county committees, under completely Irish auspices.[29]

Together the GAA and GL began the habit of participation in an intentionally alternative culture. They provided schooling in organizational techniques, fostered a communal spirit, collected funds for the overt political associations such as the IRB and gathered people together weekly, in units that could be easily and intensely propagandized.[30] The fruits of such experiences were reaped to the full from 1919 to 1921. Yet theirs was the contribution of nationalism and organization in particular, spiritualism and the willingness to sacrifice. Vitally important facets of the stimulus to revolution came from the Catholic religion. Somehow, through religion, propaganda, education and finally, through example — that is, both the overt and covert means of socialization — an ethic of sacrifice for the national cause was inculcated in many Irishmen. Yeats described this as 'something new and terrible' that had come into Irish life, — 'the mood of the mystic victim'. No one expressed this new sacrificial intent better or eulogized it more than Padraig Pearse. He wrote, there is no future for Ireland under the heel of England. The choice is one between life and a living death, between progress and decay. As long as Ireland remains in bondage so long will Irishmen be ready to face death that Ireland may live.[31]

Pearse welcomed the First World War not just because England's difficulty would be Ireland's opportunity for insurrection, but primarily in the hope that it would rekindle a martial spirit in Ireland's men. 'What Ireland wants', wrote Pearse, 'beyond all other modern countries is a new birth of the heroic spirit'.[32] In St Enda's, the school that he had established, he urged the boys to grasp 'that better is the short life with honour than long life with dishonour'.[33] Perhaps his most telling passage, part of a tract written in 1913 entitled, 'The Coming Revolution', was that where he stressed,

We must accustom ourselves to the sight of arms, to the use of arms. We may make mistakes in the beginning and shoot the wrong people; but bloodshed is a cleansing and sanctifying thing, and the nation which regards it as the final horror has lost its manhood. There are many things more horrible than bloodshed; and slavery is one of them.[34]

Finally, in his essay on 'Peace and the Gael' written in 1915 Pearse wrote,

Many people in Ireland dread war because they do not know it. Ireland has not known the exhilaration of war for our 100 years. Yet who will say that she has known the blessings of peace? When war comes to Ireland she must welcome it as she would welcome the Angel of God and she will![35]

RELIGION AND REVOLUTIONARY
POLITICS

If then Pearse's propaganda was one important strand in the
establishment of a sacrificial nationalism in Ireland, the quasi-
messianic impulse of the period was undoubtedly provided
by certain clerics, in particular, and religion in general. The
importance of Catholic clerics to the Sinn Fein cause has
never been fully analysed. Few analyses get beyond the
somewhat simplistic if traditionally accepted view that the
hierarchy of Catholic bishops was antagonistic to Sinn Fein
and threatened excommunication with withdrawal of the
sacraments, in turn, for active or dying rebels. The argument
then runs that, since the hierarchy of the Roman Catholic
Church was opposed to the rebels, then Catholicism in
general adopted a similar stance. However, the relationship
between the rosary and the gun was far more varied, complex
and individual.

The Catholic Church in Ireland was close to the people; of
that at least there is no doubt. The priest and rebel had often
shared common persecution, proscription and poverty. The
priest and peasant were both men of the soil, and common
frustration had frequently moved them both towards violent
rebellion. Often the priest was the local firebrand, the man
first to catch the initial impulse of any political movement.
Certainly he would know about it before the local policeman.
Together priest and rebel had frequently born the brunt of
English brutality. Pearse relates how the English ascendancy
once proposed in the Dublin Parliament a measure for the
castration of all priests who refused to leave Ireland.[36] The
Bill passed the Irish House and was transmitted to England
for ratification with the support of the viceroy. It was not

accepted. Similarly, as we have already seen in the seventeenth century, Irish priests were held to be responsible for the disturbed state of the country, proclaimed to be guilty of rebellion *en masse* and sentenced to death.

However, there is a danger in assuming that the Catholic clergy were of unified opinion with regard to rebellion and revolution in particular and to politics in general. There were in fact a great many nuances of opinion. Nevertheless there is conclusive evidence that in the period under discussion the younger clergy offered support and inspiration to the nationalist cause. Police reports record that,

> The steady growth of Sinn Fein from a small body to its present vast dimensions has been mainly due to the general dread of conscription — the republican programme also holds a powerful attraction for the younger men and a large number of the younger priests.[37]

A similar report somewhat amusingly emphasized that the younger RC clergy

> exercise an immense influence over the youth in their parishes and unless some means can be used to make them abstain from interereference in politics I fear that disaffection will be dangerously spread. They occasionally deliver political addresses to their congregations in the Church ... seditious songs in praise of the late rebellion [1916] have been sung at concerts in their presence without protest .... a few weeks ago, at a Concert in County Kilkenny, a curate when called on for a song by another priest sang the seditious ballad 'Who fears to speak of Easter Week' and in response to an encore repeated the offence.[38]

Of far greater importance was the fact that, coincidental with the theoretical and tactical changes in the subversive underground and the upsurge of nationalistic cultural renaissance, there occurred during the 1880s a popular religious revival. Devotion to a movement, the Sacred Heart of Jesus, had been established in the early nineteenth century with little success. However, from 1887 under the leadership of a Jesuit, James A. Cullen, 'the devotion swept Ireland in various organised forms'.[39] One branch, the Apostleship of Prayer, enrolled 8,000 members during the first four months of 1888. Organized, militant and ascetic Catholicism combined with nationalist republicanism dedicated to physical force. One religious organization in particular, the Irish Christian Brothers, acted out that fusion with dramatic effects. Little or no research has been conducted on the role of the Brothers in the metamorphosis of Irish beliefs in the nineteenth and twentieth centuries. There can be little doubt that there was a unique spirituality at work in Ireland — the problem is to determine who and what nurtured it. It seems plausible in the light of the evidence that the Christian Brothers were at least one set of the elusive pimpernels.

The Irish Christian Brothers

The Brothers were a variant of the established order of the Brothers of the Christian Schools founded by the Abbé Jean Baptise de la Salle in France in 1684. Though not formally attached to the French bretheren, the Irish Christian Brothers emulated their organization.

The Irish Brothers were founded in 1802 in the city of Waterford by Edmund Ignatius Rice, a wealthy man turned ascetic in later life. We are told that he was also 'heir to a rich and precious heritage of family traditions and loyalty to the faith and fatherland'.[40] Such religiosity and nationalism were inculcated from the beginning as the bases of the Order's teachings. They were never to leave it.

It would appear that the teaching of the Brothers was of an exceptionally high standard — so much so that the *Catholic Dictionary* reported that the altered habits and demeanour of the children who attended the Brothers' schools became a common topic of remark. The Catholic hierarchy was also impressed with the discipline they achieved as well as with the quality of their teaching. Accordingly the RC Church rewarded the Order for its good works and on 5 September 1820 granted it a prayer of memorial and a constitution by the Apostolic Brief of Pope Pius VII. Such official recognition gave the major impetus for the extension of the order throughout Ireland. The Brothers were a quasi-monastic order. Their members could not enter the priesthood proper but were nevertheless bound by monastic vows and an ascetic culture. Life membership of the Order was granted only after eleven years of probation. But teaching, especially religious teaching, was their rationale. As a result the Order's schools were imbued with an aura of pious religiosity. Icons, statues of the Virgin were prominent in every classroom, and in each school a pause was made for prayers every time that the clock struck. Not unnaturally, this committed atmosphere had a distinctive effect on boys attending the Brothers' schools. In particular, they were disciplined and dutiful. A commissioner of education who had assessed the Christian Brothers' schools in 1869 and 1870 reported that,

> in their moral aspect the Christian Brothers schools appear to me to have a tendency which is the very reverse of that which may be traced in the National System. The perfection of demeanour.... The complete ascendancy which the Brothers' exercise ... the supression of the wonted symptoms of Boyish playfulness under religious seriousness rarely developed at so early an age are parts of a

system which may be admirably adapted to make true and earnest
adherents of the Church, but is opposed to the formation of that
robustness and independence of character which a method of greater
freedom tends to promote.[41]

It was crucial too that the Brothers concentrated their
teaching on the children of the poorer workers in the cities
and the agricultural labourers in the rural areas — children
with whom Ireland's revolutionary future was to lie. There
can be little doubt, as one Brother noted, that the Order
became 'the most distinctly Irish, as they are the most
successful, of all the religious bodies engaged in education in
Ireland'.[42] Their Irishness, but above all their preaching of a
messianic, nationalistic Irishness, was their greatest contribution to the revolutionary cause. The *Catholic Bulletin,* official organ of the RC Church in Ireland, stated in May 1917
that 'In the boys of the Christian Brothers schools there is
the plastic stuff to mould a live nation out of'.[43] Contemporaries recognized the role that the Brothers were playing. A somewhat reactionary Catholic cleric, the Bishop of
Cloyne, indeed expressed the opinion that, after a thorough
reading of the Brothers' textbooks, he had come to the
conclusion that their content was, 'the most direct training
for Fenianism that I could possibly imagine'.[44]

Even so, the precise extent of the influence of the Brothers
on the emerging revolutionary consciousness is as difficult to
estimate as it was most certainly significant.[45] That they did
contribute to 'the cause' cannot be in doubt if a Catholic
cleric can write that,

The Irish Christian Brothers were perhaps the greatest human force
emerging from the gloom of the 19th century. For the redemption
of our country; they were certainly a major influence in the
moulding and fashioning of the nation. In the darkness of famine

and the maelstrom of political disaster they kindled a light that soon flared into a brilliant beacon heralding a resurrection. . . . The downtrodden Catholic mass had to be taught many virtues. They had to be emancipated from centuries of serfdom and parochial dissensions. Instruction, discipline and development of national and supranational virtues amid a people bowed down by landlords and the desolate heart stemming from dire poverty, were essential to preserve faith and nationality. Such work might take a century; and in some countries a century was not sufficient. In the space of 50 years the Brothers taught Ireland to stand erect amid the nations of the world.[46]

Another commentator goes further suggesting that,

To the making of the new Ireland that we know today no one body has contributed more than the Christian Brothers. It would well be said that the insurrection of 1916 was a Christian Brothers Easter Week. Almost all the leaders of that heroic uprising and the glorious years that followed, had been pupils of the Christian Brothers. . . . from the Brothers the 1916 leaders learned their love of freedom, and their desire for nationhood and the Gaelic way of life.[47]

Perhaps then the teachings of the Brothers were the vital link between revolutionary action and fundamental belief? Fundamental beliefs in the main had in Ireland been formed by the authoritarian, disciplined, hierarchical, conservative and proselytizing Catholic Church, itself imbued with a strong sense of national identity. These beliefs were supplemented by an equally religious, spiritual nationalism stimulated by the GAA, the GL, Sinn Fein and the Volunteers. Those who betrayed such beliefs were either excommunicated, boycotted or, later, shot. The Christian Brothers, religious men yet not of the official Church, thus possessed a degree of freedom that enabled them to perhaps synthesize,

through their teachings, religiosity and revolutionary nationalism — hence rendering the rosary and the gun compatible.

Throughout the War of Independence the teachings of the
Brothers were disseminated by their weekly publication *Our
Boys*. Again, it exhalted sacrificial nationalism. One issue
contained a message from De Valera addressed to the boys
and girls of Ireland,

> Do not wait until you are grown up [he wrote], If you wait the
> greater opportunities, when they present themselves, will find you
> unprepared. A Kevin Barry or a Terence MacSwiney is not made by
> the impulse of the moment, but by the faithful daily living in
> accordance with a rule based on the conviction and on ideal
> constantly in mind, constantly cherished. . . . Be your best selves. Be
> heroes and heroines now and later you will be the glory of the
> nation.[48]

Thus there occurred in Ireland prior to the War of Independence, a revival of Irishness and the assertion of a
distinct national identity through which the Irish political
will was regenerated. Increasingly, especially from 1916
onwards, the Irish moved towards their innate Gaelicism. One
vital revolutionary lesson they absorbed in the process of the
cultural and tactical renaissance was that a nation that is to
succeed in modern war has to convince its people that the
cause of victory is worthy of martyrdom. It was a lesson Irish
revolutionaries took to heart. By 15 August 1920 *An
t'Oglach* (the official newspaper of the IRA) could advise its
readers that 'We realise it is far more profitable to kill for
Ireland than to die for her'. It was this type of idealism that
made possible the creation of a guerrilla army and an alternative, underground government; it was this type of idealism
that Michael Collins was able to canalize and direct against
the ailing British administration. The same idealism and fer-

vour also sanctified the violence that was to ensue during the War of Independence. As a result of this kind of inspiration, many Irishmen died in the years 1919-21 with words on their lips similar to those Liam Mellows, a prominent IRA tactician and fighter, who wrote in his last letter to his mother,

I believe that those who die for Ireland have no need for prayer.[49]

This then was the background to the War of Independence. It remained for a set of contingent events, out of which it is possible to extract the three most influential, to provide the final stimulus for revolution. First there was the example of the failed 1916 Rising and the canonization of its leaders executed during General Maxwell's brief reign of terror when martial law was declared in the aftermath of the revolt. In a letter to Bryce, a former Chief Secretary of Ireland, a witness of the Rising wrote in 1916, 'Of course this is not Ireland's rebellion – only a Sinn Fein Rising'. Later she wrote,

The Sinn Fein leaders were such good men. They died like saints. Oh! the pity of it! And Ireland wanted them so much. They were men of such beautiful character, such high literary power and attainments – mystics who kept the light burning. . . . But as sure as God's sun rises in the east, if England does not get things right . . . if there's not immediately conciliation and love and mercy poured out on Ireland – all the Sinn Fein leaders will be canonised. . . . Already the tone is changing.[50]

The Rising was to prove superb propaganda for the Republican cause. It showed the Irish, or at least made Irishmen feel that they knew, where their true allegiance lay. What remained of the British administration's legitimacy perished with this act. Majority opinion now was firmly behind those seeking an end, most probably a violent end, to Dublin Castle and all that it stood for.

The second stimulus, the death of the prominent Republican Thomas Ashe from being forcibly fed while on hunger strike, aroused tremendous passion. His funeral led to massive defiance of the orders against uniformed marches. 'Volunteers' from all over Ireland gathered in Dublin to pay their last respects to their latest martyr. Michael Collins's funeral oration gave some indication of things to come when he said,, 'the volley we have just heard is the only speech it is proper to make above the grave of a dead Fenian'.[51]

Finally, the campaign for conscription of Irishmen to serve in the First World War jolted those groups who still stood with the British in Ireland into reconsidering their position. The attempt to enlist Irishmen to fight in a war ostensibly for the independence of small nations proved to be too harsh an irony. Priests, policemen and people united, at first against the conscription campaign,[52] and later against the British. A letter to the *Manchester Guardian,* 11 May 1918, from G. W. Russell (AE) poet, painter and editor of the *Irish Homestead,* reported the events and indicated their likely outcome:

> if they [the British government] persist in enforcing military service upon Ireland, if they insist on breaking the Irish will, there will not be a parish here where blood will not be spilt. There will grow up A HATE WHICH WILL NOT BE EXTINGUISHABLE lasting from generation to generation. It will be fed by tradition everywhere and our people live by tradition.

Out of this emnity the military component of the revolutionary war, the IRA, evolved.

PREPARATION FOR REVOLUTION:
THE MILITARY COMPONENT

It was the people's army, the Irish Volunteers or IRA, that emerged between 1916 and 1921 and that gave direction to the antipathy felt towards the British presence. It was the dominant organizational unit of a sophisticated alternative government. At the head of that underground government was the rebel parliament, Dail Eireann, based in Dublin. The IRA or 'Volunteers' were the fighting arm of that alternative government structure with many of the army leaders also serving as government ministers. The army was made up entirely of volunteers. At the time of the Easter Rising the police had estimated that the Volunteers were 15,000 strong.[53] However, again in the Irish revolutionary tradition, fewer than 1,800 men participated in that uprising because of organizational and leadership failures at the eleventh hour.[54]

However, the Irish Volunteers, or *Oglaigh na h'Eireann,* had a long pedigree. A volunteer organization had been formed as early as 1778, only to lapse several years later. They were reformed at the famous Rotunda Rink meeting on 25 December 1913 largely as a stimulus response to the creation of the Carsonite Volunteers in Ulster. Throughout the War of Independence 1919-21 the Army of the Republic referred to itself as the Volunteers. The title 'IRA' was never apparently, officially adopted by them though it is used here for convenience. At the heart of the Republican Army, however, was a far more clandestine and important group, the Irish Republican Brotherhood (IRB). This organization of committed revolutionaries later used not only the Volunteers but the GAA and the GL as its respectable, legal 'front'. Michael Collins, as director of organization of the Army and president of the IRB, was thus, in terms of control of the Irish underground, a far more powerful and significant man than the often absent De Valera. Collins's greatest military asset, his intelligence network, was in fact based upon the IRB structure. The IRB had been formed in Dublin in 1858 'as an oath bound secret society with the uncompromising intention of overthrowing English government in Ireland by force of arms and of establishing an Irish Republic.'[5] Members of the IRB were picked men. As an organization, it had a far more rigorous structure than the many amorphous conspiratorial groups that we have seen emerge periodically throughout Irish history. As the one effectively organized anti-government group within the state from the 1880s onwards, it was able to canalize and direct the emergent revolutionary movement. As a structure working for revolutionary war, and in terms of its function and achievements, it was a far more seminal unit to the revolutionary cause than the less clandestine political arm of the Irish underground, Sinn Fein. The IRB was the vanguard of the forces of Irish opposition, and as such it is both interesting and instructive to examine its organizational structure – a structure which, on paper at least, remained the same from the 1880s down to 1921.

The Irish Republican Brotherhood

The main unit of organization of the Brotherhood was, in Leninist fashion, the 'circle'. The circle was the basis of IRB groups in each locality. Members of each circle elected as their chief an officer who was known as 'the centre'. Each circle also had a sub-centre, a secretary and a treasurer. All were elected officials. For operational purposes each circle was divided into sections of not more than ten men, commanded by a section leader.[56] The district level was next in the ascending hierarchical structure. Each county in Ireland was divided into two or more districts. 'Centres', the leaders of the circle in each district, formed a board for directing the organization of IRB affairs in the district. Each district in turn elected a chairman, vice-chairman, secretary and treasurer. The chairman was known as the 'district centre' and was responsible to the county centre for the efficiency and discipline of his IRB unit. For the purpose of organization, operations and recruitment, each city was considered a district. It was all very democratic and organized and, in the early period, relatively easy for the RIC to penetrate. Collins, however, with his ruthless assassination of all informers, soon changed things dramatically.

Underground democracy also operated at the next level, the county. Here, periodically, local centres of the IRB held a meeting to elect the county centre, county sub-centre, county secretary and treasurer. The county centre was in turn responsible to the divisional centre of the IRB for all IRB affairs within the county. At divisional level the IRB was divided into eleven divisions:

1. part of Leinster, comprising the counties of Dublin, Wicklow, Kildare, Louth, Meath, Westmeath and Longford;
2. the remaining part of Leinster – the counties of Wexford, Kilkenny, Catlow, Queen's County and King's County;
3. part of Munster – namely Cork, Waterford, Kerry;
4. the remainder of Munster – namely Limerick, Clare, Tipperary;
5. part of Connaught, which comprised Galway and Mayo;

6. the remainder of Connaught, including Sligo, Leitrim, Roscommon;
7. part of Ulster – namely, Donegal, Derry, Tyrone, Fermangh;
8. the remainder of Ulster, including Antrim, Down, Armagh, Monaghan, Cavan;
9. southern England;
10. northern England;
11. Scotland.

The claim to have IRB organizations in the latter three areas was certainly no idle boast, especially the period of Collins's command.

At the head of the IRB was its Supreme Council. This governing body of the organization was made up of one member from each of the eleven divisions along with four additional co-opted members whose names were known only to the Supreme Council. The Council alone had power to inflict a sentence of death and give it effect. Indeed, from its inception it had regarded itself as the government of the Irish Republic and could therefore levy taxes, raise loans and carry out all the functions of legitimate government.[57]

The importance of the IRB and its Supreme Council is attested to by the fact that it was the Council that decided upon and engineered the Easter Rising. Thus the execution of the military council of the IRB by Maxwell's troops meant that, with the exception of the discredited MacNeill and the moderate Bulmar Hobson, who both survived, the Volunteer executive was also removed, since they were one and the same personnel. There was thus an interlocking directorate command structure tying the Volunteer and IRB leadership. This arrangement was to continue throughout the War of Independence with the Volunteers or IRA acting only on instructions from the IRB executive, dominated by Michael Collins.

The failure of the Rising and the execution or internment of so many of the senior personnel of both the Volunteers and the IRB made it appear, on the surface at least, that the Irish underground had been effectively destroyed. However, the work of two men in particular, Michael Collins operating among his IRB contacts and Cathal Brugha,[58] working through the remnants of the Volunteers, began quickly and effectively to reconstitute the Irish underground. Brugha, seriously wounded in the 1916 fighting, escaped execution and, when discharged from hospital on crutches, immediately began recruiting for the Volunteers. He made contact with senior IRA or Volunteer officers still in Ireland and a group of some fifty men assembled under his chairmanship at Fleming's Hotel, Dublin, in November or December 1916. It was at this or a subsequent meeting held in the spring of 1917 that a temporary executive of the Volunteers was formed.[59]

Collins, like Brugha, a member of both Volunteers and IRB, similarly began to reconstitute the Supreme Council of the IRB upon his release from internment in the Frongoch Camp in North Wales. Collins had joined the IRB in November 1909 and the Volunteers on 25 April 1914. His first allegiance was to the IRB, of which he later became president.[60]

The important outcome of both their efforts was that contact between the Dublin centre and the localities was restored and a degree of organizational unity within and between the two underground structures, Volunteers and IRB, was re-established. Thus, when the 1916 internees were released they were able to rejoin a still-intact revolutionary underground which reflected the fusion between the old structure and the new methods evolved in the internment camps. In the words of a Frongoch song,

> The last is gone back again to old Ireland
> To prepare once again for a fight to the death.

The Irish Volunteers or Irish Republican Army

Theoretically, according to plans made after the 1916 débâcle, the new Republican Army was to be a truly national force organized on the lines of the British Army and using its training manuals. It was thus in its original conception to be a conventional force. Its guerrilla component was to remain marginal until 1917 when Michael Collins and Richard Mulcahy, later chief of staff of the IRA, introduced the guerrilla style of combat. In 1917 it was decided to weld the revolutionary, guerrilla component with a stiffening spine of discipline provided by a more conventional military structure. The basic unit of the Army in 1917 became small squads of eight men. Sections of sixteen men and companies made up of four sections were also established. With a full complement of officers and some special service personnel, each local unit should have numbered eighty-seven in all.[61] This however proved to be both unwieldy and impractical. The IRA thus became territorially organized. Accordingly a great deal then depended on the cadre of committed Republicans and the local revolutionary leadership. There was little or no uniformity of unit members. For example, company strength could vary between twenty-five and a hundred whereas a battalion might be composed of three or ten companies. Everything turned upon the degree of commitment to the cause in the locality.

The year 1917 however would appear to be crucial for the military reorganization of the underground. In 1917, following the October Ard Fheis (Annual Convention), national military co-ordination began in earnest. The Convention elected a National Executive with Brugha as the chairman, Collins as director of army organization, Mulcahy in charge of training, Rory O'Connor in charge of engineering, Diarmuid Lynch supervising communications and Michael Staines in charge of supply. Although the National Executive functioned in name at least down to 1920, real power over the Army had passed, in March 1918, to the GHQ Staff and then to the Ministry of Defence when the Dail Eireann was declared an operational unit in January 1919. Nevertheless, it was Collins and Mulcahy who remained in command of both the Army and intelligence throughout the War of Independence.[6 2]

The training and organization of the Army were most thorough. The whole of Ireland was divided into brigade areas. Sometimes these areas corresponded with the counties of Ireland, but this was not a rule. Often the extent of a particular brigade depended solely upon where the writ of the local commander was enforceable. In most cases brigades consisted of four battalions, the nominal strength of a brigade being 4,000 men. Army staff headquarters was at 6 Harcourt Street, Dublin, with some of the GHQ members also seeing active service as commanders of the Dublin Brigade of the IRA. Sinn Fein and its myriad clubs, the political arm of the IRA, often supplemented the work of the army training staff by lecturing on military subjects. Similarly the Sinn Fein clubs were a most important source of recruitment and funds.[6 3]

The chief staff officer of the IRA was a brigade adjutant, while an IRA brigade quartermaster had the same functions as staff captain in the British Army, with the exception that he was also responsible for intelligence. Better-organized brigades also possessed a signals engineer and boy scout, cycle and medical officers, all holding the rank of captain. The subjects laid down for training were uniform throughout the Army and covered drill, cycling, scouting, engineering and first aid. In addition, in each section two men were detailed for the following special services: engineering, scouting, dispatch riding, signalling, transport and supply, first aid and musketry. With regard to all these spheres of military activity, a great deal of information was gleaned from demobilized British soldiers. The GHQ of the IRA in fact issued a memorandum to all units of the Republican Army instructing that every effort should be made to enlist ex-soldiers.[64]

Thus by 1919 the IRA was a unified, cohesive military force ready for action, whose greatest military assets were its political and military intelligence units. It was largely because of the efficiency of the IRA's intelligence arm that their overall plan of campaign proved to be so effective. This was Michael Collins's own empire. Collins, established the intelligence network singlehanded. He recognized at an early stage in the formulation of the revolutionary campaign that, in the light of Irish history, his twin enemies were the spy and the informer. In time he systematically removed both.

Collins's intelligence network was organized on two distinct levels – the civil and the military. The military side was by far the most important. It operated, again, mainly through the underground cells of the IRB which Collins commanded. Formally, IRA intelligence, field intelligence that is, was organized on British military lines. Each company and battalion of the IRA had an intelligence officer whose reports were passed through a brigade intelligence officer to the central office in Dublin. However, this was little more than an adjunct to Collins's own network of IRB spies operating in most Irish communities.

On the civil side of his intelligence structure Collins had men and women in post offices, on the railways, on Channel ferries, in every prison in Ireland and many in England. Similarly, dockers in all parts of Europe and the United States served in what Collins referred to as his 'Q' Division.[65] Yet by far the most important among his agents were the men working for him in the Special Branch of the DMP, men in the heart of the British administration, with access to restricted information, codes and the like. In particular four Dublin policemen — Broy, Neligan, Kavanagh and McNamara — helped turn what had been Britain's greatest security asset in Ireland against itself. It was the battle for ascendancy in the sphere of intelligence that was the critical arena of the War of Independence. The covert war between the British and Irish intelligence units in the autumn and winter of 1920 was that in which, as we shall see in the following chapters, the public security units of the British administration were broken.

Ireland's future in 1919 thus lay with the underground government, Dail Eireann, and its fighting arm, the IRA. As we have seen there occurred in the period 1880-1919 a gradual change of political allegiance on the part of the Irish people, coupled with a new military and political awareness. The legitimacy and authority of the incumbent British administration dwindled in almost inverse proportion to the growing consensus of support in favour of the underground government of the Irish Republic declared on the steps of the Dublin General Post Office, Easter 1916, and legitimized through a series of elections culminating in the Dail Eireann elections of 1918. We have also noted some of the crucial

antecedants of the revolutionary war and the preconditions
for the breakdown of public security. We have also analysed
the politico-military womb in which the embryo alternative
government grew, and have hinted at the presence of outstanding inspirational crisis leadership in the shape of the
guerrilla leader, Michael Collins. It was the coalescence of
these elements that led to the outbreak of the Irish War of
Independence — a war fought to institute a native government deriving its authority solely from the Irish people. Only
when the national consciousness was awakened, when international opinion was to their advantage, and when a sophisticated, violent militarized opposition had matured, were the
Irish able to defeat what they had come to regard as a foreign
power. Collins captured the essence of that struggle, to which
we now turn, when he wrote,

> Ireland's story from 1918 to 1921 may be summed up as the story
> of a struggle between our determination to govern ourselves and to
> get rid of British Government and the British determination to
> prevent us from doing either. It was a struggle between two rival
> governments, the one an Irish Government resting on the will of the
> people and the other an alien Government depending for its exist-
> ence upon military force — the one gathering more and more
> authority, the other steadily losing ground.[66]

Collins, the IRA and other committed Republican political
activists were to demonstrate throughout the course of the
war that the Irish were capable of creating and for the first
time sustaining a general conspiracy against the British
government. The struggle, like most other wars of liberation,
revealed that organization and human will, rather than
weaponry, were the keys to success. The Irish revolutionaries
also demonstrated that, through organization, resistance
movements can destroy both the base of compliance towards

and the legitimacy of the incumbents. Thus the Irish War of Independence was to reveal a most sophisticated, articulate and dedicated Irish politico-military underground, capable not only of outfighting but of out-legitimizing and out-governing the British in Ireland.[6][7]

NOTES

1. The term 'Irish Republican Army' was never used, at the time, by the fighters themselves. The 'Volunteers' was the popular name of the underground army. It is used here in tandem with Volunteer, since during the War of Independence the Volunteers were, in effect, a republican people's guerrilla army.

2. T. W. Moody (ed.), *The Fenian Movement* (Cork, 1968), 103.

3. Quoted in J. A. Froude, *The English in Ireland in the 18th Century,* Vol. 3, (London, 1881), 12-13.

4. Quoted in *Irish Seditions: Their Origins and History 1792-1880* (London, undated and anonymous pamphlet).

5. ibid., 22-23.

6. ibid., 23.

7. ibid.

8. T. H. White, 'The Age of O'Connell' in T. W. Moody and F. X. Martin O.S.A. (eds.), *The Course of Irish History* (Cork, 1967), 250.

9. J. A. Reynolds, 'The Catholic Emancipation Cults in Ireland' in Moody and Martin, op. cit., 22.

10. Moody, *Fenian Movement,* 102.

11. 'Rightly or wrongly the Nationalist Irish Government did not think the time ripe for an open appeal to rms. But it was hoped that these guerrilla attacks might eventually lead up to a war for independence.' P. J. P. Tynan, *The History of the Irish Nationalist Invincibles and their Times,* (London, 1894), 431.

12. It now seems unlikely that Tynan was, as he claimed, the Invincibles' 'Number One'. A Captain John McAfferty, it would appear, was organizer both of the Invincibles and of the Phoenix Park assassinations. For a detailed account of McAfferty's background see *Repeal of the Union Conspiracy* (anonymous pamphlet, London, 1886) in *Sundry Tracts on Ireland* (Central Reference Library, Manchester).

13. Tynan, op. cit., 430.

14. See Judicial Statistics, Ireland – the various numbers Cd 3112 (1905), 42; Cd 5866 (1910), 30-34.

15. Patrick Lynch, 'The Social Revolution that Never Was' in T. Desmond Williams, *The Irish Struggle* (London, 1968), 42.

16. H. B. C. Pollard, *The Secret Societies of Ireland* (London, 1922), 107.

17. Stepniak, *Underground Russia* (New York, 1891), 32.

18. Neglected that is by analysts of revolt and revolution – not by revolutionaries themselves, who have employed this particular medium to great effect.

19. L. P. Edwards, *The Natural History of Revolution* (New York, 1965), 90-91.

20. *The Workers' Republic* (12 July 1915).

21. For a discussion of the question of 'facilitation' see any of T. R. Gurr's writings on political violence but particularly *Why Men Rebel* (Princeton, 1970).

22. Gaelic League Pamphlet, No. 29 in M. P. Hickey, *The Irish Language Movement, Its Genesis, Growth and Progress* (no details): National Library, Dublin.

23. Michael Collins, *The Path to Freedom* (Dublin, 1922), 121.

24. ibid., 123.

25. Freeman's Journal (23 October 1914): National Library, Dublin.

26. ibid. (15 September 1917).

27. P. H. Pearse, 'The Coming Revolution' in his *Political Writings and Speeches* (Dublin, 1962), 92-93.

28. Collins, op. cit., p. 53.

29. F. X. Martin, O.S.A., 'Origins of the Easter Rising', in T. D. Williams, *The Irish Struggle* (London, 1968), 7.

30. CO904/102. Deputy Inspector General. Police Reports (February 1917): 'Gaelic Classes, concerts, dances, Sinn Fein clubs and GAA football matches are some of the most convenient means of collecting rebels together and formenting hatred of England.'

31. Sinn Fein Series No. 12 (pamphlet, *The Case of Ireland,*) National Library, Dublin.

32. Pearse, op. cit., 'Peace and the Gael' (December, 1915), p. 38.

33. ibid.

34. Pearse, op. cit., 'The Coming Revolution', 98-99.

35. ibid., 217.

36. Pearse, op. cit., 'The Murder Machine', p. 6.

37. CO904/107 (November 1918).

38. CO904/102 (January 1917).

39. Patrick O'Farrell, *Ireland's English Question* (London, 1971), 223.

40. *Edmund Ignatius Rice and the Christian Brothers,* by 'A Christian Brother' (Dublin, 1926), 45.

41. Pamphlet of the National Education League of Ireland in Royal Commission of Inquiry into Primary Education (Ireland) 1870, Cd 9557, Evidence.

42. *A Century of Catholic Education,* by 'A Christian Brother' (Dublin, 1916).

43. *Catholic Bulletin* (May 1917), 277.

44. Royal Commission, op. cit., 15, 620.

45. F. X. Martin O.S.A. has written in his leaders and *Men of the Easter Rising, Dublin 1916* (London 1967) that 'the leaders who emerged in 1916 and the subsequent years were largely past pupils of the Christian Brothers Schools. . . . Due recognition has not yet been given to the Irish Christian Brothers for their part in the nationalist struggle, particularly for their unqualified support of the Gaelic revival.'

46. Irish Christian Brothers, St. Mary's Clonmel, *Centenary Record 1860-1960* (Tipperary, 1960), 17.

47. ibid., 39.

48. *Irish Bulletin* VI (3) (October 1921).

49. T. P. Coogan, *The IRA* (London, 1970), 53-54.

50. MS. 11, 016 Bryce Papers 1915-1916 (i) Letter from Margaret Ashton, 16 July 1916: National Library, Dublin.

51. T. O'Donoghue, 'The Reorganisation of the Volunteers', *Capuchin Annual* (1967), 384.

52. Report from the Midland and Connaught Region, Military Intelligence Report 523/G1/E.PRO, London.

53. CSO Registered Papers, Calendar of papers relating to the 1916 Rising in the State Papers Office, Dublin Castle.

54. See F. X. Martin, 'Eoin MacNeill and the 1916 Rising', *Irish Historical Studies* (1961), 266-71.

55. F. X. Martin, *The Irish Volunteers 1912-1915* (Dublin, 1963), treats this theme fully.

56. For details of the IRB structure see W.O.32/4308, 1920, PRO London.

57. ibid.

58. Charles Burgess, later IRA chief of staff for a short while.

59. O'Donoghue, op. cit., 381.

60. Margery Forester, *The Lost Leader* (London, 1971), Chapter 5.

61. WO32/4308.

62. O'Donoghue, op. cit., 380-84.

63. CO904/105 (March 1918). A police report observed 'The Irish Volunteers, though a distinct organisation under separate control, are recruited from the Sinn Fein clubs, each club being supposed to contain a company'.

64. WO32/4308.

65. The head of the Dublin office was E. J. Duggan, a lawyer; see Sir Neville Macready, *Annals of An Active Life,* Vol. II (London, 1924), 463.

66. Forester, op. cit., 114-15.

67. Collins, op. cit., 65.

3

CONFLICT, INTELLIGENCE AND THE BREAKDOWN OF CONTROL:
The Irish War of Independence 1919-1921

In Ireland the training and drilling to the use of arms of a great part of the male population is a new departure which is bound in the not too distant future to alter all the existing conditions of life. Obedience to the law has never been a prominent characteristic of the people. In times of passion or excitement the law has only been maintained by force and this has been rendered practicable owing to the want of cohesion among the crowds hostile to the police. If the people became armed and drilled, effective police control would vanish. Events are moving. Each county will soon have a trained army far outnumbering the police and those whose control the Volunteers will be in a position to dictate to what extent the law of the land may be carried into effect.

> *A report of the Inspector General of the RIC issued to Augustine Birrell, Chief Secretary, 1915. Quoted in Cd 8279,* Report of the Royal Commission into the Easter Rising *(June 1916) p. 7.*

We have observed that by 1918 the growing momentum of political support in Ireland was behind Sinn Fein and the

Volunteers. Violent political antagonism had been focused upon the British presence represented by the Dublin Castle government. As we shall see, the events of the war of 1919-21 demonstrate just how effectively the IRA further mobilized the Irish people behind their cause. Those events also confirm and demonstrate just how effete and administratively incapable the apparatus of government had become — especially the security apparatus. Inadequate in quiet times, the administration now collapsed under a systematic terrorist attack. It will become clear too that the IRA did not confine its activities to Ireland. At an early stage Michael Collins had realized the importance of publicizing the Irish cause in the international arena. He also worked hard upon liberal opinion in England. Eventually it was the lack of support in England, for further prosecution of the war, coupled with the defeat of the British political resolve in Ireland, that led to the 1921 settlement.

THE WAR OF INDEPENDENCE:
THE EROSION OF BRITISH CONTROL

By 1919 Ireland had passed from a condition of controlled disorder into the uncertainties of a rapidly declining security situation. It was no longer clear who ruled the country. Such a situation was to continue until the final failure in 1921 of the British counter-insurgency mounted during the summer and autumn of 1920. The guerrilla war which by 1920 had already been under way for one year was waged by the Irish forces from the onset with strong reliance on intelligence, propaganda, politics and guerrilla tactics co-ordinated to make up a fully orchestrated plan of campaign in all of these arenas. The British response was altogether different. Their approach was piecemeal. There was no overall strategy and no conception of a co-ordinated counter-insurgency. The British were at their best in terms of countering the insurgency when they reorganized and developed their forces in the intelligence, political and military arenas during the summer and autumn of 1920. By that time, however, the War of Independence could not be put down without a campaign of genocide – the battle for the minds of the Irish people had by then already been won by the IRA.

The War of Independence was fought on two distinct yet intermeshing levels. First, there was the overt war between the two armies, embellished by the vital covert war between the Irish and British intelligence services. The IRA intelligence network, masterminded by Collins, was as we have seen moulded by three stimuli – the lessons learned from the débâcle of the 1916 Rising, the cultural-spiritual nationalist renaissance which inspired 'the cause', and the depressing failure of successive Irish risings. The latter in particular had taught the rebels that English dominance in Ireland rested upon English preparedness – a preparedness which in the past was the result of an efficient intelligence service provided by the RIC and the services rendered by Irish informers. O'Connor, in his biography of Michael Collins, wrote that,

> with all their faulty judgements and inaccuracies these secret police reports constituted the greatest hold of the English on Ireland. From 1789 onwards every national movement had been destroyed from within. It was typical of the romantic haze in which the Irish patriots moved that no one had realised it before.[1]

Similarly, an Irish nationalist journal had stated in 1911 that,

I think we Irish Nationalists have not devoted enough attention to the police. We want nothing less than a campaign of exterminating the police. I don't mean that we should begin a wholesale massacre of them, say tomorrow. But we should lose no time in creating such a public opinion in Ireland that the man who joins the police may be branded a traitor for all time . . . since the establishment of the RIC in Ireland one point above all else in connection with the police forces [sic] itself to the front. As soon as Irish Nationalists make an active move, either by passive resistance or otherwise against England the first body that blocks the way is not the army, but the police force.[2]

Collins's tactical priority was to discipline the members of the Irish resistance as well as to immobilize the intelligence network provided in Dublin by the 'G' Division (Special Branch) of the Dublin Metropolitan Police, and throughout the rest of Ireland, by the RIC Special Branch. In time the full momentum of the reconstituted Republican movement, and particularly its military arm, were focused on the police. The result, in purely military terms, was impressive. From 1 January 1919 to 2 October 1920, 109 policemen were assassinated by the IRA. Similarly, a further 174 were injured, 484 unoccupied RIC barracks were destroyed and some 2,861 raids for arms made primarily upon police stations.[3]

Collins had first organized an élite intelligence network around himself. He told Hayden Talbot,

Every man has been tested — tested thoroughly. First I did it myself and thus satisfied myself regarding the trustworthiness of my chief aides. Then gradually the finding of the true measure of each new man became automatic and in turn the clearing out of the ranks of the IRA of undesirables became easier and faster.[4]

Irish men ceased to talk to the police. A boycott against the police and their families was rigidly enforced in every town or village where there was an RIC station. The IRA made it quite clear what their intentions were with regard to the police. Typical of the warnings given was the following IRA leaflet issued by order of the Dail declaring,

> We hereby proclaim the South Riding of Tipperary a military area with the following regulation. A policeman found within the said area will be deemed to have forfeited his life, the more notorious police being dealt with as far as possible first. . . . Every person in the pay of England — magistrates, jurors, who helps England rule this country will be deemed to have forfeited his life. Civilians who give information to the police will be executed, shot or hanged.[5]

As a result of this type of pressure, the police increasingly became isolated from their sources of information — the people. Knowledge of the underground Republican Army and its movements became difficult to acquire. Marooned in their sand-bagged barracks, the police became a pariah caste in most Irish communities. Their difficulties were heightened when Collins's organization began selectively to assassinate detectives of the DMP 'G' division — particularly the zealots dealing with political matters. At the time the 'G' division of the DMP was perhaps the most efficient intelligence unit operating in Ireland, and, importantly, it was based in Dublin, the nub of the underground, and seen to be the epicentre of the violent covert war between the intelligence agencies.

The first victim of Collins's 'Squad'[6] was one Detective Sergeant Smith, known in IRA circles as 'The Dog Smith', the Uriah Heep of the police force. In all of the assassinations that followed, the pattern was the same — the policeman would be given a series of warnings to cease his anti-Sinn Fein activities or he would be shot.[7] Collins demonstrated that he

was a man of his word. The tactic bore fruit. An observer of
the Dublin scene in 1920 commented that,

> The situation during the winter of 1920-21 was a striking illustration
> of the manner in which a small, organised body can intimidate a far
> larger and disorganised body. The fear created in the country by this
> struggle below the surface was incredible; the boldest seemed
> numbed. A man might have been murdered in broad daylight (and
> many were) in the Dublin streets, and not one policeman have lifted
> a finger. The uniformed men on point duty would have gone on
> waving the traffic this way and that. . . . The attitude of the police
> was reasonable. While they stayed neutral they were safe; as soon as
> they interfered they became marked men.[8]

The DMP and its intelligence section in particular were
speedily rendered useless. The RIC were then subjected to
the same treatment at a more intense pitch. Already we have
seen that the RIC was suffering from the general administrative malaise of the Castle government. Sir Neville Macready,
later to be the senior security officer in Ireland, remarked
upon his arrival in the country, after a preliminary study of
the security forces, that

> the intelligence system of the RIC had become effete and unreliable
> and any reports from that quarter were now coloured with the
> political or religious leanings of its source of origin. It was like
> working in a thick fog, the only resource being to hit out at anything
> one might suddenly bump into.[9]

Faced with terror and boycott, police intelligence degenerated. Meanwhile Collins's intelligence service, relatively unopposed, developed its slickness and efficiency The removal
of informers and spies became built into IRA tactics. As late
as the spring of 1921 they were still being shot. Between

January and April 1921 seventy-three bodies, with placards round their necks announcing the removal of an informer, were taken from the Irish streets.[10] Not unnaturally, the secrecy of IRA operations became first class and Collins's intelligence agency, in strking contrast to British security forces, could act with a considerable feeling of safety. At this time Collins's most famous coup was accomplished on the night of 7 April 1919 when Broy, one of his Dublin Castle informers, arranged for Collins to have access to all the files in the Special Branch HQ. From 12.30 am to 4.30 am Collins buried himself in the documents.[11] It is not surprising that every move of the Special Branch from this point was known in advance to the IRA. Detectives in plain clothes were not immune since their identities were known. As they were systematically shot, Special Branch ceased to provide information. Like the senior Castle administrators they became cloistered men[12] not allowed out of barracks without a strong armed escort.

While the security forces were beginning to break under the strain of IRA terror, local government had already ceased to function. The Irish underground government stepped into the vacuum. A Republican police force was established. Macready wrote to the Chief Secretary, Sir Hamar Greenwood that,

> nearly every day one sees in the papers that the Sinn Fein police are able to round up malefactors where the RIC are powerless and that is because the Sinn Fein have now at their disposal the very men who formerly were used by the RIC to get their information, that is the loafers and hangers about in the various towns and villages.

He also stressed that he saw,

> No reason to deviate in the least from the opinion I originally formed of the position here, and indeed, am every day strengthened

in that opinion, and that is that the state of affairs in this country has been allowed to drift into such an impasse that no amount of coercion can possibly remedy it.[13]

The general decline of the British administration was exacerbated by the stress conditions. The authority of the Castle government began to collapse. Increasingly, responsibility for enforcement of the underground government's law was assumed by the local Sinn Fein cadre and the officers of the IRA. The records of the Dublin Brigade IRA reveal, especially by the summer of 1920, the increasing demands placed upon the IRA, 'owing to the destruction of the alleged "police" force of the enemy and the rapid development of the civil side of Republican government'.[14] The IRA General Executive in fact agreed to place at the disposal of the Dail, under officers specially appointed for the purpose, a police force voluntarily recruited from the ranks of the IRA. The force was placed under local captains with brigade officers to control all IRA police activity in brigade areas. The brigade officer sifted all charges and arranged for arrests to be made. However, a battalion police officer was the general executive officer of the IRA, and he directed all police work in his particular area. Similarly he arranged the places for custody and the operation of courts. Company officers were assisted in their local units by three or four 'specially suitable men' chosen for permanent police work.[15] The nature of the punishments meted out by this Republican police force was particularly effective — even prior to the creation of a criminal code by the Dail Eireann. Senior IRA police officers were advised by the Dublin HQ that,

Pending the development of a criminal department of the Dail no punishment will be inflicted but the convicted parties will be detained in custody until the following Sunday and publicly paraded after the principal Mass, their name and address and offence being publicly announced.[16]

However, serious political offenders were shot out of hand after a summary trial.

Realizing the gravity of the security situation and the impending collapse of the Castle administration, the British government, under Lloyd George, made a concerted effort to reconstitute the administration and pursue a vigorous counter-offensive against the IRA, particularly its intelligence units. The techniques employed in that counter-offensive as we shall see were the same as those of the IRA, that is terror based upon efficient intelligence. It was this counter-offensive that moved the war of Irish independence into its crucial and bloodiest phase.

FINAL REFORMS AND THE BATTLE JOINED

The recommendations of the Fisher Committee of Inquiry into the Irish administration ushered in the demise of the old Castle system[17] which had for so long been an anachronism. However, the reforms arising out of the inquiry themselves exacerbated the disease of piecemeal, centralized bureaucratization. On the wings of the suggested reforms came a surfeit of brigadier generals and high-flying administrators from the British wartime government.[18] With the sole exception of the security initiatives, the reforms that they brought with them, or developed on the spot, 'failed to bite'. The Castle administration remained in the same perilous predicament that had characterized it when experienced crisis managers such as Sir John Anderson were recruited. Anderson's initial reactions to the state of the administration and the condition of public security are especially illuminating and must be quoted at length. In what he described as 'a few brief notes upon the Irish position looked at from the standpoint of the civil servant whose concern is with administration rather than high policy',[19] Anderson reported that,

> (i) the ordinary machinery of civil administration in the Chief Secretary's office . . . was practically non-existent. No business that was not urgent was being attended to and business which had become urgent was disposed of in very many cases without proper consideration. The general state of this office, on which the whole civil administration of the country should pivot, was really incredible.

> (ii) The police were in a critical condition. The morning I arrived in Dublin the Inspector General of the RIC stated in my presence that he was in daily fear of one of two things, either of wholesale resignation from the force or his men running amok. Either, he said, would mean the end of the RIC. They had practically no motor transport and were stationed in many cases in indefensible barracks without means of securing aid in the event of attack. Many important questions in regard to their pay allowances and pensions were long overdue for settlement. The all important matter of intelligence and secret service had been entirely neglected.[20]

He also found the prisons very poor, most insecure and inadequately staffed. The military too he felt were present in insufficient numbers, while the rank-and-file troops were inexperienced and quite raw, 'and, for the immediate purpose of giving support to the civil authority in the task of maintaining law and order throughout the country, almost

useless'.[21] Similarly, he reported that Macready had said that
Chief Inspector Marrinan of the RIC had told him, 'in strict
secrecy that the RIC were now half informers to Sinn Fein
and the other half prepared, owing to the strain, to become
assassins — in fact the force is on the verge of a break-up at
all events in the south'.[22] Anderson later added in his diary
that the RIC

> have been paralysed by the murders of their comrades. Anyone
> passing by a police barracks with its locked doors and seeing the
> constables looking out through barred windows will at once realise
> that no body of men could preserve its morale under such con-
> ditions. . . . At present the policeman in Ireland is never free from
> the dread of being murdered.[43]

Indeed, in the eighty-two weeks from January 1919 to 31
July 1920, seventy-three policemen were assassinated. Not
surprisingly, Anderson found the police to be 'profoundly
disaffected' and the local civil service, composed entirely of
Irishmen, to be 'politically alienated and, exposed as it is to
every kind of pressure and in many places intimidation,
cannot be relied upon in the execution of a vigorous
policy'.[24]

Local government and the Irish policing system were thus
beginning to break. Yet despite the partial reform of the
Castle system and the changes in personnel, the British
forces, the police in particular, continued to be impeded and
hampered by political expediency. Antagonism, disagreement
and a general lack of cohesion not only persisted between the
British administration in Ireland and the parent body at
Westminster, but also developed within the departments in
Dublin and between the two fighting services. Macready, in
command of troops, and Tudor, heading the police, liaised
imperfectly and uneasily. In the main the policies and actions

of the British forces were limited to reaction against the moves of their opponents. There were few, if any, military initiatives. Neither was there recognition of the need to wage a counter-insurgency campaign until the summer of 1920. The British military response was thus piecemeal when co-ordination was called for; it was heavy-handed when there was a need for finesse. As a result, it was too late in the day to redeem the Irish situation when the British discovered that 'guerrilla war is far more intellectual than a bayonet charge'.[25] The whole British campaign suffered from a lack of strategic and tactical reflection. There was, for instance, no clear command structure. Sir Mark Sturgis, a senior Castle administrator during the War of Independence, noted,

> the more I see of it [the war] the more convinced I am that if it is war, we must have a virtual dictator to be obeyed by everybody, military, police, civil service etc., As it is we are a great sprawling hydra-headed monster spending much of its time using one of its heads to abuse one or other of the others, by minute, letter, telegram and good, hard, word of mouth.

He also cavilled at the half measures advocated by the British politicians:

> If we aren't to treat [he wrote], we must hit damned hard. Why does some hideous fate make all politicians love half measures which of all so-called policies is the only surely fatal one.[26]

Any co-ordination by the security forces was made doubly difficult by the allocation of certain areas of Ireland to special authorities. Many of the southern counties came under martial law but there was no blanket declaration for the whole of Ireland. An assessment of the efficacy of martial law in Ireland, interestingly made at the time of the Arab rebellion in Palestine, 1936-39, came to the conclusion that, during the Irish War of Independence,

> The declaration of Martial Law in four counties only had great disadvantage. In the first place it seemed probable that in order to avoid the penalties incurred by carrying arms in the Martial Law area, parties of rebels would make their way into adjoining counties. To prevent that it would be necessary to guard the boundaries and there were not sufficient troops to do this. Secondly, the demand for the surrender of arms was not likely to be complied with in the Martial Law area where extremists were in a majority and the morale of the IRA was therefore such as to encourage defiance of that order; whereas in 8 areas less terrorised such an order might have produced the desired result and gradually spread. . . . had Martial Law been proclaimed throughout Ireland the control of all Crown forces wouldhave been centred in one head – the Military Governor General. This woul have ensured co-ordination of effort and unification of policy. Whereas partial Martial Law led to the anomalous position of the police in the proclaimed counties being under the local Military Governors while divided control existed throughout Ireland. . . . Again, two separate forms of trial were necessary. In the Martial Law Area trials were by Military Court, whereas in other areas they were by Court Martial (instituted under the Defence of the Realm Act) and a similar offence was liable to a death penalty in one place and not in a place a few miles away.[27]

Thus both administratively and militarily the British in Ireland were proved to be deficient. This was not the case with the Irish underground. It was, however, in the military arena that the IRA had its most visible successes. The effect of its operations were such that even in Dublin, as we have seen, senior policemen, administrators and military officers were forced to live monastically within the walls of Dublin Castle. There were so many ambushes carried out by the IRA in one particular complex of Dublin streets that the British forces termed the area the 'Dardanelles'.

The major spheres of IRA activity were typically those of the guerrilla force — attacks on police barracks, army and police patrols and convoys; assassination of individuals; destruction of government property; robbery and highway robbery; the disarming of military and police to capture weapons. The aim of the attacks on police barracks was twofold; to break the hold of the police on the local communities, and to capture much needed arms and ammunition. Normally the attacks were carried out by fairly large companies of the IRA, generally one or two companies of a battalion which were either local in origin or had been dispatched from a neighbouring county. The assembly of such large groups of men was often effected by holding a sports meeting organized by the GAA in the neighbourhood. The crowds that gathered for such meetings were supposed to disarm suspicion. As we shall see, Bloody Sunday, November 1920, was an excellent example of this tactic in operation.

The arms for IRA raids were usually brought in by car and attacks were carried out after dark. The thoroughness of so many of these raids is indicated by a British War Office assessment, which noted in 1920 that,

> at a given time the attackers congregate and all roads but one are blocked with obstacles for a radius of anything up to 5 miles of the point to be attacked (a case has occurred where an area up to 20 miles has been blocked) in order to delay any relieving force. In the attacks upon patrols and convoys IRA units of varying strength were employed. Normally there were not more than 50 to 60 or fewer than 6 to 8 waiting behind a wall or in a ditch; where a small attacking force was engaging a patrol, as was often the case, they operated from the midst of an apparently innocuous crowd who shielded the attackers afterwards.[28]

The leading edge of the IRA campaign was selective assassination. Here groups of three to ten men were involved. Police, magistrates, informers and men prominent in public life were shot. There were even plans, vetoed at the last minute by Collins and Arthur Griffith, to assassinate the whole of the British Cabinet by machine-gunning the government front benches from the Spectator's Gallery in the House of Commons.[29] Assassination in fact ran the whole gamut from vengeance killings (such as that of a former British army officer, Captain Lee Wilson, who had severely mistreated Collins and other combatants of the 1916 Rising) to killings deemed expedient.[30] Redmond, Chief Inspector of the DMP, was removed because he was pressing Collins too hard; similarly, the magistrate Allen Bell, taken in daylight from a Dublin tram and shot without anyone interfering, was assassinated because he was carrying on a most successful investigation into the origin and whereabouts of the funds of the underground government, the Dail Eireann Loan Deposits.[31] Assassinations such as these, and particularly the removal of spies, Collins regarded as fundamental to the success of the IRA campaign. As he wrote,

> England could always reinforce her Army. She could replace every soldier that she lost. . . . But there were others indispensable for her purposes which were not so easily replaced. To paralyse the British machine it was necessary to strike at individuals.[32]

Police intelligence duly reported in 1919 that,

> according to information received from various sources the Irish Volunteer H.Q. has directed all county commanders to hold a certain number of men armed and in readiness to execute orders to attack barracks and assassinate police.[33]

The police were to bear the brunt of the assassination attacks and, as we shall see, they finally broke under the application of systematic terror.

Thus, as a guerrilla army, the IRA was tactically and organizationally sound. It knew its military limitations and fought within them. It was also highly mobile. By the autumn of 1920, flying columns had been organized in several of the most active IRA brigade areas. Towards the end of 1920 all brigades were instructed to create such units.[34] Militarily the success of the IRA was due to its speed, mobility and intelligence — all of which in one way or another were dependent upon the support of the Irish people. As T. E. Lawrence noted, the unsurgent force,

> must have a friendly population, not actively friendly but sympathetic to the point of not betraying rebel movements to the enemy. Rebellions can be made by 2% active in a striking force, and 98% passively sympathetic.[35]

As we have seen, by 1919 the majority of Ireland's population was behind Sinn Fein and its support was not passive but was committed to the fighting men and their creed. It was the buoyancy and success of the Irish opposition that stood in marked contrast to the inadequacies of the British administration. It was the resolute condition of the Irish political will supporting an effective guerrilla force that eventually determined that the British would lose control of Ireland. Late in the day, British attempts to regain lost initiatives succeeded in achieving little more than a massive escalation in the level of political violence. The struggle between the IRA and the police and the critical episode of Bloody Sunday, November 1920, were to prove to be, as we shall see, not only the epicentres, respectively, of the overt and covert wars but the events that finally confirmed both the political and military defeat of the British in Ireland.

THE FINAL BREAKDOWN –
BLOODY SUNDAY, NOVEMBER 1920:
A REAPPRAISAL

By the spring of 1920, the British administration in Ireland was in a deep crisis. The security forces were breaking; the political will to hold on to Ireland had all but evaporated; the IRA was in the ascendant. There was thus a dire need to resuscitate the well chewed remnants of the RIC and, above all, to counteract and combat the IRA intelligence network.[36] The police force was soon revived by the influx of Black and Tan and Auxiliary Police.[37] More importantly, during the spring of 1920, the British government began to take measures aimed at breaking IRA intelligence. In the summer of 1920 an intelligence bureau was formed in London in the charge of a Major C. A. Cameron, himself considerably experienced in espionage during the 1914-18 war. Eventually some sixty agents were trained and dispatched to Ireland. Once these secret servicemen were in the field, aided by a reorganized and far more efficient British military intelligence service, they immediately began to put the Collins organization under pressure. Collins himself was placed under great personal strain. He was systematically hunted. A price of £40,000 was placed on his head. Collins was *the* target of the British intelligence operation. Perhaps symptomatic of the pressure under which he was forced to live at this time were the periodic attacks of severe, disabling stomach pains which he developed. He described them as 'stomach trouble, not really serious but enough to prevent one doing anything more than just routine things'.[38] Some time later in 1920, he wrote, 'I have had some severe hunting . . . closer and closer it has been, but yet they have not had the ultimate success. . . . Things have been harder than anybody knows.'[39] During a period of three months in 1920, 1,745 arrests were made in the Dublin district alone. Similarly, from 16 to 18 August 1920 some 716 raids were made under curfew by the police and military.[40] Pressure was further increased under martial law when British court martial officers began resolutely building cases against IRA men. Unlike the intimidated and pro-Republican civil courts, the military courts were not afraid to convict. The situation in Dublin began dramatically to change. Collins and his men could no longer bicycle around Dublin with impunity. With the benefit of adequate intelligence, for perhaps the first time in well over a decade, the efficacy of police actions increased throughout Ireland. Yet as the overt war, from the British point of view, began to be waged with greater success, the covert war between the rival intelligence systems degenerated into a rash of reprisals and assassinations.

To minimize the effect of this far more rigorous policy on both the British press and the Lloyd George coalition government, a Propaganda Department was established in Dublin Castle with a branch at the Irish Office in London.[41] The aim of the Propaganda Department as stated by its director, Basil Clarke, was to control rigidly the activities of pressmen in Ireland, and, more importantly to distort and wherever possible to neutralise news items and descriptions of events that might be harmful to the British government.[42] This statement of intent is wildly at variance with that of Sir Hamar Greenwood, then Chief Secretary for Ireland, issued in the House of Commons:

> I have myself, gone out of my way to provide motor cars and facilities of every kind for the press of the world to see Ireland as it is, because I believe, whatever may be said against the Government,

the more publicity Ireland gets from the people who visit it, the stronger and more united will be the support, not only of the country, but of civilisation, behind the Irish Government. This is my view. As to the press generally, I welcom them.[43]

However, the evidence is quite conclusive that the Dublin Castle Propaganda Department was established to veto the provocative or harmful news coming out of Ireland in the wake of the covert intelligence and assassination campaign that the British had now operationalized. It helped create the miasma of conflicting and reconstructed reports of the crucial events of 21 November 1920.

The Propaganda Department was established by the British government and placed under Basil Clarke on 9 August 1920. Clarke had had an interesting career prior to his appointment. Educated at Manchester Grammar School and Oxford, he began a career in journalism in 1903, later becoming a war correspondent for the *Manchester Guardian,* then a war correspondent in Flanders for the *Daily Mail* and finally a war correspondent for Reuters and the Press Association based at the British Army GHQ in France. Clearly he was an apposite choice as head of the Dublin Castle Propaganda Department. He knew the military machine and was presumably on good terms with senior staff officers as well as having journalistic experience under war conditions.

The Department itself was divided into three 'stations'. The hub of the organization was Clarke himself, operating in Dublin Castle and supplemented by a station at Military GHQ in Dublin which controlled every aspect of military information. Similarly there was an office in London which Clarke supervised. In a series of memoranda preserved in the British Public Record Office,[44] Clarke himself set out 'the elementary principles underlying the chief methods of propaganda employed'. His stated aim was to suppress or neutralise 'the plethora of adverse news reports'. 'Suppression,' he stated, 'or if suppression be either undesirable or impossible, the neutralisation so far as is possible of the unfavourable factors in news having a minus or unfavourable propaganda value.'[4][5] The triple aims of the department were then, first, to mask the exact nature of the crisis situation in Ireland but particularly to deny the extent to which governability and public security had declined; second, to combat the IRA Propaganda Department; and finally, through its journal the *Weekly Summary* issued to all police units in Ireland, to boost morale and discipline the 'wild boys' in the police. (Interestingly, Palestine saw none of these tactics employed by the incumbent government, perhaps because, more geographically distant, the crisis did not seem so immediate or severe to British politicians or public. One of the consequences of this was that in Palestine the military, operating without the restrictions imposed by an ever-present, inquisitive and accusatory press, pursued their task thoroughly and broke the rebellion).

Yet rarely can there have been so many contradictory appraisals and so much controversy about the events of one day as there has been about 'Bloody Sunday' — the event that holds the key to the battle between the terrorist and the political police in Ireland.

The traditional and conflicting views of the events of 21 November 1920 suffer in the main from the fact that they have been based upon official communiqués issued at the height of the war by the combatants. As we have seen, both the English and Irish had efficient propaganda organizations doctoring the reports of the final, crucial battles of the covert intelligence and assassination war.

The British interpretation has always been that the men

shot in their beds on the Sunday morning, 21 November 1920, were military personnel serving as court martial officers. It has also been held that some of the men assassinated by what Lloyd George erroneously referred to as a 'small murder gang'[4][6] were innocents killed in error. The British account has its origins in a report on the shooting prepared by none other than Basil Clarke, head of the Dublin Castle Propaganda Department and amended by Sir John Anderson, under-secretary at the Castle.[4][7] This account also holds that, as a response to the events of that morning, British security forces surrounded and attempted to search the Croke Park football ground where a hurling match was taking place between Dublin and Tipperary. The official report, written on the Sunday evening at 11.35 pm, states that,

> the round up and search of spectators attending a football match at Croke Park, Dublin, on Sunday was carried out by the authorities according to a preconceived plan, with the object of securing Sinn Fein gunmen who had taken part in the assassinations of that morning and who, in some cases, were believed to have come into Dublin under cover of attending the match.[4][8]

When the security forces approached the ground they found IRA sentries posted; once inside the ground the first shots were fired from the crowd. In response the security forces opened fire, killing some fourteen people, among them several children and the Tipperary goalkeeper, Mick Hogan.[4][9]

The final act of Bloody Sunday involved the shooting of Clancy, Clune and McKee in Dublin while they were attempting to escape from custody. The three men were being held in connection with the shootings of the morning, although they had been arrested on the Saturday night, in Clune's case, and in the early hours of Sunday morning. McKee and Clancy, both sides agree, had helped plan the assassination. Both had met Michael Collins on Saturday evening, 20 November, at Vaughan's Hotel, to finalize the arrangements for the Sunday morning shootings. Vaughan's was a well-known IRA rendezvous. The meeting was one of the IRA élite. McKee was commandant of the 1st Battalion, Finglass Brigade, commandant of the Dublin Brigade, a member of the IRA Executive Council as well as chief of explosives supply to the IRA. Clancy, also attached to the Dublin Brigade and not long released from hunger strike in Mountjoy Prison, was known to have been involved in the attempted assassination of the Viceroy, Lord French.[50] The business that he ran, the 'Republican Outfitters Stores' in Talbot Street, Dublin, was a communications post of the IRA underground as well as a safe meeting place for senior IRA officers. These men were thus important captives for the security forces. Little seems to have been known of Clune at the time other than the fact that he belonged, according to the British, to the 1st Battalion, Clare Brigade IRA,[51] and when captured had in his possession a pocket-book in which were the names of Collins and the other members of the élite IRA assassination group, the Squad. It has since emerged that Clune had travelled to Dublin that weekend with Dr Edward McLysaght, intelligence officer with the Clare IRA.[52] Perhaps he was not the innocent clerk travelling to Dublin to audit the annual accounts of the Raheen Co-operative Society as the IRA maintained?

The Irish stance differs from that of the British in every major detail. Official IRA opinion at the time – an opinion still maintained – was that the officers assassinated on Bloody Sunday were key secret servicemen, themselves responsible for the assassination of leading Republicans; that the shooting at Croke Park was a deliberate reprisal, an attempt to redress the balance of terror; and that Clancy, Clune and McKee were not shot while escaping but to avoid embarrassing questions since all three men had systematically been tortured by the Auxiliary Police.[53]

The main body of work done on the subject either has divided into one of the two camps or has cautiously come down somewhere in between. Here, on this critical incident of the battle between the terrorists and the political police, new evidence is presented on the major bone of contention — the occupation of the British officers assassinated on Bloody Sunday. The evidence makes it quite clear that the officers shot by the IRA were, in the main, involved in some aspect of British intelligence. They did indeed belong to the group of sixty assembled in London under Cameron. Having developed a 'cover' and immersed themselves in the milieu, they formed a network throughout Ireland with its hub in Dublin. Their brief was simple — they were to break the intelligence apparatus of the IRA. The latter, however, knew all about the British operation. Quite clearly, too, Collins perceived that this was a battle that must be won if the vision of Irish independence was to retain any meaning. An IRA document captured by the RIC Special Branch affirms just how determined the IRA was to win this vital battle. The captured 'Instructions to all IRA officers commanding district areas' read as follows:

In a recent order to their troops the English Command stated their first intention was to inaugurate an extensive intelligence system. Further Macready has stated that he had covered the country from end to end with spies. On the results of this intelligence system the enemy is expecting to win. It is beyond question that intelligence is of supreme importance and that it is the duty of every Volunteer Commander to see that the lead which we have secured in this matter against the enemy is properly maintained . . . in everything keep your eyes and your ears open and your mouth shut.[54]

Here then, we must concentrate on the killings of the morning of 21 November 1920, since they determined who would win the covert war between the political police and the terrorist. The Bloody Sunday assassinations represented the acme of the chosen mode of warfare that prevailed during the Irish War of Independence — selective assassination.

BLOODY SUNDAY, 21 NOVEMBER 1920: THE DEFEAT OF THE BRITISH SECURITY OFFENSIVE AND THE IMPACT OF TERROR

Pressure had been building almost inexorably on the Dublin IRA and Collins throughout the summer and autumn of 1920 as the British intelligence apparatus became fully operational. By October the position of the IRA was extremely serious. In one of the many security forces raids in Dublin during that month, various materials belonging to the underground Irish government and the IRA propaganda department were captured. Far more threatening and alarming than the forged copies of the *Irish Bulletin* (which was the IRA Propaganda Department's journal), which was one consequence of the raid, were the crop of letters prominent Republican leaders began to receive. It is the origin of these notes, and especially the extent to which the threats contained in them were carried out, that caused Collins to move against the British intelligence officers tucked away in Dublin.

In a letter captured by Collins, Captain F. Harper Shrove,

intelligence officer of the General Staff, Dublin district, wrote on 2 March to one Hardy,

Have duly reported and found things in a fearful mess, but think will be able to make a good show. Have been given a free hand to carry on and everyone has been very charming. Re our little stunt, I see no prospect until I have got things on a firmer basis, but still hope and believe there are possibilities.[55]

The IRA has always held that the 'little stunt' was the assassination by agents of MI5 or SIS of prominent Republicans – or at least a plan for such action, conceived by the secret service and carried out by military or police forces in the form of reprisals.[56] The IRA later alleged that this policy was in fact carried out by a body of constabulary specially recruited and known as 'Igoe's Gang'. Approximately forty in number, these men served under Head Constable Eugene Igoe of the RIC who worked in conjunction with the Intelligence Section at Dublin Castle. Evidence has since come to light in the State Paper Office, Dublin Castle, that appears to confirm the IRA allegation. In a letter from C. Prescott Decie, of the No. 1 Division, Munster, one of a series of fortnightly reports to Anderson, assistant under-secretary at the Castle, dated 1 June 1920, Decie writes: 'I have been told the new policy and I am satisfied though I doubt its ultimate success in the main particular – the stamping out of terrorism, by secret murder'.[57] It is evident that this tactic had the highest official support and may well have originated with either Lloyd George, the prime minister, or, Sir Henry Wilson, chief of the Imperial General Staff. Wilson was a noted advocate of harsh methods, having declared his preference to 'Shoot all the Irish leaders by roster'. Wilson himself records Lloyd George's commitment to counter-terror in his diary, writing that the Prime Minister continued 'to be satisfied that a counter-murder association was the best answer to Sinn Fein murders'.[58] Or perhaps the initiative came from Sir John Anderson, who wrote to Wilson,

> I have been in close communication with the GOC's [of] the 4 areas in this country and as a result I must reiterate that if the present state of affairs in this country continues, some steps must be taken to regularise reprisals for outrages committed on troops. . . . It is a fact that where reprisals have taken place, the whole atmosphere of the surrounding district is changed from one of hostility to one of cringing submission.[59]

That reprisals were officially sanctioned is affirmed by Anderson later in an order to the effect that 'reprisals should be undertaken only by order of officers not below the rank of Brigadier General . . . and by police Divisional Commissioners or Chief Inspectors'.[60] Perhaps the conclusive proof of the British government's intention to assassinate prominent Republicans is contained in a note in Sir Mark Sturgis's Diary, where he records on 10 October 1920,

> Arthur Griffith has given an interview to pressmen saying that he knows we contemplate the murder of Sinn Fein leaders and that his name is top of the list. . . . He also quotes from a military document dropped by aerial post in the wrong place by incredible stupidity. Macready is furious and wants the two airmen Court Martialled.[61]

This mistake was not surprising since the Flying Corps had already dramatically erred by leaving their safe unlocked. The contents, details of the security forces courier service in Ireland as well as details of the guard arrangements in Dublin, were removed by the IRA and substituted with a note: 'Many thanks, will call again – IRA'.[62] However, within eighteen days of F. Harper Shrove's letter being written, Thomas McCurtin, lord mayor of Cork, was assassinated by a group of British police officers.[63] A short while later two other prominent Republicans, James McCarthy of Thurles and Thomas Dwyer of Bouladuff, County Tipperary, had been assassinated in circumstances that indicated the involvement of British forces. In these cases and others that followed, threats of death had been issued on captured Dail Eireann notepaper. The warning notes are further evidence of a plan of assassination by Crown forces, since in each of the death notes the capital letter 'T' and small 'L', where they occurred together, produced marked unevenness in the alignment of the two letters. An 'expert' was produced by the IRA who was 'prepared to swear' that all had been typed on an Underwood machine. The illuminating fact was that the documents captured from F. Harper Shrove had the same inconsistency of type.[64] The number of murdered Republicans increased. The police were encouraged to shoot at random anyone they suspected. One observer noted that Ireland had been,

> converted into a cross between a medieval Italian city where hired bravoes worked at street corners to stab a foe in the dark, and a more modern Balkan state, where brutalised soldier-peasants made whole countrysides reek with atrocities.[65]

One check on the activities of police had been fear of exposure by Coroner's Courts,[66] but these were replaced by Military Courts of Inquiry as a result of the Restoration of Order Act. Senior police officers undertook a whistle-stop tour of police barracks to reassure their men about their position should they be accused of the murder of innocent civilians.[67] Smyth, divisional commissioner of the RIC for

Munster, informed men at the police barracks Listowel, County Kerry, in the presence of the most senior police officer in Ireland, General Tudor, that,

> if the persons approaching you carry their hands in their pockets, or in any way look suspicious, shoot them down. You may make mistakes occasionally and innocent persons may be shot, but that cannot be helped and you are bound to get the right parties sometimes. The more you shoot, the better I will like you and I assure you, men, no policeman will get into trouble for shooting anyone.[68]

What was particularly alarming for Collins was that there coincided with this determined British policy based on reprisal a marked decline in allegiance to the IRA and Republicanism in general. Special Branch reports from the various RIC headquarters in the counties indicated that the boycott of the police was breaking. One county inspector recorded that in Leitrim,

> moderately inclined people are beginning to be friendly to the police and in addition to some of the Irish Volunteers have notified the police that they have severed their connection with the movement. The boycott of the police in Carrick-on-Shannon and Mohill has been removed. The police whose morale is excellent are patrolling and enforcing the law.[69]

Clearly the security position had begun to change dramatically. The timing in the drop of support was doubly significant since it occurred after the hanging of Kevin Barry and the death of MacSwiney in Brixton Prison after a seventy-day hunger strike.[70] One would have expected an intensification of rather than a decline in the degree of hostility shown the Crown forces. Certainly, if the RIC Special Branch had registered the change in mood, Collins's more efficient intelligence network in the localities would have first monitored and then relayed the alarming message to him in Dublin.

Thus it was by these broad fronts of pressure tha Collins was forced to act. One is reminded of Foch's dictum, 'Mon centre cede, ma droite recule, situation excellente. J'attaque.' In the light of the position in which he now found himself at this critical juncture in the war, what, for Collins, could be a better tactic to discipline IRA members and wavering Republicans than a series of assassinations which would shock the Irish people, reaffirm the determination of IRA leadership and, most importantly, remove at one blow those who were threatening the survival of Irish resistance — the intelligence agents and court martial officers assembled in Dublin? For the IRA there would be the added bonus of further violent reprisals by British forces, reprisals which in turn would harden Irish opposition. But above all, it was the pressure upon Collins that brought about the assassinations. 'Those fellows who were put on the spot', Collins is reported to have written, 'were going to put a lot of us on the spot so I got in first'.[71]

The events of 21 November 1920 were a striking cameo of the war. There was no quarter given, few if any debates, just a set of targets and resolutely organized violent action. On the morning of 21 November 1920, twenty attempts in all were made on the lives of a variety of people. Of the twenty, only one escaped physically unscathed; thirteen men were killed and six injured. Of those attacks thirteen were involved in one way or another with intelligence work. Of the remainder, two were Auxiliary policemen, two civilians, and two court martial officers administering military justice. Originally, it seems Collins had prepared a list of thirty-five men to be shot. Passed on to the IRA GHQ staff and to Cathal Brugha, this list was whittled down to fifteen names because it was felt there was insufficient evidence on which to execute all thirty-five.[72] It is necessary now to look in detail at the crucial day. The information that is revealed confirms the view that here on Sunday, 21 November 1920, was the critical battle of the war.

What of the dramatis personae of that day? Four of the thirteen intelligence officers shot were military officers – namely Captain Newberry, Temporary Lieutenant Ames, Temporary Lieutenant Angliss and Captain Bennett. These four officers, along with the judicial officer's Temporary Captain Baggallay and Major Dowling, were the only men acknowledged in the list of fatalities in the December 1920 issue of the *Monthly Military List*.[73] Though the remaining men may at one time have been military men, they were not considered serving military officers at the time of their deaths – despite their burial with full military honours and an impressive state funeral in the presence of Lloyd George.

The attacks began at 8.55 am at 117 Morehampton Road with the shooting of McLean, Smith and Caldow, who were taken from their beds to the top storey of the house before being shot.[74] The method of entry in all the assassinations was virtually the same: one or two men would knock at the door and gain entry, and the others would follow, shooting their victims in their beds or in the bedroom. It is the scale of the attacks, their precision and the number of gunmen involved that are so striking. This was a major undertaking, and clearly Collins was leaving nothing to chance. The assassination groups varied in size from twelve to twenty, there being seven groups in all. Six were detailed to carry out the assassinations, while the seventh provided cover, should – as in fact happened – a patrol of police or military be encountered.[75] There were thus approximately 120 men involved. It is most interesting, in the light of the structure of the attacking force, to note that on Sunday, 31 October 1920, in what now seems a prelude to events two weeks later, an obviously co-ordinated attack was carried out against the RIC in which nine police officers lost their lives. *The Times* referred to the incident as 'Black Sunday' and stated that the attacks occurred in seven areas of Ireland.[76] There is every likelihood that this was a rehearsal for the seven assassination squads due to go into action on November 21. Certainly the Dublin organization could not provide all the men necessary for an operation as ambitious as 21 November. Pressure was also very much on the Dublin 'Squad'. They were having to lie low. A note in Basil Clarke's hand at the Public Record Office says of the 'Dublin Murder Gang',

> they have become acutely conscious that the Crown has gained of late intimate knowledge not only of their methods and plans but also of their names and whereabouts . . . murder plans were being made in greater numbers.[77]

It was thus sound tactics on Collins's part to involve unknown groups of gunmen in the assassinations, and what better method of masking such an influx of men from the countryside than to choose the date of the GAA football match, which was to take place at Croke Park, Dublin, on the afternoon of 21 November?

Captain D. L. McLean was the first to be assassinated, at 8.55 am. McLean, with his wife and ten-year-old son, lived with his brother-in-law, John Caldow, at the house of T. H. Smith, 117 Morehampton Road. Caldow and Smith were the civilians who were shot — Caldow, it seems, having recently come to Ireland in the hope of enlisting in the police. McLean, late of the Rifle Brigade, had recently returned from intelligence work in Holland.[78] He was shot eight times. At the military court of inquiry into the assassination, McLean's wife stated that 'the men asked her husband his name and when he replied McLean, a voice said "That is good enough".'[79]

T. H. Smith was allowed to dress before being shot. McLean was shot and found dead in a sitting position by the fireplace. Caldow survived the shooting. Smith, who was found lying under a bed frame badly wounded, died in Baggot Street Hospital where all three men had been taken.

Captain Bennett and Lieutenant Ames were resident at 38 Upper Mount Street. Bennett, previously a lieutenant in the Royal Engineers, had served as an intelligence officer with the British Army of the Black Sea from 13 April to 6 August 1919. Lieutenant Ashmunt Ames was also 'specially employed'.[80] Apparently twenty men rushed into the house, asking for Ames. Bennet and Ames were both taken to Ames's room and shot — Bennet received seven wounds, one through the top of the head, one through the forehead, one in the chest, three in the back and one through the right forearm.

At Lower Mount Street were Lieutenant C. R. Peel and Lieutenant Angliss, alias Mahon or McMahon, both Irishmen. Peel was the only man to emerge without injury from the several attacks, since he was able to barricade himself in his room and survive a volley of shots through the bedroom door. He had received his 'special appointment' on 6 August 1920.[81] Angliss had been recalled from intelligence work on the Russian front to set up an intelligence group in the south of Dublin. His special appointment had been in operation since 2 October 1918.[82] He was a most experienced intelligence officer.

It was while Angliss was being killed and Peel besieged that the Auxiliaries G. A. Garniss and F. Morriss were killed. They were the Auxiliaries' first fatal casualties.[83] They had stumbled across an IRA covering party at 22 Lower Mount Road and were shot while on their way to bring Auxiliary reinforcements from their HQ at Beggar's Bush Barracks. The two men were taken round to the back of 16 Mount Street, the garden of a Red Cross nurse, and shot. Garniss received two bullet wounds, one behind the right ear and the other through the chest; Morriss was shot behind the left eye.

At the Gresham Hotel two other men were killed, Lieutenant L. A. Wilde and the Irishman Captain P. McCormack, late of the Royal Army Veterinary Corps. Neither Wilde nor McCormack appears in any of the military lists of the period. For long there have been too many questions and too few answers about these men. There is evidence, concerning McCormack at least, that it is most unlikely that, as some accounts have maintained, both men were shot in error.[84] Bloody Sunday was most carefully prepared. Given the professionalism of Collins's organization and the quality of his informants, and hence of his information, there must have been reasons for their names figuring on his very carefully checked list.

One can suggest reasons for the presence of McCormack's name on it. McCormack had recently returned from Egypt,[85] and, according to evidence given at the court of inquiry into the shootings, he was 'murdered on the eve of his departure for Egypt to take up his duties as official starter to the Cairo Racing Club'.[86] Egypt at that time was a focal point of special intelligence operations. As a veterinary surgeon and an Irishman in a rural community he had excellent cover. There is, however, the infinitely more sinister and likely possibility that McCormack was involved in some way in the use of germ warfare apparently threatened by the IRA. Early in November 1920, the RIC Special Branch had gained possession of an IRA document which detailed the methods to be used when conducting germ warfare against British troops and livestock. The note from Mulcahy, commander-in-chief of the IRA, to Collins ran:

Troops themselves

How about spreading typhoid amongst them? I know of no other ordinary disease that could spread among them with safety to the rest of the population. To get typhoid fever one must eat or drink the typhoid bacillus. It is easy getting fresh and virulent cultures. The best medium of conveying it is through the milk.

Glanders in horses

It should be possible to give horses glanders. The disease is got from harness and by putting a horse in a stable from which an infected horse has been removed. Therefore it should be possible to pass the infection by means of doctoring the oats.

Method

Any doctor or veterinary surgeon will be able to tell you how to grow the microbes. If they don't know they can look it up in any text book on bacteriology. Assume you have half a pint of active microbes, then take a hollow stick or piece of piping, get another stick to fit in this like a ramrod of a gun, put this stick down the sack of oats, withdraw the ramrod, then push in the microbes while you at the same time withdraw the hollow stick of piping.[87]

The IRA attempted to divert attention from the captured document by claiming it was a product of Clarke's Propaganda Department. As one researches further into this incident, the more perplexing it becomes. Perhaps all that one can do is present the available evidence and allow the reader to judge.

First details of the document come in a police report which states that the letter was captured in a search at the house of a Professor Michael Hayes, University College,

Dublin, at 5 am. A special courier was then immediately sent to England with the document. There would seem to be no record of a Professor Michael Hayes, although a Captain William Ivon Hayes MB, BS (Melbourne), Australian Army, MC, was chief demonstrator of anatomy in the Department of Pathology and Bacteriology at the university.[88] Both Hayes and the head of the Department of Bacteriology, which is also referred to as the Department of Preventative Medicine, were appointed on 22 October 1919.[89] The Department was likewise established at that date.

The Head of the Department was an extremely distinguished biologist, Professor Adrian Stokes, an Irishman. He apparently had little sympathy for the Republican cause, since he had enlisted in the British forces despite the furore over conscription. Born in Dublin in 1887 and educated at Trinity College, he gained his MB in 1910 and MD in 1911, becoming assistant professor of pathology there in 1913. Volunteering in 1914 and serving throughout the Great War, he 'initiated and spread new methods of treatment which saved countless lives'.[90] With the operational use of chemical warfare in 1914-18, the vague phrase only adds to the intrigue. During the war he was mentioned in dispatches; gained the DSO, OBE and Chevalier de l'Ordre de la Couronne, Belgium. He was also a member of the Athenaeum, MCC and University College, Dublin clubs.[91]

The captured document was eventually read in the House of Commons, again under circumstances that add to the mystery of its origin. One can quote the argument verbatim from *Hansard*, since this illustrates briefly the doubts as to the document's paternity: 'A question of Private Notice from a Mr. Pennefather M.P. was read asking the Chief Secretary, Hamar Greenwood, for information of a plot to infect milk and give glanders to horses.' The document, part of which I have included above, was then read and the following remarks were made.

[Mr MacVeah] Can the Chief Secretary tell the House whether one policeman or one soldier has been poisoned in Ireland and whether one Army horse has been infected?

The answer was in the negative.

[Mr Devlin] Was not the whole thing concocted in Dublin Castle?

[Mr MacVeah] It is a sheer invention. You got Pennefather to put the question. It is a put-up question.

[Mr Seeton] How is it that such voluminous and extensive information can be given on a Private Notice question within a few hours? It takes days (Hon members: weeks!) to get information on other subjects.[92]

There are thus several possibilities concerning the incident. First, that McCormack, who had been in Dublin for several months, had infiltrated the IRA and was passing them information concerning chemical warfare which Stokes and Hayes provided. This information would be incomplete but a useful front for an intelligence man to have. McCormack was thus removed since his double role was discovered. The fact that he was shot on the evening before he was to return to Egypt may mean that it was known that his 'cover' had been destroyed. The Gresham Hotel, then Dublin's finest, was certainly an expensive place for a retired captain of the RAVC to stay — one wonders where indeed his finances came from.

If this was the case the article on germ warfare would be a 'genuine' one fed to the IRA by the Dublin Castle Propaganda Department and intelligence service with the dual aim of gaining an insight, through McCormack, into the IRA leadership, as well as ultimately denouncing the IRA as a host of barbarians. The furore in the press over British reprisals would have palled alongside the use of germ warfare had the Castle propaganda staff gained maximum advantage from their material. Hence the security services tried to cover their tracks and the origin of the document by referring to the apparently non-existent Professor Michael Hayes.

A variant of this could of course be that the IRA leadership heard of the intended propaganda scoop by the British and beat the enemy Propaganda Department to the draw. They achieved this be releasing information to the Press through their own propaganda officers which implied that the whole affair was staged. Whatever the intentions of either side this indeed was the effect. The IRA Propaganda Department had nullified the potential impact of the document by casting doubts about its parentage. Despite the British messenger hurrying across from Dublin, the IRA had moved quicker.

One could of course create unending permutations over the incident. Much remained unclear until I discovered in the Dublin Record Office a note in the diary of Sir Mark Sturgis, Senior Dublin Castle administrator, clearly stating, 'Two secret servicemen were assassinated in the Gresham Hotel'.[93] McCormack was then working for British intelligence. If that fact was conclusively proved all the other possibilities gain credence. Clearly here was yet one more crucial reason for the Bloody Sunday operation as far as Michael Collins was concerned.

McCormack and Lieutenant Wilde were assassinated by a small party of IRA men while another group remained on the ground floor of the Gresham Hotel, stopping all movement in the entrance hall. McCormack was found lying on his back in bed with the newspaper in his hand — the blankets and bedclothes singed and penetrated with bullets. Wilde, shot in a separate room, was found face downwards in a pool of blood. His arms were stretched out in front of him almost cradling part of his brains which were lying in front of his head.[94]

The IRA assassins continued their work at 28 Earlsfort Terrace, where an RIC barracks defence officer, Captain P. Fitzgerald, was shot. Fitzgerald was the son of a Tipperary doctor, serving as a barracks defence officer in Clare. Prior to his assassination he had been kidnapped by the IRA, propped against a wall, shot and left for dead. Mysteriously, he survived, and had not long been out of a Dublin hospital for treatment to an arm dislocated in his previous 'brush' with the IRA when he was killed. Collins obviously wanted Fitzgerald dead. There would seem to be no immediate reason, however, unless, as a barracks defence officer, he was an important figure in the reoccupation and strengthening of surviving vacated RIC barracks – a policy that was being carried out at the time.[95]

With all this information in mind, given the now-proven occupation of the assassinated officers, the effect their unit was having upon the underground struggle between the terrorist and the political police, it is not difficult to see why Collins determined that they must be shot. Bloody Sunday, 21 November 1920, was the conclusive battle in the war of political murder. It was a question of survival too. Barrere, when questioned during the French Revolution about the actions of the Committee of Public Safety, replied with a statement Collins could quite well have issued in the aftermath of Bloody Sunday:

> We had but one sentiment, that of self-preservation, but one desire, to preserve our existence, which each of us thought to be threatened. One had one's neighbour guillotined to prevent onself being guillotined by one's neighbour.[96]

The events of Bloody Sunday were a tremendous act of reassertion by Collins. By it he broadcast Irish resolve to pursue the shooting war to a conclusion; by it he demonstrated his ability militarily to inflict serious defeats upon the security forces in Ireland – defeat which the political will in England would not tolerate. It also demonstrated the inability of England to either contain or control the war between the political police and the terrorist, short of massive repression. Thompson in a recent work on counter-insurgency states categorically that from his experience insurgencies are defeated by 'a high rate of contact in minor operations which are based on good intelligence'.[97] A cycle develops where good intelligence leads to more frequent and rapid contacts. More contacts mean more 'kills'. 'Kills' are an index of success in countering the insurgency. The public's confidence and support is given to the force claiming or seen to be achieving the greatest success. This results in better intelligence since the population, feeling more secure and relating to one of the combatants, yields more information. The cycle continues with more 'kills' and contacts. A particularly significant series of figures given in Table 4 plots the decline of the IRA in terms of successful strikes prior to November 1920. The decline is shown by the stagnation in the number of casualties inflicted, itself an index of the degree of contact. The impetus that Bloody Sunday gave to the IRA is quite clear from these data.

Thus, after a period of great stress Collins had resuscitated the IRA and reversed the situation of the summer and autumn of 1920 when the arenas of the war had been collapsing around him. As a result of Bloody Sunday he now held the initiative – particularly in the crucial sphere of intelligence. British security forces now had little hope of defeating the IRA in the immediate future. Containment

TABLE 4
Monthly Table of IRA Attacks on the
Security Forces 1920 to May 1921

Months	No. of attacks	No. of attacks	No. of casualties
1920	January	13	4
	February	11	7
	March	13	12
	April	15	23
	May	15	24
	June	24	20
	July	30	54
	August	32	69
	September	32	69
	October	42	86
	November	57	94
	December	50	76
1921	January	97	102
	February	79	95
	March	122	158
	April	211	158
	May (first 14 days)	102	92

Source: Irish Bulletin IV (93) (20 May 1921).

alone would be exceedingly difficult since the intelligence organization, crux of the British counter-insurgency, had been nullified in this single battle. A year at least to reconstruct such an intelligence unit, an additional several months before it bore fruit, and no guarantee that it would not meet the same fate made such a policy both militarily and politically exorbitantly expensive. Back in England Lloyd George was already experiencing gruelling days, but, total repression, a state of declared war in Ireland with the IRA accorded the status of belligerents, given Britain's liberal-democratic traditions, the condition of public opinion in England and the liberal ambience of international opinion in the post-Versaille period, was out of the question. Noting this the British government could do little else than seek a compromise. This they then did. The truce was eventually signed on July 9 1921.

Collins, the architect of the whole plan of campaign and the master of intelligence, summarized the whole process of the War of Independence, a battle between the political police and the terrorist when he wrote;

> England could always reinforce her army. She could replace every soldier that she lost. But there were others indispensable for her purposes, which were not so easily replaced. To paralyse the British machine it was necessary to strike at individuals. Without her spies England was helpless. It was only by means of their accumulated and accumulating knowledge that the British machine could operate.
>
> Without her police throughout the country how could they find the men they 'wanted'? Without their criminal agents in the capital, how could they carry out that 'removal' of the leaders that they considered essential for their victory? Spies are not so ready to step into the shoes of their departed confederates as are soldiers to fill up the front line in honourable battle. And even when the new spy stepped into the shoes of the old one he could not step into the old one's knowledge.[98]

NOTES

1. Frank O'Connor, *The Big Fellow – A Life of Michael Collins* (London, 1937), 89-90.

2. *Bean na h–Eireann* (January 1911), National Library Dublin.

3. Cmd 1025, June 1920, 2-3.

4. Hayden Talbot, *Michael Collins' Own Story* (London, 1923), 79.

5. *Hansard*, 129 (20 May 1920), 1721.

6. Also known as the '12 Apostles'. It was an élite group of full-time assassins also serving as Collins's personal bodyguard. At first the Squad numbered only four but was later expanded. From the outset and throughout the whole period it was commanded by Paddy O'Dalaigh. See Donal O'Kelly, 'The Dublin Scene, War Amid the Outward Trappings of Peace', in D. Nolan (ed.) *With the IRA in the Fight for Freedom 1919 to the Truce* (Kerr, 1946).

7. O'Connor, op. cit., 100.

8. J. M. Nankivell and S. Loch *Ireland in Travail* (London, 1922), 60.

9. Sir Neville Macready, *Annals of an Active Life*, Vol. I (London, 1924), 190.

10. J. Bowyer Bell, *The Secret Army* (London, 1970), 4.

11. Margery Forester, *The Lost Leader* (London, 1971), 114-15.

12. Sir Frank Sturgis reported in his diary, 10 July 1920, 'Ordered into the Castle to live', PRO 30/59 Part I. And there the administrators were to stay until Sir John Anderson insisted they show their faces on the Dublin streets to improve morale.

13. CO904/188/1, Sir John Anderson's Papers, 17 July 1920.

14. General Order, New Series No. 9, 19 June 1920, IRA GHQ Brigade Orders 1919-21. MS.900: National Library, Dublin.

15. ibid.

16. ibid.

17. For an account of the Castle in this period see J. W. Wheeler-Bennett, *John Anderson, Viscount Waverley* (London, 1962), Chapter 3.

18. Sir Ormonde Winter, *Winters' Tale* (London, 1955), 288.

19. CO904/188/1, which contains both diary and papers on the period written by Anderson, 1-4.

20. ibid., 20 July 1920.

21. ibid.

22. ibid.

23. ibid., 6 August 1920, 91.

24. CO904/188/1, 25 July 1920, 76.

25. T. E. Lawrence, 'The Science of Guerrilla Warfare', *Encyclopaedia Britannica* (London, 1948), 953.

26. PRO 30/59, op. cit., 3 August, 1920.

27. CO733/315, Secretary of State to High Commission (Palestine) on Martial Law.

28. WO 32/4308, Sir Hamar Greenwood on Sinn Fein.

29. Forester, op. cit., 114-15.

30. ibid., 286.

31. CO904/177/1.

32. Michael Collins, *The Path to Freedom* (Cork, 1968), 69-70.

33. CO904/109(3), Inspector General's Monthly Report, September 1919.

34. F. O'Donoghue, 'Guerrilla Warfare in Ireland' *An Cosantoir* (May 1963), 299.

35. Lawrence, op. cit., 953.

36. Much of the following material is taken from my 'Bloody Sunday – a Reappraisal', *European Studies Review,* II (1) (1972).

37. The Auxiliary Division was inaugurated on 27 July 1920. Its members were contracted to serve for six months with an option on a further six months. They were paid £1 a day, all found but had no pension rights. Cmd 1618, 'The RIC Auxiliary Division', 2-7. The first British recruits for the RIC arrived in Ireland 25 March 1920. R. Bennett, *The Black and Tans* (London, 1959).

38. Forester, op. cit., 104.

39. ibid., 188.

40. WO 35/70, General File HQ Dublin District, 10 October-31 December 1920.

41. CO903/168, Intelligence Summaries 1920, 'Government Publicity'.

42. ibid.

43. *Hansard,* 134, (1-19 November 1920), 719.

44. See PRO, CO904/168, for complete documentary evidence.

45. ibid.

46. *The Times* (10 November 1920), 12.

47. See CO904/168.

48. ibid., 51.

49. ibid.

50. ibid., 71.

51. K. J. Browne, 'They Died on Bloody Sunday', a souvenir of the Conor Clune Memorial, November 1970, 5.

52. ibid.

53. Reports would indicate that the men had been tortured. An ex-British officer named Pearson who saw the bodies and examined the wounds described as 'ridiculous' the opinion that they were received whilst escaping. ibid., p. 12.

54. Police and Crime Reports No. 5 471/192 OC RIC, 13 December 1920: State Paper Office, Dublin Castle.

55. *Irish Bulletin,* IV (53) (April 1921), and *Watchword,* (25 September 1920) and *Irish Bulletin* II (8) (10 September, 1920).

56. Collins, op. cit., 67.

57. Fortnightly report, 1 June 1920, Chief Secretary's Office. Crime Branch (Special) 1920: State Paper Office, Dublin Castle.

58. Major General Sir C. E. Callwell, *Field Marshall Sir Henry Wilson: his Life and Diaries* Vol. II, (London: 1927), 251.

59. CO904/188/1, 2-3.

60. ibid., 5.

61. PRO 30/59, Vol. 2, 1 October 1920.

62. ibid., Vol. 1, 30 August 1920.

63. *Irish Bulletin,* II (27) (27 October 1920).

64. ibid., II (8) (10 September 1920).

65. 'Last Days of Dublin Castle' *Blackwoods Magazine* (212) (July/December 1922), article by 'Periscope', p. 165.

66. *Irish Bulletin,* II (50), Supplement (13 July 1920): 'no police-man would be held up to public odium by being pilloried before a coroner's jury'. Attributed to divisional officer of Cork, RIC.

67. *Hansard,* 136, (13-23 December 1920), 1606.

68. Sturgis notes in his diary that Smyth was hastily called to London to explain his remarks: PRO 30/59, Vol. 15, 15, July 1920.

69. CO904/113, November 1920 Special Branch Reports.

70. CO904/168 contains detailed reports on the condition of Mac-Swiney's health in Brixton.

71. Winter, op. cit., 321.

72. Browne, op. cit., 7. Cathal Brugha (Charles Burgess) was at this time IRA chief of staff.

73. Army Monthly List 2815a, December 1920.

74. CO904/168, 58.

75. Ibid.

76. 'Black Sunday in Ireland', *The Times,* (2 November 1920), 12. It is interesting that Black Sunday followed Sir Hamar Greenwood's assertion that the situation was improving while Bloody Sunday followed Lloyd George's 'We have murder by the throat' speech at the Guildhall, 9 November 1920.

77. B. Clarke, CO904/168, 51.

78. Army Monthly List 2756, November 1920. McLean was edu-cated at Sherborne and Magdalene taking honours in law. See *Manchester Guardian* (22 November 1920).

79. Details of the injuries the officers sustained are contained in CO904/189/1 British Officers and Auxiliary Police Cadets assassinated in Dublin.' The Court and Inquiry Record, Dublin Castle, 2.12.1920.

80. Army Quarterly List, 1421, October 1920.

81. Army Monthly List, November 1920, 2756.

82. ibid.

83. ibid., 2350.

84. *The Times* (23 November 1920).

85. K. Hawkes and G. Lindley, 'Bloody Sunday', *Observer* (21 November 1970).

86. CO904/168, 58. See also J. Gleeson, *Bloody Sunday* (London, 1962), 124.

87. CO904/189/1.

88. CO904/113, Special Branch Reports; *Hansard*, 134 (18 November 1920), 2067-8.

89. *Dublin University Calendar 1920-21* (Dublin 1920), 38.

90. ibid.

91. *Who Was Who 1916-1928* (London, 1929), and *Concise Dictionary of Irish Biography*, (Dublin, 1923), 240.

92. *Hansard* (18 November 1920) loc. cit.

93. PRO 30/59 Part 2, 21 November 1920. Sturgis Diaries.

94. CO904/189/1.

95. CO904/113.

96. Winter, op. cit., 321.

97. Robert Thompson, *Defeating Communist Insurgency*, London, 1966), 88.

98. Collins, op. cit., 70.

II
PALESTINE

4

DEFENDING THE MANDATE:

The Condition of Public Security Prior to the Arab Rebellion

Just Palestine Policemen a' doin of their job,
We come from every walk of life there be
We're pretty slick an' slippy, an we 'avent got a bob
But we're known from Tel Aviv to Galilee

There's Christian, Jew and Arab in this ruddy 'oly land,
As matey as a bunch of rattle snakes
But if you'd give us coppers just a day or two's free hand,
We'd guarantee we'd give the lot the shakes.

Now there's Hussein El Mohammed and Moses Moshevix
Plus Parliamentary members safe in Tooting,
Whats mucking up the country with their rotten politics
And leaving British coppers to the shooting.

We don't do no complainin and believes a lot in Fate
And verily we trust we're sons of Mars;
But we're sent in open pick-ups in the manner of live bait
While the Army tours the hills in armoured cars. . . .

Our brothers in the Army, they know the game as well
And don't do all their fighting by the book
So its 'Use your boots and butts boys go down and give 'em hell
They've knifed a British copper in the souk.

So Palestine Policemen they gets it in the back
And at the Golden Gate they stand and stare
And gaze upon St. Peter as he pops up from his shack
With 'Well me boys, what 'ave you to declare?'

We're only common coppers, sir, we never 'ad a bob
We 'ave a few kind deeds, sir, and some vice
But in the so-called Oly Land we always done our job
so now we'd like a bit of Paradise.

Roger Courtenay, Palestine Policeman,
Epilogue, *(Herbert Jenkins, London 1939)*

This chapter, which opens the Palestine case study, has, like the initial chapter on Ireland, a limited set of aims. First, it seeks to indicate in broad strokes the prevailing security conditions in Palestine from the inception of British control in 1917 to the onset of the breakdown of that control in 1936. Second, it is intended here to detail and examine the public security structures in Palestine during that period — that is both the Mandatory police forces and the Jewish self defence units — including the extra-legal Haganah, which at times acted as an adjunct to the British security forces. Finally, and seminally, the chapter concentrates upon indicating and analysing some sources of stress, both within the police structure and acting upon it. It also examines the various and unsuccessful attempts to reform that structure and to rationalize the arrangements for maintaining law, order and a degree of justice.

THE CONDITION OF PUBLIC SECURITY IN PALESTINE, 1917-1936: THE VIOLENT AND DISTURBED BACKGROUND TO THE ARAB REBELLION

Palestine under the Mandate in particular, and the Middle East generally, have throughout their histories consistently revealed patterns of endemic and violent political disturbance. The period under review here was exceptionally disturbed. Throughout the 1930s Palestine was one of the seismic zones of political life. Any history of the Mandate reveals that the maintenance of internal security was a perennial problem. Freed from an already faded Turkish control during the 1914-18 war, Palestine was an incohesive agglomerate, an inherently fissiparous structure riven with racial, religious, tribal, economic and political cleavages. Within the territory there was no accepted, legitimate, authority referent with a moral title to rule. The expedient substitute erected by the League of Nations was the superimposed Mandate administration governing in truly colonial style. Spontaneous allegiance towards that particular central authority was minimal. Rather was it traditionally, freely given, in the Arab case to antagonistic and often openly feuding micro-societal groups like the Arab brigands, the religious authority of the local mukhtar and the Mufti of Jerusalem. The Jews in their turn gave allegiance to the Jewish Agency, the Haganah

underground from 1920 and, or, the myriad off-shoots of the
first *Aliyah,* the developing kibbutz movement. Throughout
Palestine, authority was thus fractionated and political allegiance dispersed. Episodic violence in time became institutionalized as the dominant expressive mode of discontent.
The Mandate administration was unable to mobilize support
throughout the political community. Thus, during the period
1920-39, and again in the later period of the Jewish independence struggle, an analysis of governing Palestine provides a
case study of a regime operating almost continuously on the
very margins of survival. Successive administrations were unequal to their daunting task, attempting to govern, or at least
to rule, without the tacit support of the governed and in the
face of serious intra-administrative conflicts. Indeed, Mandatory control of the country was lost completely at times
and in certain areas between 1936 and 1939, when the
anaemic public security apparatus collapsed under continuous, violent, widespread pressures. Given the degree of
alienation from the Mandatory authority and the extent of
the cleavages in the social and political fabric, it is not
surprising that disturbance was endemic and the government's hold on security little more than tenuous. Even so,
the government did survive, functioning for a considerable
length of time in a continuum of disequilibrium — especially
between 1936 and 1939.

Yet for most of the Ottoman period of occupation and the
early Mandate period — that is, prior to the injection of the
additional stress of illegal and sanctioned Jewish immigration
— Palestine had remained comparatively quiet. It is possible
that this resulted from a lesser number of stressful elements
in the system, particularly Jewish immigration, but more
probably it was a product of exceedingly harsh and swift
Turkish justice. Graham and Gurr, in a comparative study of

political violence, found that public security was weakest and political instability greatest in systems that fulfilled two preconditions.[1] First, where inconsistency in the response to disorder proved counter-productive; second, in countries that exercised intermediate degrees of control. Both factors go towards establishing an image of authority. In Palestine the contrast between the British and Ottoman images could not have been sharper. The comparatively low-profile response of the British and their inconsistency in the prosecution of offenders cannot have failed to have had an effect on the Palestine Arabs in particular. Perhaps British moderation was interpreted as tolerance and support for both their cause and methods? Whether this was the case or not the Turks had ruled Palestine with a mere two squadrons of mounted gendarmerie. Their security posture was simple, barbaric, but effective.

> Any bother anywhere and they would ride in and string up a random number of locals to their own olive trees. If they could identify the miscreants so much the better, if not, anybody would do.... Whatever the ethics of the system those two squadrons were ample for the job and peace reigned from Dan to Beersheba.[2]

In similar fashion the Turks reduced the political powers of the local native élites, particularly the sheikhs, and substituted their own loyal nominees. Young Arabs, often the most potentially disobedient and politically active segment of the community, were taken away to serve in the conscript Ottoman Army. It was a formula that made for quiet times.

However, as the Ottoman Empire itself decayed into crisis, political stability and public order at that empire's periphery also declined. This was particularly the case in Palestine after the Turkish revolt of 1908. Palestine remained disturbed but under control until the inspiration of the Lawrencian revolt in the Hedjaz exacerbated existent tensions and broke the fragile public peace.

The British thus inherited a divided community and a security problem of considerable dimensions. The latter was partly of their own making, since they had financed the Lawrencian adventure to embarrass the German-Turkish alliance. Britain's problems were compounded and her credibility affected by the fact that, if she had not promised Palestine to both Arab and Jew in the heat of battle, there was evidence of a somewhat less formal, dual commitment in the shape of the Balfour Declaration and in between the lines of the McMahon correspondence. Palestine for both Arab and Jew was a twice-promised land. A cartoon in the Arab newspaper *Falastin* for 23 July 1936[3] captured the mood brilliantly. The cartoon showed John Bull with two wives standing before a judge, represented by an archbishop. The Arab wife is standing aside. Her style of dress is restrained and decent, her hair is falling over her shoulders but her face registers gloom. The Jewish wife looks like a harlot, is half-naked and disdainful in appearance. Yet, she looks content. John Bull, the bigamist, stands between the two wives rebuking his Arab wife. The Archbishop is admonishing the husband. Under the cartoon was the following dialogue.

[John Bull] My Lord I married first an Arab woman and then a Jewess and for the last sixteen years I've had no peace at home.
[Archbishop] How do you come to have two wives? Are you not a Christian?
[John Bull] It was the pressure of the Great War.
[Archbishop] Well, my son, if you are sincerely looking for peace you must divorce your second wife, because your marriage to her is illegal.

Palestine was then an inherently disturbed, fractured country in which periods of quiet were interspersed with endemic rioting in the cities or brigand incursions from the desert and hills. The Great War particularly made the latent cleavages manifest as well as, in itself, becoming an additional source of instability. Indeed, the effects of that war went so deep, particularly the stimulus to pan-Arabism of the revolt in the Hedjaz, that Sir Herbert Samuel, high commissioner of Palestine, felt that as late as 1929 Palestine was still 'disturbed by the groundswell that followed storms of war'.[4] Paradoxically, public order had, by Palestine's standards, been reasonably well maintained during the immediate period following the Great War when Palestine was ruled, temporarily, by a British military administration. However, in the transitional stage from military to civil government serious disturbances erupted. For example, in May 1929 there was widespread rioting in protest against the official acceptance of Jewish immigration into Palestine. The Arab city of Jaffa was the epicentre of the disturbances in which some 95 people were killed and 219 seriously injured – most of them Jews. At the time of the rioting the security forces that were operational consisted of three infantry battalions, three cavalry regiments, artillery and attached troops and a somewhat hastily constituted and ill-prepared police force. Indeed, the Mandatory government's hold on the internal security situation was so tenuous that the High Commissioner saw fit to order detachments of the Royal Navy into Haifa and Jaffa. It was an early example of the fragility of the public peace in Palestine.

Despite episodic incursions and spasmodic outbursts of traditional tribal banditry the period 1921-28 was comparatively quiet. However, as in Ireland during the superficially quiet days from 1890 to 1910, changes were taking place within the Palestinian Arab community. The Palestinian Arab cause, ill-organized and internally divided, was maturing. Similarly, fed by multiple frustrations and rumour, tension between the Arab and Jewish communities was growing. A dispute concerning the Wailing Wall, holy ground to both Jew and Arab, proved to be the catalyst of a most serious set of disturbances which changed the nature of the internal conflict pattern.

On 15 August 1929 a Jewish demonstration was held at the Wailing Wall, and on the following day the Arabs held a counter-demonstration. On 17th August a young Jew was stabbed to death by an Arab into whose garden he had followed a lost football. His funeral stimulated serious anti-Arab demonstrations. However, on 23 August Arabs armed with knives and clubs came out of the Old City and invaded the new, killing many Jews. On the following day 65 Jews were killed at Hebron and for many days after Jewish colonies throughout Palestine were attacked. The police opened fire on Arab rioters in Nablus and Jaffa while in Safad, Arabs attacked the Jewish quarter killing and wounding 45 people. In all some 133 Jews were killed, 399 wounded and 6 Jewish colonies destroyed along with 116 reported Arab deaths, most of the latter at the hands of the police and military.[5] The 1929 riots were in fact a turning point in the internal security of Palestine, since for the first time the focus of violent Arab discontent turned on to the Mandatory administration as much as on to the Jews. It was also the point at which both Jewish and Arab communities began systematically to arm themselves in preparation for a battle of survival. Similarly, it saw the beginning of the end of the Haganah policy of *havlagah* or restraint. Above all, in terms of the condition of internal security, the riots demonstrated the weakening effects of the economies of state carried out on the police force during the preceding nine years. The police, particularly the Arab section, collapsed in the face of the 1929 Jerusalem riots. For the first time they revealed their redundancy as an effective instrument of control in crisis.

The period 1929-36 following upon the riots in Jerusalem saw the continued if gradual escalation of the intra-community conflict; the rise of civil disobedience and the demonstration of the inability and, or, reluctance of the Mandatory authority to suppress both. In August 1930 there was a further crop of rioting in Nablus. Throughout 1930 and 1931 there were a series of Arab terrorist murders of Jews. All of this was set against a backcloth of endemic agrarian crime and concerted, violent attempts by Arabs to curtail illegal Jewish immigration. In October 1933 Arab demonstrations and riots targeted against both government and Jews took place in Jerusalem, Jaffa, Haifa and Nablus. Sniping, abduction, assassination and boycott commenced. Political committees, many with revolutionary intent, were formed in the major towns. A sub-culture of violence began to develop and aided the growth of internal conflict to such a level that in 1936 it was directly challenging, physically, the existence of the Mandate government. Rebels appeared in the hills and brigand gangs took to sabotage. In November 1935, with the police attack on and the destruction of the armed gang of the revolutionary religious leader Al Qassam, a martyr for the revolutionary cause was created. His sacrifice became an example to Palestinian youth. Guerrilla warfare was organized in the hills and urban terrorism in the streets of the major towns. By 1936 in the cities and the countryside a rebellion was under way. Public security, never a robust creature in Palestine, lapsed. The political debate took to the forum of the hills and the streets where it was to remain for some three years.

THE FUNCTION OF THE PUBLIC
SECURITY APPARATUS

As we have begun to see, the condition of public security in
any given system is not only the produce of the cleavages,
frustrations and opposition groups at work within that
system's boundaries. Importantly, and the basic thesis of this
book, the condition of the police, its detective, preventative
and restraining arms, directly affects the process of conflict
resolution and ultimately the condition of public security.
Within a limited time scale an efficient police can help detect,
prosecute and cauterize political discontents and subversion.
Throughout this book the emphasis is upon the failure of
police forces under stress as much as upon the nature and
causation of the threat. David Easton has observed, when
discussing the tolerance levels of stress-given regimes, that,

> stress would prevail only if we were limiting our observations to a
> given time interval. If a system had all the time in the world to deal
> with an increased volume or time-consuming content, there would
> be little reason for an overload to evolve. Alternatively . . . one of
> the ways of coping with overload is to extend the available time.[6]

One of the prime functions of the police in a crisis situation is to extend the time for the peaceful resolution of
conflict by detecting and then constraining unchannelled
discontents as well as the more overt assaults on the public
peace. In Palestine, far more than in Ireland, the police failed
to achieve this end largely as a result of the deficiencies in
their intelligence structure and operations. As in Ireland, so
too in Palestine the police and their detective or intelligence
units were a critical variable in the equation of revolt.

THE STRUCTURE OF THE PUBLIC
SECURITY APPARATUS IN PALESTINE

It is extremely difficult to compile an acceptable picture of the overall structure, content and distribution of the police forces in Palestine prior to the Arab Rebellion of 1936-39 primarily because the police organization itself was unstable. It seldom continued the same for more than three years at one time. Almost continual crisis conditions, rapidly changing administrative personnel on short tours of duty, chief administrators holding radically differing notions as to the precise role that the police should play and major reform attempts in 1921, 1922, 1925, 1926 and 1929, followed by minor ones in 1931 and 1935, all effected changes in the shape, condition and complement of the Palestine Police Force. Reforms during the period of the Arab Rebellion 1936-39 altered police structure even more.

It is important to note at the outset that the Palestine Police Force, which came into being in 1925-26 as a result of Lord Plumer's reorganization,[7] was composed of the disparate police units which had policed Palestine from 1920-21 onwards — that is, the separately recruited British and Palestine gendarmeries, the ghaffir forces and the almost purely Arab force guarding Trans-Jordan. Throughout both the early and later period, the British force was the élite unit.

Each constable recruited into the Palestine Police Force was to serve five years after an initial six months' training at the police school. A salary of six pounds per month (clothing and equipment free)[8] did not attract high quality recruits. The Force HQ, located in Jerusalem, was divided into two segments: the Administrative Department, which concerned itself with general police matters and the prison service, and, as a separate unit, the Criminal Investigation Department. Throughout the period under discussion the force was distributed into the following seven districts:[9]

District	Division
Jerusalem	Urban, Rural, Hebron
Southern (Jaffa)	Jaffa, Ramat Gan, Tel Aviv, Ramle
Gaza	Gaza, Beersheba
Northern (Haifa)	Urban, Rural
Nazareth	Nazareth, Tiberias
Nablus	Nablus, Tulkarm, Jenin
Frontier	Northern Frontier, Safad, Acre

Each of the divisions was divided into areas controlled from stations and posts. A superintendent and deputy superintendent were in charge of each district and a deputy superintendent and assistant superintendent in charge of each division, which took its divisional name from that of the headquarters town, with, of course, the exception of the Frontier.

The British section of the police was composed of a curiously mixed personnel. An officer serving in the force noted that:

> Between us we represented every conceivable situation of life in the British Isles, from the heir of an impoverished Earl, products of exclusive public schools, and graduates of famous universities to professional bruisers, coal miners, regular soldiers and really tough Tyneside Geordies who played a better game of football in their bare feet than they did with boots on.[10]

The British section could perhaps best be caricatured as an agglomerate of adventureres, escapers and marginal men with a salting of professional colonial service policemen from Ireland, India, Ceylon and elsewhere. The native Palestinian element of Jews and Arabs was drawn, in the main, from the uneducated, poorer sections of the community. The two sections of the force were kept apart, almost segregated. In the early period of the Mandate the British police were discouraged from learning either Arabic or Hebrew. As one serving British police officer noted, 'Obviously we were at that time intended to be used not as real policemen but as tough shock troops'.[11] Like the RIC, the Palestine Police were then a gendarmerie, a 'police of the Prince', though again like the RIC they were seldom allowed consistently to fulfil their role. Such role conflict created in Palestine the same problems experienced by the RIC.

INTELLIGENCE

As we have observed in the Irish context, an efficient intelligence structure is an essential prerequisite, in the short term at least, for the containment of subversion. In Palestine the collection of political intelligence in particular was completely inadequate from 1920 to 1938 — that is until the restructuring of security during the counter-insurgency campaign of 1938. In detailing the whole intelligence staff working for the Mandate government, it is as well to remember that it seldom, if ever, functioned as a cohesive unit. A picture emerges in Palestine of mutually exclusive and warring intelligence departments.

The CID of the Palestine Police was the largest operational intelligence section covering the whole of Palestine. In addition, the intelligence section of the Trans-Jordan Frontier Force (TJFF) operated in Trans-Jordan, while a third intelligence agency, that of the Army Defence Headquarters Staff, operated in both Palestine and Trans-Jordan. There was thus much duplication of surveillance. However, the bulk of the 'hard' intelligence, as opposed to hearsay, manufactured tales and rumour, came from Special Service officers.[12] During the period 1920-36, a mere four Special Servicemen covered Palestine.[13] Prior to the 1936-39 rebellion they were stationed in Jerusalem, Haifa and at Amman and Ma'an in Trans-Jordan. As the rebellion escalated other Special Service officers were appointed to Jaffa and Nablus, key centres of Arab discontent, as well as to Nazareth and the Jordan Valley. Their duties were 'to procure information of a military, political and topographical nature and to keep in touch with feeling in the country by touring their districts'.[14]

Yet, despite the impressive array of information-gathering units, the quantity and quality of information received were both extremely poor. Sir Herbert Dowbiggin, reporting on the Palestine Police in 1930, designated the CID as 'the weakest spot in the force'.[15] Similarly, the Committee of Imperial Defence had noted in 1929, with reference to police intelligence,

> we are informed that little information is forthcoming from it. For example, in 27 days out of 33 days during September and October [of 1929 – immediately after the August riots in Jerusalem and elsewhere] the police had no information to publish in their daily situation reports. . . . Not only must the police, owing to the nature of their present organisation, rely largely on rumour for their information, but it has been reported that since the August outbreak the Palestinian personnel of the junior ranks of the police have shown a tendency to withhold information regarding events in their districts from their senior officers.[16]

Dowbiggin's recommendations for a new CID were not acted upon until two years later. In 1932 the CID was both thoroughly reorganized and strengthened.[17] The staff was further increased in 1934 to cope with the growing problem of illegal Jewish immigration. By 1935 there were some fifty-one CID officers operating within the Palestine Police alone. However, the reforms appear to have had little appreciable effect upon the collection and collation of hard political intelligence. Police intelligence remained inadequate down to 1936 and almost completely dried up thereafter as a result of the Arab terror and boycott. Selective assassination of Arab CID officers, usually the zealots, effectively neutralized the Arab CID as a reliable source of information. The Arab CID became politically unreliable; if they did not actually transmit sensitive information to the Arab rebels, they often sat upon information until it was of little use to the security forces. One incident, one of many documented, is worth detailing. Joshua Gordan of the Jewish Agency, reporting a meeting with Rice, deputy inspector general of police in 1936, observed that,

> I inquired whether he [Rice] was directly informed of the information which was being given to the British Crime Investigator Corporal Fisher by an Arab fellah woman with whom we [the Jewish Agency] had placed the police in contact. I understand that she had been giving valuable information about the movement and actions of a certain gang and I said that if Corporal Fisher was merely passing this information on to Abdin Bey, his superior officer, the British might spare themselves the trouble of obtaining this information. . . . he [Rice] had not been getting the information at all and as we had not heard any results, it would appear that the information was merely buried by Abdin Bey.[18]

It was an incident that typified a general pattern of action throughout the Arab section of the Palestine Police.

THE AUXILIARY POLICE

Auxiliary Police units were established in Palestine to bolster the existing public security apparatus in times of crisis. Similarly, they enabled the release of trained policemen from passive routine to the more offensive, anti-terrorist actions becoming daily more necessary after the serious riots of 1929. There were, however, vital differences between the composition of these Auxiliary units and the force proper. They were in fact composed predominantly of Jewish personnel. It was because of this fact that both the civil and military command kept a very tight hold on the activities of the Auxiliaries. Both feared partisan policing, but above all offensive action, by a Jewish force operating under the imprimatur of the Mandate. The overall attitude of the Mandate administration to the question of auxiliary policing by the Jews is effectively summarized in the following statements from the High Commissioner's Office. First it is documented that in the War Office 'There was general agreement with the High Commissioner's opinion that Jews should be employed for defensive purposes only and only in areas mainly Jewish'.[19] The same document also revealed the fear of offensive action by Jewish police units, many of whose men were simultaneously members of the illegal Haganah underground army. 'Arrangements might well be made', the document continued,

> for their training now in limited numbers with a view to using their services for protective work ... if the need arises. Any such training should be carried out with the utmost discretion in order to avoid giving the impression in Palestine or outside Palestine, that HMG already foresee that after the publication of their decisions upon the

Report of the Royal Commission (Peel Commission) a state of affairs will inevitably prevail in which the forces of authority will be ranged against the Arab population. As regards the employment of Jews even for defensive purposes in predomenantly Moslem areas, it was agreed that this would be politically most undesirable. . . . It was further agreed that in view of the possibility serious relations which might thereby be provoked in neighbouring Arab countries, the GOC should not, in any circumstances, decide to use Jews for offensive purposes without prior approval of HMG.[20]

Though it was eventually realized that there was a distinct need to utilize Jewish forces to preserve the Mandatory regime, the most rigid controls were always imposed upon their actions. It was only later, at the height of the Arab Rebellion, that Jewish Auxiliary units were granted more freedom of action.[21] At first, they were specifically restricted to guarding fields, villages and their own settlements. Later they were allowed to accompany Jewish workers wherever they were required and ultimately they became mobile units policing whole districts. From 1938 onwards, they became an important component part of the public security structure. Yet how were they composed? What was their complement and distribution? The few who have written about the Auxiliary Police have loosely referred to 'ghaffirs', 'settlement police' and 'supernumaries' as if they were one cohesive unit. By 1938 there were in fact five distinct classes of Auxiliary Police in Palestine. They are detailed below:

The Temporary Additional Police

This was a body of men enlisted for six months and having the same rates of pay and serving under the same regulations as the police proper. Most of the men were employed on general protection duties.

The Railway Protection Police

This self-explanatory unit guarded and patrolled stations, block-houses and vulnerable and important bridges on the main railway line from Haifa to Lydda. The force was administered by an élite of British officers but was otherwise composed entirely of Jewish personnel.

Jewish Settlement Police

This unit was composed of temporary additional police as well as volunteer, unpaid, special police enlisted after the onset of the Arab Rebellion in 1936. Its complement was something of a barometer of crisis since it rose and fell according to the level of internal disturbance. In effect, it was the core of the Auxiliary Police units. Reorganized in 1938, they became a much more flexible, articulated unit with a unified administration and command. Similarly, they were organized into ten companies, each commanded by a British police inspector seconded from the regular police. They were thus a mobile reserve as well as guardians of the Jewish settlements.

Supernumary Police

These were private police officers, paid for by individual firms such as the Palestine Electricity Corporation, to guard private industrial property.

Ghaffirs

The ghaffirs were those auxiliaries, often from the Jewish Settlement Police, who were exclusively employed as night-watchmen.

THE HAGANAH (IRGUN HAGANAH HA'IVRITH BE ERETZ ISRAEL): THE HEBREW DEFENCE ORGANIZATION IN PALESTINE

Given the focus of this book, little more than a superficial analysis of the Haganah can be provided here. However it is essential to outline its role in the security pattern in Palestine.

The Haganah was built upon deep traditions of self-defence in various Jewish communities throughout the Diaspora but particularly among the Russian Jewry. The Odessa pogroms of 1881 and the Kishinev pogrom of spring 1903 demonstrated to Jews in Czarist Russia the need to organize their defence. However, it was not until the second *aliyah,* or wave of immigration, into Palestine in 1905 that self-defence units were established in Jewish communities there. Others had conceived of such defence units, men like Michael Halperin who in 1886-87 expressed the idea of a Jewish force throughout Palestine based upon a union of labour and military training later to characterize the Haganah. Halperin's notions were seized upon and improved by the Hashomer, or 'Watchmen', of the Shomrin, an élite group of Zionist settlers including the late Ben Gurion, Eliyahu Golomb, founder and head of Haganah, and Dov Hos.

It was they who created the first systematic Jewish defence organization. By 1919 this force had demonstrated that it possessed a zest for organization and had already achieved a union of social, economic, political and military thinking. With these developments and Trumpeldor's First World War Jewish legion, the Zionist Mule Corps, as military antecedents, and with the *Gdudim* (group) as the base of the political component, the Haganah was formed on 25 June 1921 as a response to calls for unity in Jewish defence made throughout 1920. To begin with the Haganah held strictly to its policy of restraint (havlagah) and worked with the British government, often it would seem through the auspices of the Jewish Agency. The policy of restraint was not unopposed, however, and caused friction and schism within the Haganah until, faced with the 1929 riots and the 1936 rebellion, it went on to the offensive. By 1937 it had within its national structure some 17,000 men, 4,000 women, 4,000 rifles, 10,000 small arms and 230 light machine-guns.[22] It was a sophisticated underground army but it is particularly important to note here the efficiency of its intelligence section. In time the British, and particularly Orde Wingate, came to rely upon Haganah information concerning the location of Arab gangs and urban terrorists. The High Commissioner, Wauchope, in July 1938 specifically asked for the help of the Jewish Agency's intelligence section in tracking down terrorists. Moshe Shertok of the Agency reported that 'He [Wauchope] knew that the Intelligence Department of the Jewish Agency was at least as good as that of the Government, if not much better.'[23] The Haganah was thus an appendage of the formal security apparatus.

SOME PROBLEMS OF POLICING.
STRESS IN THE PUBLIC SECURITY
APPARATUS 1920-36

The police apparatus in Palestine reflected in miniature the complex problems that the Mandate government faced. It was a creature of crisis, lacking legitimacy and internal cohesion and without a definite notion of what its precise role was to be. From its inception the Palestine Police was conceived of as a somewhat inadequate second-best to the military apparatus. The major advantage of a quasi-military police force under civilian control was, for the Colonial Office, that it was cheap. Both HMG and the Colonial Office had stressed in 1920[24] that, at £500 per man per annum, the military, operating as an internal security force, was too expensive. Civil policing in Palestine was thus instituted as an economic expedient, and it suffered under the continued application of economies down to 1929. Hastily recruited, organized and centralized under the British military government in July 1919,[25] the police had, from their inception, little status and authority among Jews, Arabs or, indeed, British communities. Their stature was not increased under the military government since they were not even allowed to investigate cases thoroughly — this was regarded as the preserve of the courts and the public prosecutor. The police in fact operated as little more than drilled, uniformed, native errand boys for the military. Organized into district units, they were also, from the outset, highly susceptible to local racial and religious influence. It was the British component, many of them ex-Royal Irish Constabulary men or Black and Tans, who gave the force its backbone. By contrast, the native force possessed little unity of organization and no

systematic training, had not effected any significant formalized co-ordination between districts, and possessed no reserve
upon which it could call in times of stress. Conditions in the
force were at first so poor, and the job held in such low
esteem, that in 1921 sixty per cent of the force resigned on
the grounds of bad housing and low pay. This crisis, and the
inadequate manner in which disturbances in Haifa and Jaffa
were combated, forced both an inquiry and the first in a long
line of piecemeal reforms[26] — none of which alleviated the
major flaws in the police apparatus.

The force was improved organizationally in 1921 by the
establishment of an HQ staff in Jerusalem. The security
situation was also eased somewhat by the institution of a
mobile strike force, the Palestine Gendarmerie. A similar
unit, to be known as the Arab Legion, was created for
Trans-Jordan. In 1922 these reforms were extended with the
creation of a British Gendarmerie of 35 officers and 724
men, mostly transferred from the still disturbed but now
independent Ireland. The Palestine Gendarmerie, officered in
the main by British policemen but composed of Jews and
Arabs, was financed from Mandatory funds, while the British
Gendarmerie was maintained directly from the United Kingdom. As an exercise in financial pruning, the substitution of
these forces for the military garrison was clearly a success.
The cost of the garrison as a whole, standing at £3 million in
1921-22, had by 1923-24 been reduced to £1½ million. It
was thus merely an extension of the prevailing policy when in
1925 the mounted squadron of police and one company of
the recently established British Gendarmerie were disbanded;
the apparent calm in Palestine during 1924, 1925 and 1926
made it appear good policy to reduce the defences. Sir
Herbert Samuel, the High Commissioner, was over-optimistic
when he saw the country so pacified in 1925. He wrote that
year that,

The spirit of lawlessness has ceased; the atmosphere is no longer electric; there have been no more raids from Trans-Jordan; all the brigands have been hunted down and either shot, executed or imprisoned.... For some time past Palestine has been the most peaceful country of any in the Middle East.[27]

His report neglected the continuing brigandage in the hills and the disturbances in Jaffa, Nablus and Tulkarm as well as the two small-scale revolts and incursions from the desert in 1922 and 1924 when both the Wahabis and Druzes from the Nejd had raided Mandatory outposts. There was a consistent undercurrent of antipathy, which was sure to revive when Jewish immigration escalated. The quiet was misleading.

However, in April 1925 the Security Conference held in Jerusalem[28] continued the policy of economies. Both Samuel, the High Commissioner, and the secretary of state for the colonies felt that the British Gendarmerie should be reduced by some 200 men and its mounted cavalry unit disbanded altogether. Since Samuel was retiring it was decided not to apply the reforms but to leave Lord Plumer, his successor, to assess them. Plumer not only reviewed Samuel's proposals but suggested sweeping reforms of his own which weakened the security apparatus still further. That reforms of such scale should follow those of 1920, 1921, 1922 and 1925 added to the aura of uncertainty in public security work, itself part of a wider feeling of impermanence. In his diary, Colonel Kisch of the Jewish Agency had written,

MacNeill [Brigadier General A. J. MacNeill] who commands the British Gendarmerie is very sore with the Authorities who cannot come to any decision as to the future of his force. As a result over 200 of his best men have announced their intentions of resigning on completion of one year's service.[29]

Plumer had in fact recommended that both the Palestine and British Gendarmeries and the Arab Legion be abolished. This represented a radical change in the style of policing since it ended the aggressive, para-military stance of mobile gendarmeries and substituted for them an essentially static and defensive single unit, the Palestine Police. The bulk of the personnel of the Palestine Gendarmerie was to be absorbed into the Palestine Police. The remnant was to be organized into three new detachments making up a Camel Corps, later known as the Trans-Jordan Frontier Force (TJFF), with those British Gendarmerie officers who remained being absorbed into the Palestine Police Force. In practice, the reforms merely compounded the operational weakness of police units, not only because of the implicit force reductions but also because of the disarray the recommendations created. Plumer's recommendations remained in force from April 1926 to August 1929, when the riots of that month demonstrated just how inadequate internal public security forces had become. Kisch again wrote in his diary,

> On the subject of public security I unfortunately found myself in serious disagreement with Lord Plumer in respect to the measures he was introducing into the reorganisation of the gendarmerie and the police. . . . It was doubly difficult to make criticism effective, partly because of Lord Plumer's great authority as a Field Marshall, in matters of security, and partly because during his tenure of office Palestine in fact remained absolutely quiet. However, I was convinced that the security arrangements were dangerously inadequate and even if they might seem satisfactory in Lord Plumer's time, they could not be relied upon to keep the peace in Palestine, unaided by his great personal prestige as head of government.[30]

Thus 1926 was a major turning point on the public security front in Palestine. It was a year that also saw the

Arab component of the force becoming increasingly predominant — despite their reluctance to prosecute rebellious
fellow Arabs. The rearrangements of 1926 exaggerated the
existing ethnic imbalance of the force. The Zionists were
vociferous in their complaints. Kisch again stressed that,

> the new scheme does not take sufficiently into consideration the
> situation which would develop in Palestine in the event of any wave
> of Islamic fanaticism . . . Arab police cannot be relied upon for the
> protection of Jewish life and property. . . . the Government is taking
> an unjustifiable risk in regard to the Jewish lives for which it is
> responsible.[31]

Chaim Weizmann also wrote at the time about his anxiety
'as to the possible effects of the far-reaching changes now in
progress in the arrangements for defence and security of
Palestine'.[32] Assessment of the data on the rearrangements
makes this concern understandable. For instance, the disbanded Palestine Gendarmerie had been fifty per cent British,
fifteen per cent Jewish with a larger contingent of Jews in the
officer corps. It was replaced by the TJFF, a predominantly
Arab force. By the end of 1926 the TJFF consisted of 31
British officers, 35 Jews in technical work and 700 Arab
officers and men. Similarly, the Palestine Police made up of
1,752 officers and men had a Jewish contingent of only 212
officers and men — 1,300 being Arabs. The Jerusalem Police
Force, focus of so much rioting and political violence, was
particularly affected. In a city where Jews made up sixty per
cent of the total population, out of 300 serving officers and
men in the police, only 41 were Jews and of these 25 were
employed in the police band.[33]

Yet the imbalance of the force ethnically or religiously was
not solely a product or reflection of prevailing government

policy moving, as it seemed at the time, increasingly towards Arab self-government.[34] It was also part product of self-exclusion from the force by so many members of the Jewish community. A member of the Jewish Agency reported that,

> As regards the enlistment of Jews in the police, the actual situation is: Jews will not go into the police force for the sake of the job. In times of distress, unemployment, some may go, and they will leave again at the first opportunity. Only those will remain who have no prospects for other employment or who have no greater ambition than £7 a month for them and family for their lifetime. It will be agreed that those with such mentality are not the elements to build up the back-bone of the Jewish section of the Palestine Police. Already now there are loud complaints of the Jewish population about the 'element' of the Jewish policemen. . . . A better element we will be able to get into the police only if we will be able to reach that part of the Jewish youth who will go into the police not for the job's sake, but for the sacrifice.[35]

The Jewish community in Palestine thus perceived their policemen as unskilled workers, poorly paid, intellectually inadequate and marginally criminal. European Jewry in Palestine also expressed a marked reluctance to serve in the exposed, dull and dangerous rural areas. Tel Aviv and Jerusalem had more to offer.

The religious and ethnic imbalance in the force had serious effects upon policing. Successful civil policing is dependent upon the establishment of a mutual if somewhat distant respect between police and public. With so few Jews in the local forces, Jewish citizens were most reluctant to go to Arab officers, with whom, very often, they could not even communicate. Many complaints in the available police records evidence this state of affairs. One such complaint from a local council to the Jewish Agency emphasized that, the number of policemen and officials in the Nazareth District is decreasing to a very noticeable degree. . . . Previous to the disturbances [of 1929] two Jewish officials were employed in the District Administration and these either resigned or were discharged, so that today there is no Jewish official. The situation is such that a person not knowing English or Arabic cannot negotiate with the government. In the Nazareth police station there are four or six Jewish policemen and one Jewish officer up to the time of the disturbances. . . . At present there is no Jewish policeman in Nazareth.[36]

Thus both the position of Jews within the police force and the attitude of the Jewish community towards it was unsatisfactory. Of 439 Jewish constables enlisting during the years 1932-36, 255 were discharged or resigned.[37] Even those Jews and Arabs who remained in the force, working together reasonably well in quiet times, revealed their underlying mutual suspicion and distrust in times of crisis. Thus the police force, supposedly one of the supportive structures of the Mandate government, was itself infected with the same fundamental cleavage that ran, like some massive geological fissure, through the social, economic and political life of Palestine.

During the period 1920-36 the Arab section of the police became increasingly and dangerously unreliable in times of crisis. There were of course glorious exceptions, but in the main there was or could be little empathy with, or lasting allegiance to, the British administration, when men of their own religion, blood, tribe and class were in direct opposition to that administration. A history of the Arab section of the Palestine Police is one of episodic collapse in the face of politico-religious tests and targeted terrorism. The stamina of the Palestine Police in no way matched that of the RIC.

One of the contributory factors in the total collapse of the Arab section of the police in 1938 — they were eventually disarmed — was their inadequate training under stress. The riots of 1929 and 1936 and the rebellion from 1936 to 1939 all clearly demonstrated this failing. Again, Kisch, probably the most prolific and perceptive writer of the period, wrote in the aftermath of the 1929 rioting that,

> During the recent disturbances it has become apparent that when faced by an actual Arab rising against Jews, the Arab police cannot be relied upon for offensive action. In some cases there is evidence of actual collusion on the part of the police. . . . The rising in its earlier stages having been almost exclusively Moslem, the Christian Arab police were less affected than the Moslem Arabs. . . . None of the police, however . . . appear to have been equipped as regards training and discipline for effective action under fire. Both during the period of active rioting and during the subsequent period of tension, it became abundantly clear that the British police are effective out of all proportion to their number in dealing with such a situation.[38]

In Palestine the native Muslim policeman was in the unenviable position of being something of a 'Levantine man' — a man of the East serving the sophisticated, alien, litigious codes of a modern industrial state. Is it not then valid to suggest that it was,

> too much of a detached idealism to reckon with the hope that a native police officer who has hardly seen any Western government, who hardly conceives the Western maxims of objectivity and impartiality, even when he hears about them, will suddenly rise to the lofty heights of an umpire when it goes against his own flesh and blood, friend and benefactor . . . cease to be what he is only because he wears a uniform . . . it has to be realised that the ordinary policeman is drawn from the poorer classes of the population and possesses a very scanty education. He can read and write even in his own tongue with not too much ease. He does not know any foreign

language at all. The subject of civics is something unknown to him. Soon after entering the police force he is bound, owing to the conditions offered to him, to continue in his free hours, the mode of life he has led before. He associates with the same people, reads or hears the same papers, and holds the same opinions. . . . Under such circumstances there is not much probability of abandoning his Eastern conceptions of life and relations in favour of a people strange to him and suddenly, together with his uniform, acquire a Western sense of duty or *esprit de corps.*[39]

Many of the Arab police thus held an allegiance alternative to that feeble one they felt for the Mandate.[40] By 1936 the Arab police were so deficient in allegiance to the Mandate that they had become much more of a threat to, than a guarantor of, public security. It was a picture that parallelled that of Ireland in 1920 and 1921.

It is strange though that, while as early as 1929 the police force was seen to be deep in crisis after the riots in Jerusalem, the reform proposals failed to touch the heart of the problem – the question of allegiance. Had the native Palestine force been placed in barracks as were the Royal Irish Constabulary in Ireland they would perhaps have been insulated from some of the pressures they faced from extreme nationalists working in their communities. Dowbiggin's police reorganization plan of 1929-30 was to be the last systematic civilian attempt to rescue the security situation prior to the belated but eventually successful military reform undertaken during the counter-insurgency campaign of 1938.

Dowbiggin, described as 'the star police turn of the British Empire',[41] had been provided with his brief by a Government Imperial Defence Committee paper of 20 December 1929. Compiled by the formidable triumvirate, Trenchard, Madden and Milne, it emphasized that,

We are convinced that no addition to the military forces in Palestine
would have the same preventive effect as a well organised and
efficient police backed by an adequate intelligence department ... we venture to express our strong conviction that reorganisation required must amount to considerably more than
merely an increase in the British section of the police force, which is
now under consideration. We feel most strongly that the whole
police force requires reorganization and that in particular, arrangements should be made to instil British influence, mentality and
methods into the native force.[42]

Once in Palestine, Dowbiggin quickly confirmed his repu-
tation. His report, had it been speedily and efficiently implemented, might well have revitalized the security apparatus.
He made a set of seminally important suggestions. Primarily,
he stressed that there should be not only a clear conception
and precise statement of the role of the police, but also that,
in terms of the administration itself, there should be precise
delineation of the respective powers of civil and military
authorities. These problems were never satisfactorily resolved
until the near-collapse of the Mandate in 1938 concentrated
the minds of those involved. The problem of allocating civil-
military responsibilities, particularly with respect to the
rebellion, led to a most bitter intra-administrative wrangle
during the period 1936-38.[43] Dowbiggin also recognized the
lack of an *esprit de force* as a major weakness. He indeed
suggested that housing the police in barracks would be
partially remedial, alleviating the boycott and ostracism of
Arab officers. Barracks, on a national scale, were not con-
structed until 1939, by which time the rebellion had already
been broken. Dowbiggin also advocated an increase in the
British section of the police to 650 men, recognizing it as the
vertebrae of the force; the reconstitution of a mobile strike
force of 100 men which Plumer had destroyed; the need for a

permanent Special Constabulary Reserve; and, again in con-
tradistinction to Plumer, an increase in the number of sealed
armouries for Jewish colonies. Above all, he identified as the
greatest weakness of the force its CID and intelligence
section. Little was done to effectively remould this apparatus
other than by increasing its personnel.[44]

Thus, Dowbiggin's was the final, failed reform of the
public security apparatus prior to the rebellion of 1936-39. It
has been pointed out elsewhere that,

> The maintenance of public order everywhere requires the constant
> intervention of law enforcement agencies ... their absence or
> neutralisation even in the well ordered society is conducive to
> violence and mob action.[45]

Palestine was not a well ordered society. The experience on
the public security front 1920 to 1936 confirms the assessment above that a policing vacuum induces disorder. In
Palestine the police apparatus was seriously flawed prior to
the onset of the Arab Rebellion 1936-39. Indeed, the flaws,
particularly in the intelligence sphere, led to a failure to
monitor or check subversion, to growing brigandage and to
the organization by the Arab guerrillas of alternative
authority structures. By 1929 the police were incapable of
dealing adequately with a rash of spontaneous, disorganized,
essentially urban riots. By 1936 little had been accomplished
to make the force either detect, prevent or withstand the
Arab Rebellion with its vigorous campaign of guerrilla warfare in the hills, assassins in the cities and nationalistic
extreme political cells in most villages. The result was the
almost complete collapse of the Mandate government in
1938. It is to assessing the rebels and detailing the collapse of
public security that we now turn.

NOTES

1. H. D. Graham and T. R. Gurr, *The History of Violence in America: A Report to the National Commission on the Causes and Prevention of Violence* (London, 1969).

2. Bernard Fergusson, *The Trumpet in the Hall* (London, 1970), 77.

3. Translations of the Arabic Press. State Archive, Prime Minister's Office, Jerusalem.

4. Cmd 3530, 'The 1929 Riots in Jerusalem', 12.

5. Cmd 6808, 'Report of the Anglo-American Committee of Inquiry, into the problems of European Jewry in Palestine' (Lausanne, 20 April 1946), 69.

6. D. Easton, *A Systems Analysis of Political Life* (Chichester, 1965), 67.

7. Lord Plumer was the high commissioner of Palastine.

8. Palestine Police Manual, 2: State Archive, Prime Minister's Office, Jerusalem.

9. ibid., 16.

10. Lionel Morton, *Just the Job: Some Experiences of a Colonial Policeman* (London, 1957), 19.

11. ibid., 20.

12. See Air 5/1244 PRO, London, for details.

13. ibid.

14. Ibid.

15. Cd 5479, Peel Commission (1937), 191.

16. CAB 24/209 Committee of Imperial Defence (20 December 1929): PRO.

17. Cd 5479, op. cit., 194-95.

18. Central Zionist Archive (CZA) S.25/183 – Miscellaneous documents on security 1933-1939. 1/7/36, Central Zionist Archive, Jerusalem.

19. WO32/4178, Respective functions of High Commissioner and GOC (PRO).

20. ibid.

21. CZA S.25/46 Keren Hayesod document, 'Security in Palestine and Defence of the Yishuv', Jerusalem (25 July 1938).

22. Yehuda Bauer, 'From Co-operation to Resistance: The Haganah 1938-1946', *Middle East Studies,* II (3) (April 1966), 183.

23. CZA S.25/46 Ben Gurion-Moshe Shertok. Interviews with the High Commissioner (26 July 1938).

24. Cd 5479, op. cit., 185.

25. CZA S.25/6167, Arms to Jewish Colonies.

26. Sir Charles Jeffries *The Colonial Police* (London, 1952), 155.

27. Cd 5479, op. cit., 187.

28. Cmd 3530, op. cit., 14.

29. F. H. Kisch, *Palestine Diary,* 14 February 1923 (London, 1938), 31.

30. ibid., 235.

31. CZA Jewish Agency Memorandum 2 March 1936, 3. Kisch to the Chief Secretary of the Mandate Administration on behalf of the Zionist Executive.

32. ibid., Weizmann's letter to the Annual Meeting of the Permanent Mandates Commission, 1 May 1926.

33. ibid., 4.

34. The Mandate government had also begun to withdraw the sealed armouries in 1926 from the Jewish colonies in which, for protective purposes, they had been established. The withdrawal was almost completed by 1929.

35. CAZ S.25/6170, Joshua Gordon to Kisch, 17 July 1931. Jewish numbers in the police force, 1927-33.

36. CZA S.25/4374, Local Committee of Afuleh Bloc to Kisch 8/12/1929.

37. Cd 5479, op. cit., 197.

38. CZA S.25/6167, Police Reorganization, Dowbiggin Plan, 1929-30.

39. ibid.

40. ibid. Joshua Gordon of the Jewish Agency.

41. The description, it seems, is W. G. A. Ormsby-Gore's, colonial secretary. It was related to Kisch by Namier. See CZA S.25/6167.

42. CAB.24/209, PRO.

43. See my 'The Politics of an Arab Rebellion' Parts I and II in *British Army Review* (44) (August 1973) and (45) (December 1973) for a detailed account of the Rebellion.

44. Cd 5479, op. cit., 'Public Security'.

45. C. Leiden and K. Schmidt, *Politics of Violence and Revolution in the Modern World,* (Englewood Cliffs, NJ, 1968), 20.

5

THE ARAB REBELLION 1936-1939:

From Brigandage to the Brink of People's Revolutionary War

> The Arab rebellion was in fact a peasant revolt drawing its enthusiasm, its heroism, its organisation and persistence from sources within itself which have never been properly understood and which now will never be known. Like Feisal's revolt in the desert it was one of the blind alleys of Arab nationalism doomed like the desert revolt to failure, and destined, unlike the desert revolt, to oblivion for lack of a Lawrence to immortalise it.
>
> *John Marlowe,* The Seat of Pilate *(Cresset Press, 1959),*
> *pp. 137-8.*

The nature of the overall threat to public security in Palestine was less sophisticated and thorough than that which occurred in Ireland. In Palestine, by way of contrast to Ireland in 1916-21, the guerrillas lacked a formalized political component and coherent, binding political objectives. Neither was there a united politico-military leadership cadre or the structures of an alternative underground government.

Throughout its three years the Arab rebellion was essentially acephalous and riven with internecine, inter-tribal quarrels. Only the Mufti of Jerusalem, Haj Amin, through periodic injections of finance and the constant religious inspiration of his office, was able to superimpose a degree of unity and direction upon the rebellion. Nevertheless, as this chapter demonstrates, the revolt did mutate from simple banditry through rebellion to the brink of people's revolutionary war before declining, under stress, into banditry again. Here then, through comparison with the Irish case, the value of a sophisticated political component to the insurgents will be developed.

THE NATURE OF THE ARAB REBELLION

The Arab Rebellion in Palestine, when assessed overall, appears as a protracted yet sporadic peasant war. In essence the rebellion was made up of an integral set of smaller wars, resulting in the main from the lack of a single, binding political objective. The revolt had not one but several component targets. It was a peasant war where Arab gangs fought against Jews, the Mandate government and among themselves. Almost as many Arabs were killed by Arabs – some 494 – as the total number of Jews killed during the course of the rebellion – some 547.[1] Friendliness to Jews, support for the Mandate government and reluctance towards the Mufti's faction and/or the Arab guerrillas motivated many of the shootings. As early as 1929 British intelligence had noted that, a secret committee called the Boycott Committee has been formed for terrorist purposes with a view to the assassination of persons considered to be acting against Arab nationalist interests. After one warning, anyone who continues his activities is to be killed by members selected by the committee. Said to have been formed with knowledge of the Supreme Moslem Council (SMC) and the Arab Executive who have subscribed to expenses. . . . It appears to have organised its murder campaign quite effectively. In this connection it may be mentioned that in a recent letter Sir John Chancellor [the High Commissioner] reported as a disquieting feature of the situation, that the sources of information hitherto available to the police had completely 'dried up'. This may be an indication that the terrorist party of the Boycott Committee is meeting with some success.[2]

The internal sanction apparatus of the terrorists, which 'removed' informers, waverers and fellow travellers, was composed of hard, zealous, wild young men known as the *shabab*. Even the most prominent and respected men in Palestinian Arab public life were not immune from its actions. By 1937 the security situation was so unstable that a friend of Weizmann's noted that,

the entire Arab community lives in constant dread of these terrorists. No one dares to open his mouth in criticism of the Mufti, so much so that Ragheb Bay Nashashibi[3] said the other day that if the Palestine Government arranged for fresh elections for the Presidency of the SMC he would certainly vote for the Mufti because it was as much as his life was worth to do otherwise.[4]

The tactical similarities with the Collins organization are, at this point, striking. However, in contrast with Ireland, Arab was also killed by Arab to resolve long-standing personal disputes. Blood feuds, or *fasad*, were settled under cover of the rebellion. Political differences were frequently used as a medium for the pursuit of personal rivalries. John Marlowe indeed noted that 'Arab life in every village and town in Palestine is honeycombed with personal feuds, often of an extremely bitter kind, and political views are usually decided by local and personal sympathies and antipathies.'[5] This internecine conflict particularly affected the Palestinian Arab political élite where a bitter and intense struggle for Arab political hegemony in Palestine was fought between the two dominant Arab families, the Husseinis and the Nashashibis.[6]

However, most of those assassinated by Arabs were known or suspected opponents of the Mufti. Some indication of the extent of the powers and the effectiveness of the internal sanction apparatus can be gained by detailing a short list of some of the Arabs prominent in public life who were killed by the shabab. The disciplining and terrorizing psychological effects upon the Arab community of the assassination of community leaders was traumatic. If not moved as a result actually to participate, Palestinian Arabs at least ceased to display openly any disaffection towards the Arab cause.

Some Victims of the Internal Arab Terrorist Apparatus

1. the Mayor of Hebron, Nasr El Din Nasr, assassinated 4 August 1936;
2. Ibrahim Yousef, member of Tiberias Municipal Council, assassinated April 1937;
3. the Mukhtar of Balad Esh Sheikh, assassinated September 1937;
4. the Mukhtar of Shah Mata, assassinated December 1937;
5. the Mukhtar of Ein Razal, assassinated August 1938;
6. the Mukhtar of Beth Mahsir, assassinated August 1938;
7. Hasan Sidki Dajami, a member of the Jerusalem Municipal Council, assassinated November 1938. As a leading opponent of the Mufti and a member of one of the four leading Arab families,

his assassination prompted all the Arab members of the Jerusalem Municipal Council to flee the country.[7]

The rebellion of 1936-39 was thus possessed of hexagonal dimensions. It was a racial, religious, colonial, familial and peasant struggle intermingled. Similarly, it could be classified chronologically as being at one and the same time both medieval and modern: modern in the sense that it was only the second of the series of 'colonial' conflicts to be fought within the crumbling British Empire of the twentieth century (the first being Ireland 1916-21); medieval partly because of the familial elements in conflict, but more importantly because of the nature of the Arab military campaign, fought as it was by what were little more than feudatory retinues of bandit marauders only marginally inspired and motivated by loosely held, inchoate notions of liberation and jihad. It becomes quite clear that in Palestine, in contrast to Ireland, the political component of the struggle was thus intrusive rather than intrinsic.

POLITICS, PARTIES AND THE ARAB GUERRILLAS

Individually and in comity, the Palestinian Arabs were politically underdeveloped. Not only did they lack traditions of even moderately sophisticated political structures, but in both the preceding historical period and the period under analysis there appears to have been no spontaneous community of Palestinian Arabs able to act in concert for any significant period of time. The fellahin fought for territory, to preserve their link with the land, to retain in reactionary fashion what they had. They had little or no empathy with the futuristic symbolism of revolution. The fellahin too were fettered to the immediate moment in time. Only the effendis, economically comfortable, articulate and educated, were able to juggle mentally with the conceptual symbols of national independence. It was men of their class who were able to conceive a brotherhood of Arabs and to work towards gaining that independence which their compatriots were achieving or had gained in Syria, Iraq and Egypt. Even so, it was only during the latter part of 1935 and particularly during the six-month period of the General Strike in Palestine that intra-Arab schisms, at the level of the political élites, were temporarily sunk in a common cause. Again, it was not a spontaneous unity, but more a tactical expedient, part product of the application of terror and boycott. The Peel Commission could thus report in most interesting fashion that,

> As in Ireland in the worst days of the war [1919-21 – the War of Independence] or in Bengal, intimidation at the point of a revolver has become a not infrequent feature of Arab politics. Attacks by Arab on Jew, unhappily, is no new thing. The novelty in the present situation is attacks by Arab on Arab. For an Arab to be suspected of a lukewarm adherence to the nationalist cause is to invite a visit from a body of gunmen.[8]

This is not to say that a potential revolutionary situation did not exist in Palestine by 1936. Social, economic, religious, political and racial tensions were both multiple and manifest. A high percentage of the Arab population was armed. The Mandatory government's authority was becoming increasingly void; its structures were weak and inefficient while it quite clearly lacked a consensus of support among the populace for either its political institutions or intentions. Similarly, opposition groups of either quasi- or wholly military complexion were forming throughout the country. A police report compiled in 1929 by an 'observer' of the General Assembly of the Arab Congress held in Jerusalem noted that:

> Great enthusiasm and determination to 'save the country' even at the cost of their lives was manifested. Judging from the attitude of the Assembly, it was apparent that the people were in a state of extreme excitement that approximated to a revolutionary disposition. . . . The least spark is sufficient to set the country in flames.[9]

Even so, the Palestinian Arabs, unlike the Irish, were not able to construct either the political or politico-military instruments capable of exploiting, developing and then sustaining such a situation. Efforts were made to construct a political infrastructure, but they were conceived too late in the day, almost when the rebellion had begun. Yet the rebellion did mutate. At the high point of the rebellion in 1938 the opposition of the Palestinian Arabs had passed from mere brigandage and peasant banditry to a median position on the boundary of peasant rebellion and a people's revolutionary war. That it did not develop further resulted from the inadequacy of its political arm and the failure to establish complete political direction of the urban and especially the rural guerrilla campaigns. Clausewitz is pertinent here since he stresses that, 'If we reflect that war has its roots in a political object, then naturally this original motive which called it into existence should also continue the first and the highest consideration of its conduct.'[10]

The Arab rebellion lost impetus and deteriorated into marauding primarily because it lacked this disciplining spine of a developed political underground. Deep Arab fighting traditions asserted themselves.[11] As Sir Alec Kirkbride noted,

> War has always been regarded in Arabia as the most honourable profession a man can follow because the social structure of Arabia has been on a tribal basis since the dawn of history, it is natural that the organisation of war has taken similar lines.[12]

The lack of developed political structures within the Palestinian Arab community was not a phenomenon limited merely to the period under discussion. There were in fact few deep traditions or organized and developed political institutions. Under both debilitating Ottoman paternalism and the British Mandate, political participation was purposively kept minimal. Cohen noted that,

> Like all the millions of Arabs in the Turkish Empire, the Arab population of Palestine lacked not only national and political autonomy but also the most elemental cultural and natural rights such as Arabic language schools and recognition of Arabic as an official language.[13]

Thus when terrorist groups such as the *al-Feda'jah* (suicidal fighters or commandos) and *al-Kafas-Sauda* ('the Black Hand') commenced operations in Palestine in 1918 and 1919 in the hope of sparking off a revolt similar to the Lawrencian one in the Hedjaz, they found little or no support. In fact, throughout the first three decades of the twentieth century what political direction there was came mainly from outside Palestine. Kedourie sustains this assessment, noting that 'the Muslims of Palestine neither had political organisation exclusively their own nor were they accustomed to negotiate with the government through representatives duly elected and formally appointed.'[14] Thus the 'Arab awakening', a muted one in Palestine, was largely controlled and influenced from Syria through the deliberations of the General Syrian Congress which met some seven times from 1919 to 1928. Later, from 1928 to 1934, the Congress was represented in Palestine by the Arab Executive Committee (AEC). Recognized by the Shaw Commission as representing Arab opinion in Palestine, the AEC, elected by the third Arab Congress in Palestine (in Haifa, December 1920), was dominated by Mussa Kazim-al-Hussain[15] until his death in 1934.[16] After his death the Committee split and four political parties, again mainly familial holdings, emerged. Only two of the parties, the Istiqlal or Independence Party, and the Arab Young Men's Congress Executive, or Youth Congress Party, had programmatic content. Both of them were representative of the most youthful and radical elements in Palestinian Arab politics. Of the other parties the National Defence Party (formed in 1934), the Palestinian Arab Party (formed March 1935), the Reform Party (formed June 1935) and the National Block (formed October 1935) were all created in the aftermath of the breakup of the AEC. Doctrinal differences between them were few. Again, familial allegiances and quarrels provided the major dividing lines. One contemporary observed that,

> A dominant characteristic of the Arab parties of Palestine is the mixture of programmatic party with the feudal, patriarchal clan. There exist, also, parties consisting of leaders, cliques, and parties without any definite character.[17]

Politically the Istiqlal Party alone was the standard bearer of the Arab cause. Similarly, it was the first party to advocate and invite systematic civil disobedience and to attempt formally to relate the Palestinian struggle with a wider pan-Arabic quest for independence. In short, it was perhaps the one 'modern' party organized according to a platform, that of pan-Arabism, and eschewing ascriptive criteria as the rationale of all policy and membership.

Yet the AEC had given the first systematic impetus to Arab nationalism in Palestine in 1929 when it set itself the task of bringing about a revival of Arabic language and culture.[18] As a result Muslem cultural societies, often politically active, were established in many towns. One further sign of impending unity and a degree of political development was the fact that in the 1930s Christian and Muslim Arabs began to appear together on the same political platforms.[19] Similarly Arab newspapers appealed for the subordination of all intra-Arab disputes to the national cause.[20] At the same time the Arab youth of Palestine were becoming increasingly politically involved through a radical Arab youth movement, led by a wealthy orange-grower Yacoub Ghussein, Bey of Wadi Hanin. The movement quickly established young men's societies in most of the major villages and towns. Events were to demonstrate that, in the cities at least, it was the Arab youth, zealous and unified behind an idea, who were capable of propelling the fatalistic fellahin towards rebellion. The newspaper *Es Sirat,* as early as 8 August 1929, recognized this in an editorial, 'Youth with a Future', when it suggested,

> There is one category in the country from whom we expect something. This is the young generation. They only are the ray of the dawn of the revival expected, they only are the flesh of hope . . . let the whole world realise that there is a young generation in Palestine who is willing to serve, who hates humiliation and servitude and accepts nothing in lieu of independence.[21]

By 1936 it would appear that the young Arabs had taken to

heart Thiebault's dictum in Louis Madelin, the 'French Revolution' that 'When a man is eighteen he belongs to any party that will attack.' Typical of the inspirational rhetoric of violence and willingness to sacrifice of those times was a song the Arab youth frequently chanted, which ran as follows,

> Swords renew the youth of age
> and blood erase the life of disgrace.
> Students of Palestine it is now the time,
> Wake up and die to redeem your fatherland.
>
> . . .
> . . .
> . . .
>
> Walk on the edges of swords
> and sell your blood in the way of your country
> Swords shall judge
> Palestine never give up
> We shall all die for your prosperity.[22]

Here at least was an emergent, potentially cohesive, revolutionary vanguard. However, the youth movement, an essentially city-based phenomenon, failed to develop a liaison with the rural guerrillas in the field or to influence their attitudes and structures in any meaningful way. There was little or no cross-fertilization. Structurally, strategically and tactically, the guerrillas revealed themselves as peasant units each operating after its own lights in its tribal fief — that area of territory within which it had won or coerced authority and allegiance. It is the guerrillas, the leading military arm of the rebellion, who demonstrated the rebellion's political immaturity. They were exceedingly parochial. The village and the family were the twin centres of the guerrilla fellahin's world.

Accordingly, his military organization was in the microcosm. A peasantry such as this typically has several factors operating unfavourably against it in terms of the possibility of organizing a unitary revolt. Since a peasantry is not a homogeneous and undifferentiated mass, its different sections have different aims and different social perspectives. Each of them is thus confronted with a different set of problems. Similarly, as Teodor Shanin notes, the 'inescapable fragmentation of a peasantry into small local segments and the diversity and vagueness of their political aims considerably undermine their potential political impact'.[23] He adds,

> the political impact of the peasantry has been generally marked by its basic socio-political weakness. The vertical segmentation of peasants into local communities, mass and groups, and the differentiation of interest within these communities themselves has made for difficulties in crystallising nation-wide aims and symbols and developing national leadership and organisation.[24]

Certainly the picture of the typical peasant community, of disparate, parochial units, is borne out in Palestine at this time. Writing of the Palestinian peasantry in the nineteenth century, E. A. Finn stressed that,

> Just as the wild Bedaween are divided into distinct and generally hostile tribes, so the fellaheen, are divided into clans governed by their respective sheikhs. They speak a common language; they possess a common religion; their manners and customs are generally the same all over the country. Yet of national unity there is absolutely none. They never combine for any purpose, except when occasionally some clans make alliances for raiding each other in their faction fights. . . . There is nothing among them approaching the co-operation of patriots as a nation ready and willing to join hand-in-hand for the mother country. . . . They have no national life. Every

district lives in and for itself and wages its own petty wars with its
neighbours, but it has neither interests in common with any other.[25]

It was in this remnant feudal society that the coterie of
landed aristocrats, their class symbolized by the Mufti,
attempted to politicize a rebellion which was for most of its
combatants an affair of the heart, the seasons, and above all
the soil. Peasant rebellions generally tend to be traditional,
localized and ritualistic rather than political, universal and
revolutionary[26] – Palestine was no exception.

The Palestinian Arabs were certainly ideological innocents.
For the fellahin the loss of his land as the *Yishuv* expanded
was the most important seed motive of rebellion. Similarly
the fellahin translated calls for 'independence' into terms he
could conceputalize – namely, the independence of his own
person, his family and his village. Encroachments, violation
of his territory in the Ardrey[27] sense, mixed with a general
pressure on his community life from both modernization and
the immigrant Jews, angered the fellahin and increased his
xenophobia. He fought therefore to maintain his intra-
community boundaries. Once this had been achieved, no
matter how temporarily, the guns were hidden away until the
next real, imagined or rumoured encroachment. Commitment
to the rebellion by the fellahin was thus sporadic rather than
total; incident rather than ideologically inspired; self-centred
rather than selflessly patriotic; social and psychological rather
than purely political or economic.

However, the Palestinian Arabs were not totally devoid of
political structures. As we have seen, they were developing
politically. From at least 1929 through to 1936 the Arab
youth and educated townsmen were organizing politically. A
loose political infrastructure of local 'national committees',
modelled on the central Arab National Committee (ANC),

began to appear throughout Palestine in 1936. The ANC was formed in Nablus on 20 April 1936. By the end of April, subsidiary committees had been formed in all towns and large villages. Political centralization of a kind was achieved five days later with the formation of the Supreme Arab Committee (SAC), which embraced all Arab political parties including the previously maverick Christian Arab and Istiqlal Parties. Yet the gestation period of these new structures was minimal before the revolt commenced. Hence their impact on the matrix of society was transient and the temporary unity they brought subsequently shattered in the heat of the revolt itself. Although the Peel Commission reported in 1936 that the revolt was 'sustained by a far more efficient and comprehensive political machine than existed in earlier years',[28] it is worth emphasizing that political organization in those years had been minimal.

Yet by 1936 the Arab Nationalist movement in Palestine had made progress. There was an active, nationalistic, propagandizing press and a fund, the *Sanduk-ul-al- Arabia*[29] (the Fund of the Arab Nation) set up in 1932 obstensibly to 'rescue' Arab lands from the Jews but no doubt in 1936, like the *Waqf* funds, being used by the Mufti to pay the men in the hills and thus sustain the war effort.

Similarly, the movement possessed a group of established political spokesmen and a leader, the Mufti, acknowledged and received in the chancellries of the world. Most important of all, the Palestinian Arab cause had gained its first revolutionary martyr of stature in 1935 when the millenarian revolutionary Sheikh Izzed Din El Qassam was killed by police, along with several members of his gang, in an engagement in the hills of Galilee. Qassam's vital lesson to the Arab cause was that he transformed speech into action. A short time before his death in 1935 Qassam had sent one of the members of his gang, Mahmoud Salem, nicknamed Abu Ahmad, to Haj Amin, the Mufti, to announce to the Mufti Qassam's wish to begin a revolt in Palestine with the intention of destroying the Yishuv. His aim was to open hostilities in the north while the Mufti began a second front in the south. Haj Amin, however, vacillated and eventually replied that 'the time is not yet ripe for such a thing'.[30]

Qassam's sacrifice and its subsequent impact upon the youth of Palestine demonstrated that the Mufti had perhaps not read the times right. Almost overnight Qassam became the symbol of violent resistance. Arab newspapers presented him as a martyr to both faith and nation. One commentator wrote, 'Dear Friend and Martyr, I have heard you preach from a platform resting on a sword. Today . . . you are, by God, a greater preacher than alive you ever were.'[31]

It was Qassam's example that was taken up in 1936. Like him, many of the rebel leaders came from outside Palestine and seemed to believe not in any sophisticated notions of political independence, but in vague apocalyptic missions and eschatological futures.

Thus the twin components of the Arab rebellion, the political and military, failed to coalesce. In Ireland, by contrast, the military and the political arms were indivisibly fused. For a time at least in Palestine there was a vague communion of spirits, but this evaporated under pressure. The two essentially disparate segments returned to more natural concerns – the guerrilla fellahin to their marauding and brigandage; the politicking townsmen and educated youth to petty politics, bombastic rhetoric and episodic urban terrorism.

The Arab Rebellion had by 1938 reached only that stage in the maturation of revolutionary tactics and structures which Irish partisans had achieved during the Land League

period of the 1880s. The period1936-39 in Palestine remained a rebellion writ large, possessing only some of the
structural and ideational requirements of a protracted
people's revolutionary war. In its military component it was a
peasant rebellion, retarded perhaps above all by traditional
Islamic fatalism − a fatalism which, we are told,

> In Islam exists only in polarity with rebellion. The constant tension
> between these two poles indeed explains why fatalism can exhibit
> itself with dignity and why rebellion has so often been merely
> momentary, impulsive and unsure.[32]

THE ARAB GUERRILLAS IN THE ARAB
REVOLT − PERSONALITIES AND TACTICS

Assessment of the Palestinian Arabs as military units in the
field again reveals a picture of deep tribal, peasant-style
loyalties and formations ineffectually papered over by a
brittle, Arab nationalism. The rebels were true to the bandit
type. First, the bandit fellahin were not economically tied to
the land. The land had no tyrannical hold on them. They
were potentially mobile. Similarly, the bandits were, in the
main, escaped or ex-criminals: ex-servicemen or deserters
from the Ottoman conscript army and mostly youths or
bachelors. They were then 'marginal men' seeking to establish
personal respect through military exploits. The Palestinian
Arab guerrillas of the period can in fact be satisfactorily
equated with Hobsbawm's category of 'Haiduk bandits' −
that is, a bandit operating as 'a more serious, a more ambitious, permanent and institutionalized challenge to official
authority than a scattering of Robin Hoods or other robber

rebels'.[33] Throughout the course of the rebellion the fighting men in the hills remained essentially a banditry, unlike their compatriots in the cities. Periodically under the leadership of men such as Fawzi Kauwakji, or Abdul Rahim el Haj Mohammed, some structure and training was appended to their innate warrior skills. Yet a return to tribal modes of fighting was never long delayed. In contrast to the Irish experience, the Palestinian insurgency lacked a sophisticated, underground, cellular base in which it could regroup and recharge itself when under stress and from which it could draw continuous support. In Palestine there was no systematic cadre-training and hence no vital second echelon leadership to sustain a protracted struggle in which heavy losses would be encountered. Guerrilla tactics and strategies were strictly limited to armed action. There was no attempt to establish alternative authorities other than a few hill courts; no attempt to create a potential infrastructure of an alternative government through institutionalized or even ad hoc liaison between the fighting units in the hills and the political component in the cities and towns. Without unitary politico-military leadership, random, unsystematic warfare remained the norm. It was a style of rebellion that not only stood in stark contrast to the highly articulate Irish insurgency, but compared unfavourably with sophisticated Jewish efforts at nation-building at this time.

Of the seven basic structural elements that seem necessary for a fully fledged people's revolutionary war — a headquarters as the locus of formal power giving overall politico-military direction to the campaign while at the same time allowing local units autonomy and hence creating an articulate force; an intelligence organization; adequate communications; a propaganda department; a training programme with reserves at all levels but especially trained so as to be able to replace the leadership cadre; a fighting arm of guerrilla and sabotage units in towns and country; and a political department concentrating on the international arena[34] — the Arab rebellion possessed only three — intelligence, propaganda and military units. The Irish underground forces possessed all seven. But the greatest weakness of the Arab in contrast to the Irish underground was their lack of political direction and a politico-military department. Clausewitz, and the conduct of some of the successful people's revolutionary wars of this century, argues that in military combat a clear statement of political objectives, or a creation of them, is essential, since war is merely an extension of politics and politics determines the outcome of war. Hence bad, clouded or non-existent policy results in unsuccessful war. Palestinian goals on the ground so often consisted more of attempting to mobilize mass support to remove the Jews from Palestine than attempting to achieve national independence — 'National independence meant nothing to the peasant but he knew a Jew when he saw one'.[35] Thus one of the few consistently clear statements of Arab intent throughout the period was anti-Zionism. Typical of many inflammatory tracts is the following editorial from the Arab newspaper *Al Dif'a* — again seeking to mobilize the youth of Palestine.

> You were the sole master in your country which was occupied on the understanding that you would have a free hand and would be annexed to Syria after a few years and later to the Arab Federation. Everything has been late, no supremacy, no Syria, no Federation. Do you know who is responsible for this?
> Jews and Zionism.
> You possessed lands, towns, villages, mountains, plains, valley and coast. You were the sole master of your country. But today Tel Aviv is larger than Jaffa. The Jews form the majority in Jerusalem and form half the population of Haifa. . . . If you were young, you had a

brilliant future. If you were a merchant, your trade would have prospered; a farmer you would have retained your land and your produce increased . . . a youth you would have realised your dreams in military schools, navy army and other aspects of public life. All this has been lost.

Do you know the cause?

It is Jews and Zionism.

And now your country is in danger of being judaized. You are threatened with eviction. Your language is in danger of being exterminated. The past is detestable, the present bad and the future gloomy. . . . For this we have pledged ourselves to suffer death in the defence of our country and have determined not to retreat or relent. We want Palestine a purely Arab country. We want to recall always the cause of its calamity so that we may hate and abominate it for ever. Do you know what it is? It is the Jews and Zionism.[36]

With this xenophobic, racialist and essentially negative ideology dominating the actions of the Arabs, it was difficult for the rebellion to develop either politically or militarily beyond the point of mere protest and to advance to seek definite revolutionary changes.

The dominant fellahin tradition was, quite simply, brigandage. Herbert Samuel, the High Commissioner, had reported in 1925 that,

the majority of the people are illiterate, placid, and, as a rule, easily led by men in whom they place confidence: they are prone to fierce and personal family quarrels, and . . . are occasionally liable to be swept by passion or panic into excitement and unreasoning violence. Strangely credulous as they often are, the most unfounded stories may find ready acceptance and give rise to sudden riots. Here and there, among the villagers and in the Bedouin tribes . . . are to be found individuals who are attracted by the adventure and the profit of a life of Brigandage.[37]

Throughout the course of the rebellion spontaneity over-whelmed any superimposed systematization. The lesson of the Irish experience was that an amalgam of both was appo-site.

Militarily, the British appear not to have held the Arab guerrillas in any great esteem. A disparaging memorandum by an anonymous military commentator noted that,

> the Palestinian Arab is not a fighting man; even when led and reinforced by trained and experienced individuals from Iraq, Syria and Trans-Jordan, the rank and file still retain their characteristic carelessness, lack of enterprise and wholesome regard for their own skills. They had none of the military qualities of, for instance, the tribesman of the North West Frontier in India. As a rule they were indifferently armed and invariably poor marksmen. Traditional Arab Warfare is an affair of much noise and the minimum of casualties and many an Arab was content to 'do his bit' by firing off his ammunition at night at long range with the least possible risk to himself but as often as not without any defineable target. Even the more offensive and energetic showed themselves remarkably con-servative in habit; a site where an effective hold-up or successful sabotage had been achieved assumed a lasting popularity and was used time and time again, often in exactly the same way and at the same time . . . on the whole it would be difficult to find a more obliging adversary and risks could be and frequently are taken which would have been quite unjustifiable in any other country.[38]

Whether or not the Arab guerrillas qualified as good soldiers according to the lights of the British Army, the gangs were most successful in taking control of several major towns, including the old city of Jerusalem and large areas of the country.[39]

Although there had been intermittent gang warfare carried out by groups such as the Green Hand Gang, under Ahmed

Tafish,[40] around Safad in 1930 and El Qassam's fighters in 1935, it was only under cover of the civil disobedience of 1936 that individual gangs began to coalesce into units, attract widespread support and recruits, and hence begin to pose a serious threat to public security. With urban riots, sabotage and individual assassinations as tactical constants, it is possible to chart the escalation of the rebellion during the six-month period of the General Strike. The increasing scale of violence, the onset of systematic targeted assassination and a generally more organized guerrilla plan of campaign are detectable. The rebellion appears to have escalated through the following five stages in the six months of the strike.

1. Violent rioting in the cities. The riots were unco-ordinated and incident-orientated with Jerusalem as the main focus of disturbances. However, the riots were soon followed, or in some cases accompanied, by widespread mobilization in support of the strike itself.

2. The onset of the General Strike and campaign of civil disobedience fostered by the Youth Congress and Istiqlal Parties in particular.

3. The beginning of systematic, targeted terrorism and intimidation on a Palestinian scale — in both rural and urban areas. Arab police officers and pro-Mandate *mukhtars* are singled out for assassination.

4. The beginning of the sabotage of communications and other services as well as periodic running battles between guerrilla gangs in the hills and security forces.

5. Finally, the coalescence of several existent armed bands leading to the commencement of a protracted campaign of guerrilla war in the hills coupled with urban terrorism in the cities.

In September 1936 Fawzi Kauwakji had been invited by Arab leaders, the Mufti in particular, to come to Palestine and lead an armed rebellion. On 2 September 1936 a crucial meeting was held in the Jenin area at which the various major gang leaders such as Hassan Sadeh, Sheikh Atiyah, Aref Abdul Razzik, Hassan Salameh, Fakhri Abdul Hadi and Mohammed As-Saleh (nicknamed Abu Haled) swore a binding allegiance to Kauwakji and recognized him as the supreme leader of the revolt. It was Kauwakji's leadership and training schemes that gave the revolt the degree of planning, not evident elsewhere in the revolt. In an interview given to a correspondant of the extremist Syrian newspaper, *Al Kabas*, Kauwakji detailed how his expeditionary force was formed and moved into Palestine.

> I relied [he stated] upon my friends in the Syrian revolt who were living in Syria and Trans-Jordan. Afterwards I started to constitute an Iraqi band of young men who were trained in the Army, in order that the 'expedition' should be organised in military methods, in order not to repeat the anarchy that had prevailed in the Syrian revolt. The party was constituted in spite of the strict eyes of the Iraqi Government and the British Intelligence Service. One part of it was despatched by cars by a remote route and I remained in Bagdad. When I received the news that the party had reached Palestine safely, I started with the remaining party. . . .[41]

In 1936 the rebellion was thus in its initial organizational phase. Bases were being established in the hills and political committees in the towns — but not as parts of a cohesive whole. Mobilization of the Arab populace was in its infancy. Thus the security forces still maintained a rather tenuous grip on most areas of Palestine. The opinion of both police and military chiefs at this time was that, had they been allowed to pursue the rebels in the hills and continually harass them, the rebellion would have met an early defeat. However, towards the end of 1936, with the termination of the General

Strike, the rebel bands were allowed to disperse to the utter chagrin of the military command. Sir Charles Tegart, recruited into the Palestine administration to advise on public security when it had become almost non-existent, remarked in 1938, at the beginning of a concerted counter-insurgency offensive, that 'there was no question this time of letting the bands retreat with flags flying . . . and the District Officers standing to attention and saluting, the way it had happened in 1936'.[42]

Thus in 1936 the guerrillas retained their arms, and the resultant apparent calm was, as Kisch of the Jewish Agency reported, 'a facade behind which armed bands were still being maintained for use on a word to be given by the Arab Higher Committee'.[43] Political expediency applied to public security work thus allowed the guerrillas to escape un-prosecuted.

During the uneasy truce of several months' consequence upon the termination of the General Strike, political violence and lawlessness continued. To keep the peace the Mandate decided upon a low-profile security stance. It was counter-productive. As in Ireland after the Easter Rising, guerrilla forces were allowed to regroup unhampered. The outcome was that the rebellion ignited again in 1937 and reached a crest of sustained violence throughout 1938. So serious had the security situation become in 1938 that the High Commissioner, MacMichael, wrote to the Secretary of State for the Colonies, Ormsby-Gore, that,

> there is no doubt that the position here is deteriorating rapidly and has reached a stage at which rebel leaders are more feared and respected than we are. The civil population is being terrorised by their ubiquitous activity, and, having to choose between two dangers, prefer the side which retains their sympathy on nationalist grounds. They see the rebels, in spite of our activities, harbouring

villagers, etc., and naturally regard them as being in the ascendant at present.[44]

A serving officer in the Palestine Police commented upon the transference of authority when he wrote of Fawzi Kauwakji,

> he was the great Arab hero. His portrait was everywhere, from places of honour in the houses to convenient positions in the driving cabs of lorries . . . over a large area, the Jenin, Nablus, and Tulkarm district, his influence became far greater than that of the British administration. Indeed that region became a sort of kingdom which Fawzi was the ruler.[45]

Yet it was not until 1938 that the rebellion became really militarily effective. The High Commissioner, MacMichael, observed on 14 July 1938 that considerable progress had been made by the gangs and that it was,

> notable that during the last three months the tactical skill of the armed bands has developed. They now operate according to a plan and under leaders whose instructions they understand, trust and obey, they have, as is only natural, excellent 'intelligence' and many of their schemes owe such local success as they have achieved to a discipline and sense of tactics which are, for instance, in the concluding stages of the disturbances of 1936.[46]

It was during 1938, the apogee of the rebellion, that further unsuccessful attempts were made to create some of the basic units of an alternative government infrastructure. Arab courts operated in several areas. All issues of law within Arab communities had to be taken to these courts if a visit from the shabab was to be avoided. The edicts of these courts rather than those of the Mandate were adhered to. National traditions were revived. Arabs were instructed to and began wearing the *keffiyeh* and *agal*. Even so, there is no evidence of an effective *ersatzgemeinschaft*,[47] or substitute community of rebels, being created. Even where they were strongest and in control of a region, the rebel gangs and their leaders continued to feud.

The number of activists involved in the rebellion was small. It would appear that at no one time were there more than 1,000 to 1,500 permanently active rebels broken into small, self-contained bands. These men were the backbone of the rebellion, the permanent nuclei of otherwise evanescent gangs. The regular fighting cadre would, for any one engagement, be reinforced by temporary detachments of armed fellahin, often from villages close by the target to be attacked. However, in practice, despite the eulogies of praise and allegiance given to Kauwakji, there was no central command of the Arab guerrillas. Those who signed the Jenin agreement soon went back on it — one signatory, Fakhri Abdul Hadi, even fought for the British against Kauwakji. There was thus no charismatic leader of the politico-military stature of Michael Collins. However, there were several self-styled titular heads of the revolt such as Fawzi ed Din El Kauwakji and Abdul Rahim el Haj Mohammed. Fawzi Kauwakji, essentially a soldier of fortune, epitomized many of the Arab guerrillas in his career pattern. Firstly, he was not himself a Palestinian but a Syrian who had served with distinction in the Turkish Army during the 1914-18 war. After the French occupation of Syria, offering his services now to the other side, he obtained a Legion of Honour for his work as an intelligence officer. At the outbreak of the Druse revolt in 1925 he again had a change of heart, joined the rebels and was eventually sentenced to death. Escaping to his Hedjaz, he became military advisor to King Ibn Saud.

Finally, he gained a commission in the Iraq Army which he resigned in 1936 to begin his operations in Palestine. There he appointed himself 'generalissimo' of rebel forces.[48] Most guerrilla leaders, however, were independent in their own areas and 'ploughed their own furrow' — though some gangs and their leaders did adhere to the Mufti's cause and follow his commands. It is an interesting exercise to examine in some detail two of the principal guerrilla leaders, one representative of the 'independent actor' type and the other of the 'soldier of the Mufti'.

Abdul Rahim el Haj Mohammed, another self-styled commander-in-chief of rebel forces, and Aref Abdul Razzik both operated in Samaria. Razzik was the Mufti's man, el Haj Mohammed the independent.[49] Typically, the two men loathed each other. Mohammed, operating from his base at Tulkara along with rebels Yousef Abu Dorrah and Issa Batat from Hebron,[50] was a man of good family and some education. He was also a more honest and genuine patriot than many of the rebels. Certainly he was neither as coldly ruthless nor as criminally inclined as some. A British Army bulletin noted of him, obviously with a wistful eye on the passed chivalry of Agincourt ethics in battle, that 'within his lights his campaign is conducted on decent lines'.[51] Because of its comparative humanity, his campaign was used to symbolize the Arab guerrillas for external propaganda purposes — perhaps in an effort to mask the fact that guerrilla warfare is an unmannerly form of war.

Abdul Razzik was more typical of the Arab guerrillas both in his attitudes and background. He began his activities as a highway robber taking money and goods from his compatriots, the fellahin. In 1923 he was arrested and imprisoned for three years after operating as a brigand, with seven other men, in the Nablus-Tulkarm hills. Released in 1926, he

became a land-broker and sold more than half of the land of
the Taiba village, Tulkarm, to Jews.[52] During the rebellion
most of his power came to him as the leading military arm of
the Mufti's political wishes. Based in Taiyibil, Samaria, he
became the chief exponent of the terror directed against
uncommitted or wavering Arabs. Similarly, he treated as his
personal booty a high percentage of the subscriptions to rebel
funds.[53]

Gang leaders such as these chose their headquarters as
close to the Palestine border as possible – hence facilitating
escape, recruitment from outside Palestine and the shipment
of weapons. Fawzi Kauwakji, for instance, was based in a
village north of Nablus conveniently placed for receipt of
arms from Syria via the Samakh neighbourhood or from
Trans-Jordan along unobtrusive routes. This site also offered
posssible escape across the Jordan.[54] From this base and
arsenal he would sortie out from time to time attacking
villages and communications. Like other rebel leaders, he
possessed a limited number of villages specifically allocated as
the collecting point for arms often brought into Palestine by
hashish smugglers, who knew the most secret routes and
hiding places.[55]

At the beginning of the rebellion, the gangs were com-
posed of mixed contingents of Palestinians, Syrians, Iraqis,
Druses and Trans-Jordanians. For example, the gang of
Abdullah al Asbah Fawzi Raschid was composed of thirty
Syrians and twenty Palestinians, while that of Ibrahim
Yousef Abu Dorrah contained a regular core of fifteen
Syrians and ten Palestinians.[56] Hence it is not surprising they
lacked from the outset a cohesive motivating nationalistic
ideology – they were men more in the style of mercenaries
than true partisans.

The gangs appear to have evolved in a well-defined cyclical

pattern. Their formation began with small, personal, ill-organized followings confining their activities to petty robbery and minor acts of terrorism. Because of their size and mobility, they were able to avoid contact with the police and the military. Hence operating with what must have seemed to some fellahin as apparent impunity, their prestige grew and with it their numerical strength. The gang's terrorist activities then began to increase in direct proportion to their size. At this stage several gangs would begin to coalesce and operate as one large marauding unit. In doing so they became less mobile, more easily identifiable and hence easier targets. As a result they suffered severe defeats when located. Dispersed into smaller gangs by such pressure, the recruitment cycle would then begin again.[57] The whole process was spontaneous. Neither the Mufti nor the Palestinian political élite could regulate the size, structure, targets or tactics of the gangs.

In terms of their fire-power, the individual gangs were not particularly hard-hitting. Their weapons were often unreliable. The weapons used in the 1936-39 rebellion could in fact be broadly categorized into prewar and 1914-18 war stock. The prewar rifles were often treasured family weapons. Indeed, on one occasion security forces descovered an eighteenth-century Portuguese musket, still in use and functioning well. Prewar weapons were mostly Turkish in origin although Japanese, Russian, English, and German guns were all in use. Many of the weapons appear to have been curious amalgams rebuilt from available spare parts. A British Army communique duly noted, 'Quite a number [of the weapons] bear no resemblance to any one type of manufacture but consist of component parts of many rifles which, when fired, must be a distinct cause of uneasiness to the firer'.[58]

Ammunition too was tailored to fit the piecemeal

weaponry. The same report observed that 'the Arab is not a connoiseur of armament and has no compunction in filing the round to make it fit the rifle he owns'.[59] The greater proportion of Arab armaments was made up of Great War weapons abandoned by either the retreating Turks or the British on the battlefields of 1916-17. Again, many of these weapons were assembled from available parts, probably by ex-Turkish armourers serving with the guerrillas. One interesting phenomenon of the rebellion in terms of weapons supply was the 'returnable weapon'. Many of the arms used in the period 1936-39 had originally left Palestine for the Syrian revolt of 1925-26, only to begin returning to Palestine from 1929 onwards.[60]

It was in fact in 1929 that the turning point came in the arming of the native Palestinian communities, both Jew and Arab. During the course of the 1929 riots in Jerusalem it was apparent that there was not a great number of arms in the country because they were neither extensively used nor extensively carried. Weaponry used in 1929 was more often the primitive home-made cudgel or the knife. It was only after 1929 that Jews and Arabs began systematically to arm themselves. The reorientation in the type of weaponry was a crucial variable in the escalation of the threat to public security. Knives are far easier to deal with than bombs and bullets, and their effect is individual rather than multiple. Table 5[61] indicates the reorientation in weaponry revealed in the changed techniques of taking or attempting to take life in the period 1934-38. The rise in the number of shootings naturally parallels the decline in public security.

The rebellion was not entirely random and scattered. It was patterned in that, in addition to the urban-rural dichotomy, there were three distinct theatres of conflict based upon the differing scales of rebel and security forces activity.

TABLE 5

Reorientation of Weaponry: Incidents of Murder and Attempted
Murder in Palestine, 1934-38

Year	Murder		Attempted Murder	
	Shooting	Stabbing	Shooting	Stabbing
1934	30	46	35	67
1935	37	41	31	73
1936	146	49	353	86
1937	128	24	166	53
1938	502	33	409	39

The original impetus of the revolt had come from the towns
— particularly Jerusalem, Nablus, Jenin and Tulkarm. In
these urban areas there were two broad 'types' of rebel. First,
there were those of the effendi class, men with some education and often a profession. It was a category that also
included educated youth. Second, there were the poor, illiterate, displaced and often unemployed fellahin — the
lumpenproletariat. The effendis, politically aware, were the
'administrators' of the revolt in the urban areas since they
conceived and provided both organization of and personnel
for the rebel committees. The fellahin were the 'labourers' of
the revolt in the towns, providing its violent arm. They were
the assassins, the abductors and the interrogators. In many
revolutionary struggles this group has provided the dispens-
able vanguard of the movement in its organizational phase
where disciplined violence and disciplining by violence act
simultaneously. Strangely, in Palestine, it was the effendi
class, the 'administrators', who succumbed to the fellahin. As
the rebellion evolved the politically aware cadre was dominated and then displaced by the men of terror in both urban

and rural areas – a state of affairs that might well explain the eventual decline of the political component of the revolt which, though present and developing early on, had become almost invisible by the end of 1938. Eventually it was the agents and squads of terrorists from the local guerrilla gangs who alone kept villages and towns in rebel hands. In Jaffa, Abdul Rahim el Haj Mohammed, Aref Abdul Razzik and Hassan Salameh all had groups operating. The towns in fact presented a separate security problem, since in Jerusalem, Haifa, Jaffa, Tel Aviv and Jenin superimposed on the current of rebellion against the Mandate was the extra dimension of interracial and religious conflict between Jew and Arab. As Haining, the GOC, noted, 'Trouble in the towns differs from that in the rural areas in that it may be started by either Jew or Arab organisation'.[62]

Within the umbrella dichotomy of urban-rural guerrilla activity were the three rural theatres and styles of war. The major theatre of activity was in northern Galilee and Samaria. It was there, as well as in the towns, that security was most severely tested, and eventually broken. In the northern Galilee district the gangs had less well defined areas than the gangs in Samaria. A further point of contrast was the large number of minor chieftains, owing to the lack of an outstanding single leader. In Galilee too the general direction of the rebellion was less controlled though no less extensive in scale.[63] Most of the Arab attacks took place at night and consisted of well-organized sabotage against the IPC pipeline [64] roads and the Tegart Wire,[65] as well as attacks on Jewish colonies and military and police patrols and random sniping at military and police billets. Owing to the proximity of the frontier giving easy access to Syria, gangs frequently drifted in and out of the area. However, it is possible to detail some of the main gangs, their leaders and centre of operations in the Galilee district.

1. Fawzi Raschid	Strength of gang twenty to forty men, with his centre of operations at Tarshiha. Raschid was probably the most important leader in the area and may have exercised a loose control over some of the other gangs and leaders in the area who are listed below.
2. Mbada Farhat	Strength of gang ten to fifteen men. Area centre Majdal Kurum.
3. Rabbah of Ghabsiya	Strength of gang eight to twelve men. Area centre Bassa-Wadi Kassim.
4. Abu Ibrahim	Strength of gang twenty to forty men. Area centre Deishum-Safsaf.
5. Mohammed (Schoolmaster of Arraba)	Strength of gang five to ten men with centres in Majdal Kurum and Beit Jann.
6. Abdullah Shair	Strength of gang twenty men, based in the Safad area.
7. Aref el Hamdan	Strength of gang fifteen to twenty men. Based in Arraba-Sha'ab.
8. Riad El Khatib	Strength of gang five to ten men based in Nahf-Mughar.
9. Abdin Bey (a Turk)	Strength of gang thirty men operating in Safad south of the Acre-Safad Road.

In the second theatre, the Samaria District, fighting was also intense and contained three principal gang leaders operating in more or less well-defined areas detailed below.

Abdul Rahim El Haj Mohammed

Abdul Rahim was a Palestinian of Dennebeh village near the epicentre of the rebellion, Tulkarm. His gang was composed of between fifty and eighty men, twenty of whom were Syrians.

Area of operations
(main centre)   Umm Al Fahm-Yabad-Yamun

Boundaries   North : Lajjun-Affule
                        East : Affule-Jenin-Nablus
                        South : Nablus-Tulkarm
                        West : Tulkarm-Karkur-Musmus Pass

In addition to his own gang, Abdul Rahim also exercised general direction and financial control over the gang of Yusef Abu Dorrah (below). He also possessed a Lewis gun which was greatly prized.

Yusef Abu Dorrah

Yusef Abu Dorrah was a Palestinian of Silet El Harthiya, the normal strength of his gang fluctuated from 30 to 100 or 120 men. Captured documents revealed that his gang was divided into some eleven detachments with a nominal strength of five to ten men each.

His main area of operations was similar to that of El Haj Mohammed but also extended over the Carmel Range and east of the Jenin-Nablus road as far as Beisan.

The following sub-leaders of the gang were known to security forces:

Number 1 Detachment	Faiz el Haj Mohammed
Number 2 Detachment	Hussain el Qadr
Number 3 Detachment	Suleiman el Buri
Number 4 Detachment	Fathallah
Number 5 Detachment	Ali Ibn Ali el Faris of Umm Al Fahm
? unknown ?	Massoud Nassar of Izzim
? unknown ?	Ahmad al Aso of Sanur

Aref Abdul Razzik

Razzik was a Palestinian of At Taiyiba, the normal strength of whose gang consisted of a permanent nucleas of thirty to forty men who, with the exception of five Syrians, were all Palestinians. However, local reinforcements on the eve of an operation often raised the strength of his unit to some 200 men.

Area of operations (main centre)	near At Taiyiba
Boundaries	North : Tulkarm-Nablus Road
	East : Nablus-al Lubban
	South : A line al Lubban-Ras El Ain
	West : Ras el Ain-Tulkarm

The third centre of the rebellion, much less disturbed than these two major theatres, was composed of the Jerusalem-Hebron-Beersheba-Gaza-Jaffa district, where for much of the time effective control could be maintained by routine patrol and flag marches by both police and military.[66]

The Arab Rebellion was thus a peasant rebellion of considerable duration and scale. For a time it ended Mandatory control in certain areas of Palestine and threatened it and the Yishuv everywhere. The concern here has been to describe in detail the nature of both the rebellion and its combatants; to draw out the contrasts between it and the Irish revolutionary underground. The Arab rebellion was unsystematic, unstable and prone to anarchic lapses. The differences in the condition of the respective rebel forces in Ireland and Palestine was one of the crucial variables in determining the extent of the breakdown of public security in those areas.

Similarly, a detailed description of the nature of the rebellion confirms that it was not solely the product of the Mufti's machinations, attempting, as some would have it, to establish a caliphate with himself as Caliph. The control the Mufti exercised over the rebellion, and especially the guerrillas in the field, was minimal. From beginning to end the rebellion possessed a spontaneity which most of those who have so far written about it have neglected to point up. There is, I think, impeccable, and possibly incontrovertible, evidence from Jewish, Arab and British sources that substantiates the thesis of spontaneity. This is particularly true of the period at the beginning of the revolt, the General Strike and the campaign of civil disobedience. For instance, the High Commissioner, Arthur Wauchope, writing in October 1936, noted that,

> it is incorrect to say that various Arab parties united to declare a general strike on 22 April 1936 . . . the strike was begun independently and spontaneously in various places by various committees and groups, who, on the 20th and 21st April issued calls for a strike. The committee of Arab leaders did not issue their manifesto calling for continuation of that general strike until 25 April.[67]

That Wauchope was not deceived as to the spontaneity of the
beginning of the revolt is also evidenced by the remarks of
the Arab leader Ragheb Bey Nashashibi, a member of the
ANC, in meetings with Wauchope. In April 1936 Nashashibi
stressed that 'the disturbances were quite unexpected',[68] and
on 5 May 1936 he again emphasized that,

> the tension in the country was great and the attitude of the leaders
> was dictated by the pressure brought to bear upon them by the
> nation. The people . . . at the present time were ruling the leaders
> and not the leaders ruling the people.[69]

That Nashashibi was not merely indulging in rhetoric for the
benefit of Wauchope is evidenced by a phone call from
beduin sheikhs assembled at Beersheba. The call, made to the
Mufti on 20 April 1936, was monitored by Haganah intelligence and a report was submitted to the Jewish Agency.
During the conversation the sheikhs asked the Mufti for
guidance — how and when were they to act? The Mufti
replied vaguely that there was no definite system and everyone could do as he liked.[70] It is worth emphasizing that this
was just four days after the supposedly Mufti-inspired first
incident of the revolt — the disturbances in Jaffa on 19 April
1936.

Militarily the rebellion could not hope to defeat the
security forces of the Mandate government. Lacking overall
political direction, given the British commitment to the Balfour Declaration and, above all, the most determined and
thorough pioneering of the various Aliyah, it had few chances
of political success. As one authority has noted, rebellions
'have lacked the elements of political organisation on the
objective level and of individual-national commitment on the
subjective level which could create new administrative structures and increase political participation'.[71]

The Arab rebellion was in no way a thorough-going general conspiracy against the government as was the Irish War of Independence. Rather was it deeply rooted in tribal brigandage. As the Irish Volunteers successfully demonstrated — in a struggle such as the Palestinian Arab political élite attempted to wage — the first axiom should be that,

> armed action is by no means the whole struggle, it is just one of several kinds of resistance; in order to win the struggle we have to assault the Czar's Government from every possible side, cause every possible damage to all its offices, all its activities. Such a constant assault and constant distraction will be the general conspiracy against the government.
>
> Such a conspiracy is terrible for the government. It is terrible because in every other fight, the government can get at its enemy, imprison, kill, punish — but with the general conspiracy it can do nothing. The enemy is everywhere and nowhere; strikes blows but is constantly elusive.[72]

For the fellahin, unlike the Irish volunteers, it was sufficient that they had revolted and taken up arms for a time. The Arab Rebellion was dogged by its traditional morés. Unlike the Irish War of Independence, it was an inarticulate rebellion fighting in only one of the five major arenas of people's revolutionary war — the military. As a result the breakdown of public security in Palestine was total only episodically. Nevertheless, the rebellion, as a politico-military phenomenon, does stand as an interesting example of the development and decline of politico-military disobedience from a base of primitive banditry, through rebellion, to the brink of people's revolutionary war. Initially, its effect on the condition of public security was as dramatic as the Irish attack. The difference between the two breakdowns of public security lay in the fact that in Palestine the guerrillas were incapable of fighting in all the arenas of revolutionary war and failed to unite their people behind them.

As we shall see with regard to Palestine, though the process and pattern of collapse was similar to that occurring in Ireland, the Palestine rebellion lacked the resolution and organization of the Irish assault. Spontaneity was an inadequate susbstitute for methodical zeal. Hence public security, though broken for a time, was re-established by the Mandate government and not, as in Ireland, by the alternative, one-time underground government.

NOTES

1. Aharon Cohen, *Israel and the Arab World* (London, 1970), 215.

2. CAB 24/207, Police report for the week ending 26 October 1929.

3. A member of one of the most prominent Palestinian families.

4. CZA 508/125/5 1937-39, Documents on Public Security. B. Joseph to C. Weizmann, 12 September 1937.

5. John Marlowe, *The Seat of Pilate* (London, 1959).

6. 'It was the Husseinis who decided the political strategy of the Palestinians until 1947, and they led them into ruin.' For a brief treatment of the familial disputes see Eli Kedourie, 'Sir Herbert Samuel and the Government of Palestine', *Middle East Studies,* V (January, 1969), 44-68.

7. Moshe Pearlman, *The Mufti of Jerusalem: The Story of Haj Amin el Husseini* (London, 1947), 21.

8. Cmd 5479, Royal Commission on Palestine (July 1937), 135.

9. CAB 24/207, op. cit.

10. See R. A. Leonard (ed.), *A Short Guide to Clausewitz on War* (London, 1967), 57.

11. 'That intermittent dispersed way which is characteristic of Arab Warfare.' George Antonius, *The Arab Awakening* (London, 1961), 110.

12. Sir Alec Kirkbride, *A Crackle of Thorns: Experiences in the Middle East* (London, 1956), 71.

13. Cohen, op. cit., 44-45.

14. ibid., 148.

15. Kedourie, op. cit., 48.

16. CO 814/10, Arab Executive Committee, 1935.

17. Michael Assaf, *The Arab Movement in Palestine* (New York, 1937), 38.

18. Cd 5479, The Peel Report (1937), 67.

19. ibid.

20. There were four main daily papers in Arabic: *Alliwa* (3,000-4,000 circulation), official organ of the Palestine Arab Party; *Falastin* (4,000-6,000 circulation), supporting the National Defence Party; *Al Dif'a* (4,000-6,000 circulation), supporting the Istiqlal Party; *Al Jamia al Islamica* (2,000) — Independent Party. See ibid., 153.

21. Commission of Enquiry into the Disturbances in Palestine 1929. Colonial Number 146. Evidence. Vol. I. Exhibit Number 45. p.l. 053.

22. *Falastin* (18 November 1936). Translations of Arabic newspapers, State Archive, Jerusalem.

23. Teodor Shanin (ed.), *Peasants and Peasant Society* (Harmondsworth, 1971), 253.

24. ibid., 255.

25. E. A. Finn, *Palestine Peasantry — Notes on their Clans, Warfare, Religion and Laws* (no publisher quoted), C2A, 22818, 3.

26. E. M. Kourie, *The Pattern of Mass Movements in Arab Revolutionary Progressive States* (The Hague, 1970), 21.

27. R. Ardrey, *The Territorial Imperative* (London, 1967).

28. Cd 5479, op. cit., 132.

29. Cohen, op. cit., 44-45.

30. Subhy Yassin, *The Great Arab Revolt in Palestine 1936-39.* (Damascus, no date), 21-22. An Arabic text kindly translated for me by Shay Lachman of the Hebrew University, Jerusalem.

31. Colonial Number 148, op. cit.

32. Manfred Halpern, *The Politics of Social Change in the Middle East and North Africa* (Princeton, 1963), 220-21.

33. For a detailed treatment of the bandit 'type', see H. J. Hobsbawn, *Bandits* (London, 1969).

34. For a similar assessment see J. K. Zawodny 'Guerrilla and Sabotage; Organisation, Motivations, Escalation' in *The Annals,* CCCXLI (May 1962).

35. Marlow, op. cit., 76-77.

36. *Al Dif'a* (September 1936).

37. Report of the High Commissioner 1920-25. Colonial Number 15, (1925), 13.

38. Air 5/1244, Operations in Palestine 1937 – Vol. 2.

39. See the final chapter of this case study.

40. CO 733/190, 'The Green Hand Gang'.

41. *Ha'aretz* (Jewish newspaper of the period) (13 September 1936). Translation in the State Archive, Jerusalem.

42. Note of an interview with Sir Charles Tegart, 10 October 1938. Shertok Papers, C2A.S25/4951.

43. F. H. Kisch, Note on an interview with Brigadier Simon and General Dill, November 1936. CZA S.25/188. Miscellaneous Documents on Security.

44. Air 2/3312, Palestine Disorders 1938. Letter dated 5 September 1938.

45. Roger Courtney, *Palestine Policeman* (London, 1939), 69.

46. CO 935/21, Narrative dispatch on the Palestine situation 20 September 1937 to 31 December 1938. Despatch Number 3. 14 July 1938.

47. Philip Selznick, "Institutional Vulnerability in Mass Society", in J. R. Gusfield (ed.), *Protest, Reform, Revolt* (Chichester, 1970), 264.

48. Cd 5479, op. cit., 100.

49. WO 32/4562, Appreciation of the Rebels by GOC Haining.

50. ibid.

51. ibid.

52. Moshe Pearlman, *Mufti over the Middle East* (London, no date), 21.

53. WO 32/4562, op. cit.

54. Air 5/1248, Monthly Summaries of Events 1938-39.

55. Air 2/1568, Illicit Arms Traffic in Palestine and Trans-Jordan.

56. Air 2/1244, Operations in Palestine 1938, Vol. II.

57. Air 2/1248, op. cit.

58. Air 2/1568, op. cit.

59. ibid.

60. ibid.

61. CO 814/14/1939, Annual Report of Administration.

62. WO 32/4562, op. cit.

63. See 'General Note on the Gangs in the Galilee and Samaria Districts', File 8283 State Archive, Jerusalem.

64. Iraq Petroleum Company Pipeline, later guarded by Orde-Wingate's Special Night Squads. It was a magnet for terrorists.

65. The wire, named after the counter-insurgency expert called in to assess the situation in Palestine, Sir Charles Tegart of the Indian Police Service, was an attempt to stop the infiltration of arms and men. It was erected on the north-east frontier from the Sea of Galilee to Rosheinna without serious opposition but as it progressed from east to west determined efforts were made to destroy it. For example, on the night of 28-29 June 1938, six kilometres were completely destroyed. See WO 32/9497. Report of Military Operations, 20 May 1936 to 31 July 1938.

66. For this detail on the gangs, see File 8283, op. cit.

67. WO 32/4178, Memo by High Commissioner Wauchope on the GOC's report of events in Palestine 15 September – 30 October 1936.

68. CO 733/310, Minutes of interview with Arab leaders, April 1936.

69. ibid., 5 May 1936.

70. Information given to the author by a former intelligence officer. I am given to understand, however, that a transcript, in Hebrew, exists in the Haganah Archive, Tel Aviv.

71. P. J. Vatikiotis (ed.), *Revolution in the Middle East* (London, 1972), 12.

72. Edward Abramowski, 'The General Conspiracy Against the Government' in R. Malinowski, 'The Pattern of Underground Resistance', *The Annals,* CCXXXII (March 1944).

6

THE BREAKDOWN OF SECURITY
AND
THE RECAPTURE OF CONTROL

Back from the Brink of
People's Revolutionary War

... desperately sorry I was for Arabs and British policemen alike. Both were too obviously the victims of a Government wavering between fawning and cruelty, always unable to make up its mind. . . . Resolute action at the beginning of the disturbances, one single volley, would have quietened matters. It is rather repugnant to consider at all, but, if force had to be used, then how much better to use it effectively, with one keen, smashing, bitter blow, than to dally along until near a thousand men had been killed and twice as many maimed. A dozen deaths at the commencement would have closed the matter. It is certain that we cannot rule Palestine by winning the love of the Arabs: they hate us. Then let us either rule by fear, which is the beginning of respect in Arab countries, if we intend to rule at all, or let us evacuate the land which our palsied fingers and insincere policy is ruining, and whose children we are sacrificing by our weak, misunderstood kindness far more ruthlessly than if we governed in the Roman fashion.

Douglas Duff, Palestine Picture *(Hodder & Stoughton, 1936), p. 205*

Both prior to and after the inception of the Mandate, Palestine was a disturbed polity. Under the Mandate, government was especially weak since Palestine became something of a backwater of the colonial civil service. The Mandate itself was an impermanent system. Interestingly, it resembled the situation of Ireland after 1914, when, with the Home Rule Bill on the Statute Book, there was an air of foreclosure surrounding the apparatus of government. Less of a 'lame duck' than the Dublin Castle administration, the Palestine administration nevertheless failed to attract the cream of the colonial service, most of whom were reserved for India. Marlowe wrote that,

> Palestine cannot be said to have been uniformly fortunate in its administrative officers. At the outset they consisted largely of men of little or no administrative experience, war-time officers who had received temporary positions under the Military Administration and had been taken on by the Civil Administration in order to achieve some sort of continuity. Few of them acquired that command of either Arabic or Hebrew which is necessary in order to establish adequate personal contact with the inhabitants of the country.[1]

The administration was remote and failed to root itself in the milieu — perhaps because of its impermanent status. Of greater consequence was the fact that it demonstrated a marked preference for Arab against the Jew. Shertok of the Jewish Agency repeatedly spoke of,

> the hostile attitude of certain officials influencing the views of large sections of the Administration, which comes very near to regarding the riots as a blessing in disguise in as much as they will probably teach the Jews a good lesson, clip the wings of their high hopes and reduce their impossible claims on the Government. This attitude is 'felt in the air' but it also revealed in conversations and reflected in official communiques.[2]

Though there were some Zionists within the Mandate administration, greater weight of support was given to the less thrusting, less sophisticated and more supplicant Arabs. As orientals, they, to the colonial mind, resembled far more closely the stereotyped colonial subject than the immigrant European Jew.

An academic visitor to Palestine was of the opinion that,

there can be little doubt that the general sympathies of the English officials in Palestine have been 'Asiatic' rather than 'European'. In most cases their previous service has been in Eastern countries like the Sudan, where the population accepts the British official as belonging to a different order of human beings. They were not used to the European settler, and it is probable that the first Jewish immigrants showed a certain aggressiveness comprehensible to anyone who knew the conditions under which they had been living and the ideals which they hoped to realise. A thousand little difficulties arose between the early settlers and the British officials and the rift was widened by a policy which almost amounted to dualism. The Zionists had their own 'nation building' services and the British officials came to look upon the Arabs as their special charge. This encouraged a natural tendency to consider Palestine as a pleasant Asiatic country which we could have administered very comfortably, if the Jews had not formed an unnecessary complication.[3]

One arm of the Mandate government, the judiciary, and particularly its Chief Justice, Michael F. J. McDonnell, displayed overt partisanship towards the Arabs and the Arab cause. It was a liaison that had serious repercussions upon both government and public security. The antagonism between the civil administration, particularly Wauchope, the High Commissioner, and the Chief Justice was one of the three major areas of the failure of intra-administrative communications on both a personal and institutional level.

CIVIL-JUDICIARY RELATIONS

It is perhaps stating the obvious in terms of the instinct of survival that the law cannot afford to be neutral when faced with a direct, violent, widespread challenge to the authority which both created and maintained it. Imagine then a situation where the civil administration had to tolerate within itself for several years a chief officer of the law who was directly antagonistic to that authority, to its senior administrator and to the policies that both he and his Whitehall superiors sought to enforce. One direct consequence of the Chief Justice's stance was to exacerbate both the tardiness of the Palestine magistracy and their partisan interpretation of the law. Again, Shertok of the Jewish Agency wrote to Wauchope that he,

> could not understand how it was tolerated that at a time when the Government was engaged in such a hard struggle for the maintenance of its authority and prestige it should be so let down by its own courts.[4]

The structure of civil justice in Palestine, its partisanship aside, was under McDonnell a feeble creature. There was a general lack of systematization. There was no effective central supervision of magistrates or the sentences which they imposed. Liaison between the police and the magistracy was poor. Similarly, there were extensive areas of Palestine where there was no effective, Mandatory judicial authority — a consequence of the failure to operate travelling magistrates' courts.[5] Together these flaws added up to a general failure to enforce the law and the growth of the large backlog of unprosecuted cases detailed in Table 6. Ironically, McDonnell had himself written to the High Commissioner in April 1930 stating that he felt,

TABLE 6

The Processing of Civil and Criminal Cases in
Palestine Magistrates Courts, 1923-29

Year	Number of civil cases tried	Number of criminal cases tried	Total number of cases pending at the end of each year
1923	28,000	17,000	519
1924	32,000	20,000	783
1925	39,000	21,000	537
1926	53,000	23,000	1,352
1927	58,000	27,000	1,491
1928	60,000	27,000	2,344
1929	61,000	24,000	3,082

Source: CO. 733/190/77269 Magistrates — Non-enforcement of the Law

very strongly that if confidence in the system of government is to continue, prompt justice is most desirable in magistrates courts which bring the administration into contact with the vast bulk of the population, especially the poorer classes.[6]

The effects of the failure to prosecute cases were multiple. For instance, the fellahin, unavailingly seeking civil redress of grievances in Mandate courts, were effectively alienated from that system. Similarly, the police were frustrated both by the backlog of unprosecuted offenses and by what they regarded as the inadequate sentences handed out by the courts. Those fellahin who were active in brigand bands against the Jews and/or the Mandate could not have failed to notice the discrepancy between the Ottoman style of governance and

that of the Mandate. Its moderation may have been interpreted as sympathy with their cause and tactics, especially in
the light of McDonnell's behaviour. Whether or not this was
the case, anti-system violence matured in the unprosecuted
vacuum between the letter of the law and its non-
enforcement. A government memo to Wauchope indeed
suggested that 'the continued terrorism has been possible
only on account of the failure of criminal justice'.[7] Similarly,
Shertok, in an incredibly scathing letter to Chaim Weizman
concerning the Judiciary in general and the Chief Justice in
particular wrote,

> Another piece of information which has come through today is that
> the imposition of Martial Law is again under active consideration. If
> this is so it can only be in order to brush aside the civil courts which
> under the guidance of that inveterate Jew hater, the Chief Justice,
> have taken up an obstructionist attitude *vis a vis* the government in
> the present emergency. If the government has been dilatory in
> resorting to strong measures to suppress disorders the courts have
> been doubly so in bringing to book that small proportion of crimi-
> nals which has been caught by the police. Cases of murder have been
> tried by District Courts and not by Courts of Criminal Assize which
> alone can impose the death penalty. Generally the courts could not
> be got to act swiftly and have shown extreme reluctance to mete out
> exemplary punishment. The Special Regulations issued by the High
> Commissioner laying down severe penalties and fixing a minimum
> term of imprisonment for certain offences, have been openly flouted
> by the Courts. Judge Plunkett, President of the District Court,
> Jerusalem, declared on two occasions that he does not consider
> himself bound by these regulations.[8]

When the judiciary did not quite blatantly impede prosecution of known terrorists, it indulged in almost farcical judicial
hair splitting. Again the government was undermined.

Yet, the most debilitating aspect of the crisis between the civil authorities and the judiciary was the attitude of the Chief Justice and his bitterly antagonistic relationship with the High Commissioner, Wauchope. Wauchope wrote of the Chief Justice in 1936, 'McDonnell has allowed his views to become known amongst his Arab acquaintances and his presence in Palestine may constitute a serious danger . . . so long as he remains in the country he will be a source of some embarrassment.'[9] Later, he added more strongly, in a letter to W. G. A. Ormsby-Gore, Secretary of State for the colonies, that,

> for the good of Palestine and for the good of the Arabs whose cause the Chief Justice now pretends to have at heart, I trust he will accept your suggestion and tender his resignation. I look upon his influence as having a baneful effect among all the Judicial Departments, among all the Arabs of the towns and even among some Englishmen.[10]

Wauchope had also emphasized that,

> it seems hardly possible that any judge holding such extreme and partisan views can administer, even-handed justice between Arab and Jew. . . . Everyone has consistently given all the help possible to the Government in an effort to end these lawless and dangerous disturbances. The Chief Justice alone has provided a hindrance.[11]

One of the origins of the schism between the Chief Justice and the High Commissioner had been an investigation into the condition of the judiciary and magistracy in 1933-34. The report of that investigation clearly indicated that there was no supervision of the magistrates' courts; while they were theoretically supervised by the Chief Justice, through his aids, the superintendants of courts, the president of district courts and a triumvirate of British magistrates, in practice there was no supervision. Thus, in 1934, the Palestine government proposed that supervision of magistrates' courts throughout Palestine be the responsibility of the attorney-general — thus effectively bringing them within the high commissioner's orbit of influence. The Chief Justice felt this would greatly reduce his powers of control and that the changeover was actually conceived with such an end in view. This was not the case. The transfer, effective by 1934, was an attempt at improving administration. The rationale behind it was not to transfer the administration of justice in the subordinate courts from the judiciary to the executive but to improve the supervisary machinery, which, if it had ever functioned, had now clearly broken down. The Chief Justice, however, felt threatened. The reform of 1934 thus exacerbated what antipathy he felt to the High Commissioner and the Mandate government's policies. Perhaps this was also because in 1934 there had been tacit personal criticism of the Chief Justice? Wauchope, endorsing the criticisms made by Spicer, inspector general of police, and by the Jerusalem Bar Association concerning the inordinate delay in the disposal of cases confessed that he was 'not satisfied that under the existing system the courts are so organised as to deal efficiently and promptly with the administration of justice', adding 'in the seven years he has been in Palestine the Chief Justice has done little to improve the efficiency of the magistrates courts and I feel sure that if left to himself, he never will.'[1][2]

No doubt McDonnell was acting according to his own conscience in all of this. What one could quite clearly doubt, in the light of evidence presented in this text and elsewhere in archival sources, is whether both McDonnell's known personal attitudes and his practice in office had anything to do with the strict and literal interpretation of the law, whatever he believed of the Palestine Mandate. W. G. A. Ormsby-Gore wrote in September 1936 that 'we were all agreed in Cabinet that the Administration of Palestine had been seriously inconvenienced by the delay in bringing the criminals to justice and by the very inadequate sentences imposed in the civil courts.'[13]

Palestine had in effect by 1936 become something of a haven for brigands, revolutionaries and escaped criminals seeking to avoid the comparative severity of justice in the neighbouring French territories. There was every chance that a criminal or subversive could escape capture, or, if captured, avoid prosecution, or, if prosecuted, serve no more than one or two years. As in Ireland the forces of opposition to the system were able to muster relatively unhampered. Brigands indeed prospered. While it has often been said that no government will watch willingly and passively over its own demise, in a Palestine dominated by appeasement and reconciliation the Mandate government, perhaps unwittingly, did just that. Again, as in Ireland, it rallied only when it had become quite apparent that, not only had public security collapsed, but the government too was on the brink of breakdown. In such a power vacuum, with no tangible authority referent to enforce the law, the civil government was to all effects suspended and superseded by the military. General Dill, GOC, had angrily written in September 1936, after some 300 had been killed and 1,300 wounded, that despite this,

No sentence of death had been imposed and it was notorious that justice had been only tardily and ineffectually imposed. . . . the garrison had risen to twelve times the normal. This large increase was not in my view due to the military requirements of the situation but rather the disinclination of the civil authorities to make full use of their powers or of the military forces at their disposal because they feared that strong repressive measures would leave bitterness.[14]

In purely clinical terms, the failure to make the rebels feel the full strength of the British Mandate was a grave error. It was only after the removal of McDonnell to the Seychelles with a fat sinecure and the imposition of military courts for the trial of all offences connected with the carrying and possession of illegal arms — and, indeed, for all crimes of a political nature — that some progress began to be made on the judicial front. Even so, it had taken the assassination of the promising district commissioner of Galilee, Andrews, to provoke stern measures. The military courts established in the Northern Area, with their headquarters at Haifa, and, in the Southern Area, with their headquarters at Jerusalem, both had jurisdiction throughout Palestine. In December 1937 four officers, a member of the judge advocates department and five clerks came out from England to further assist the enforcement of the law. For a time prosecutions had been conducted by the police whose divisions were involved or by military officers selected by the area commander. However, these methods were replaced by the institution of permanent military prosecutors — a technique also employed in Ireland. The inception of these courts not only greatly improved the processing of cases and the deliverance of salutory death sentences but, crucially, centralized all judicial work and also improved relations and liaison between the judiciary, the police and the local administration.

Civil-judiciary relations were then one of the major areas of administrative failure. Civil-military antipathy compounded that failure. Not only was there a series of acrimonious debates between the civil and military officers over allocation of powers, but the test of political expediency was applied by the Mandate government to all military and police activities. Operating in tandem, these administrative flaws greatly reduced the efficacy of the government. In the vacuum rebellion grew.

CIVIL-MILITARY RELATIONS AND THE POLICE – THE APPLICATION OF POLITICAL EXPEDIENCY TO PUBLIC SECURITY WORK

While the Arab rebels were handicapped militarily by a lack of politico-military co-ordination, both the British military and police suffered, under the restraints of an altogether too accommodating political directive towards the Arab guerrillas. One authority noted that,

> Events in Palestine in 1936 made the attitude of the civil power still more difficult to understand. The government of that country seemed to be always trying to prevent the police and His Majesty's Forces from ever doing more than just defend themselves. It seemed to have no desire to stop sub-war and re-establish British authority in the country.[15]

The British government was particularly anxious not to disturb the tenuous peace of the Muslims in India by repressing the Palestinian Arabs. Mandate policy was thus one of restraint and minimum response. It was a stance that was grossly counter-productive in the long term. Both police and military commands found the policy of minimum response distasteful. They saw only defects in the strategy of benign defence adopted by the Mandate government. It is particularly instructive here to detail some of the attitudes of the Inspector General of Police, Spicer, with reference to the way he felt the rebellion should be tackled and the advice that he gave his men, and then to set these against the actual policy adopted. One can then assess the impact of political expediency.

Spicer, speaking on the telephone, in the presence of B.

Joseph of the Jewish Agency, to the District Superintendant of Police, Nablus, said that,

> he knew it was un-British to use terrorist methods buy the situation would never be got in hand otherwise. When one party used terror the other party had to retaliate with the same methods. . . . In his view if a village was believed to have been involved in an act of terrorism the police should place a detonator in one of the houses, remove the inmates and blow up the house and then warn the villagers that if they were involved in further acts of terrorism a second time, the police would blow up five houses. If they did not pay fines which were imposed on them he saw no point in selling their furniture at public auction because the Arabs would not buy it and the Jews would not come from Tel Aviv to buy it. He would in place thereof take a ton of produce from the threshing floor, sprinkle it with petrol and burn it and warn the villagers that next time the police were required to act they would burn five tons. In his opinion that was the only way of dealing with the situation.[16]

Similarly, Spicer had given all his officers instructions that, in so far as the law required them to make a baton charge in a riot situation before opening fire, their baton charge should be very short so that they could quickly use their firearms. He in fact advocated 'shooting as many as need to be shot for them to abandon their violence'.[17] Spicer, like the military command, had also recommended early, swift and harsh action to cauterize the rebellion. The rebellious outbreaks had been sporadic and patchy at first, but the government had chosen not to act decisively. No co-ordinated initiatives had been taken to deal with the rebellion until 1938. Thus the police and military had been restrained while the judiciary had malfunctioned. Frustrated by such restrictions, Spicer responded that,

If only they would give me two weeks as I desire, I could enforce order and quiet. The situation is horrible. I am in despair. I am exasperated and at my wits end with these Arabs out of control. . . . I would have the murderers very soon but they [the Government] render me helpless, they will not let me act.[18]

The government's policy was thus the converse of the stance that the security forces wished to adopt against the rebellion. The rationale of the government was minimum force. Typically, civilians in security roles seek first to prevent, then to tame, pacify and preserve. The military way, from the point of basic training upwards, involves killing as a fundamental ethic and destruction or defeat of the enemy as a goal. In crisis situations the solutions presented by civilian and military thinkers are thus frequently antagonistic. Palestine 1936-39 can be viewed as a classic demonstration of such a conflict.

In 1936, against the advice of the air officer commanding, Air Vice Marshal Pierce, the civil government decided to 'continue our present policy, after the reinforcements have arrived, of endeavouring to protect life and property without adopting strict repressive measures'.[19] In July 1936 restrictions were placed on the opening of fire by the troops — albeit not because of unfounded complaints, but because, on more than one occasion, troops had fired on and killed or wounded innocent Arabs.[20]

The situation deteriorated further with the decline in the operational efficacy of the Arab section of the Palestine Police. By 1936 the Arab section of the police, that is the bulk of the force guarding the main towns and villages, had become completely redundant. The incidence of crime and violence had escalated dramatically, as the date in Table 7a indicate. Similarly, political crimes of violence, assassinations and sabotage had also escalated as the comparative data in Table 7b reveal.

TABLE 7

Some Data on the Incidence of Crime in Palestine Prior to and During the Arab Rebellion, 1936-39

(a) Serious Crime

			Year		
Nature of crime	1934	1935	1936	1937	1938
Murder and manslaughter	109	115	254	192	594
Attempted murder	122	115	508	250	569
Highway robbery	32	32	122	221	600
Theft by breaking into premises	337	858	1,194	935	835
Animal theft	499	393	463	543	211
Agrarian crime	425	443	688	439	314

Source: CO 814/13/1938, Executive Council Decisions

(b) Summary of Crime, 1922-37 (Palestine)

Year	Indictable offences	Other offences	Murder	Attempted murder	Highway robbery	Theft by breaking in
1922	699	12,832	142	–	180	83
1926	971	18,098	95	56	94	146
1929	4,723	22,084	178	232	34	128
1935	1,753	10,525	115	115	32	858
1937	2,653	14,399	192	250	221	935

Source: CZA 1435, Vol. II, Anglo-American Committee of Inquiry, 585

By 1938, the weaknesses in the internal security situation were acute. A War Office assessment of the condition of the police force during the period 1 August to 31 October 1938 stressed that the Arab section of the police had deteriorated almost to the point of complete disintegration and had become little more than an easy source of supply of rifles and ammunition for the rebels. Police stations with their store of arms were a bait to the rebels. MacMichael, who had replaced a battle-weary Wauchope as High Commissioner, wrote in August 1938 that it was impossible to place any reliance on the Arab police. Since they could not be dismissed *en masse*, it was decided not to recruit any more and to transfer as many as possible from duties requiring the use of firearms to those not normally requiring them; to end their CID duties and to reduce their numbers gradually, filling some of the vacancies with Jews.[21] Indeed an Executive Council Minute had noted in September that 'special arrangements for the rehabilitation of police dispositions in rural areas had to be abandoned owing to the fact that the Arab personnel of the force could no longer be regarded as reliable'.[22]

It had indeed become quite apparent that the majority of the police had been demoralized by conflicting loyalties, by the strain of almost continual combat from 1936 to 1938 and, above all, by the strain of unrelenting intimidation and terrorism to which both they and their families had been subjected. As a result of the failure of the force proper, rearrangements in hand to create a strike force, a composite rural mounted force of British and Palestine police, were abandoned. The Eastern Frontier Division, predominantly composed of Arab personnel, who also disbanded some three-and-a-half months after its establishment. Thus, as general public security collapsed, many police posts and stations were closed and their personnel withdrawn to Jerusalem, hence exacerbating the vacuum of authority. In Palestine as in Ireland, police posts were yielded from a position of weakness. Again, the city that received them, Jerusalem, was the administrative centre and like Dublin was itself particularly insecure. Indeed, by October 1938 the Old City of Jerusalem was completely out of Mandate control. No 'European' could safely go inside the walls. The police had been driven out in September and there was no security even for Arab shopkeepers. Murder, assassination, arson and looting took place unimpeded. Rebel gangs from the hills had also infiltrated the city and used a school of the Muslim Council, *Rowdat al Maarif*, as the terrorist command head-quarters in the city. One Muhammed Mahmud ad Durzi seems to have directed the rebels in the Old City, many of whom were *fedayeen* brought from the north of Palestine. It is not surprising, in the light of the impotence of the Mandate government, that the prosecutor of the Jerusalem Military Court, Lt C. V. Watson-Gandy, conceded that the civil administration had been 'making a mess of the situation for over two years', and that control should have been given to the military before the riots had bee widespread. He emphasized that 'the situation was too bewildering to cope with and even if the military were to take complete charge they will need at least six months to restore order'.[23]

Palestine was also full of firearms. The North and Galilee in particular had become a virtual independent kingdom of the rebels. People were killed in daylight. The government's authority and prestige had vanished. Loyal Arab officials throughout the country complained of the collapse of public security. The mukhtars and elders of Tiberias town in particular pointing out that they were 'under the mercy of thieves who are numerous nowadays'.[24] A leader in the Arab newspaper *Al Sarkhah* in January 1937, well before the peak of the rebellion in 1938, stressed that,

Incidence of Terrorism in Palestine, 1937

Nature of incident	Jan.	Feb.	Mar.	Apr.	May	Jun.	Jul.	Aug.	Sep.	Oct.	Nov.	Dec.	Total
A. Robbery													
Highway robbery	13	6	2	—	—	1	4	2	1	2	2	2	34
Robbery from buildings	3	6	2	7	6	3	2	5	2	6	9	8	59
Robbery in open country	6	2	9	8	3	2	5	6	7	3	4	3	58
B. Use of bombs and firearms:													
Against police or military	—	1	3	8	14	13	2	7	3	23	11	24	109
Against Jewish settlements	5	18	16	8	4	4	12	1	10	37	13	13	143
Against Jewish transport	—	1	1	1	—	2	1	1	—	9	6	37	38
Against Arab transport	—	1	4	—	—	—	—	—	1	10	2	5	23
Against British houses	—	1	—	—	—	—	—	—	—	—	1	1	2
Against Arab houses	6	16	7	10	7	17	10	12	12	2	12	10	109
Attacks on shepherds at work	1	1	4	3	—	1	—	1	1	—	1	—	11
Attacks on ploughmen at work	—	—	1	1	—	—	—	—	—	—	1	—	3
Attacks on quarrymen at work	—	—	—	—	—	—	—	—	—	—	2	—	2
C. Sabotage of government and municipal property													
Sabotage of railway lines	1	—	—	—	—	—	—	—	—	—	2	—	5
Sabotage of telegraph wires	—	1	4	2	3	2	4	4	2	33	12	15	82
Sabotage of roads	—	—	—	—	—	—	—	—	—	—	1	—	1
Sabotage of other government property	—	—	—	—	—	—	—	—	—	—	2	1	3
D. Sabotage of private property													
Jewish-owned	2	1	2	—	3	3	1	2	2	2	—	2	18
Arab-owned	9	4	6	9	6	13	2	3	3	2	2	3	61
E. Assassination and Attempted Assassination													
of British Officers	3	—	—	—	1	—	1	—	1	—	1	—	5
of Arab officers	—	5	4	1	4	2	2	7	6	6	12	8	61
of Jewish officers	—	5	4	—	3	3	1	1	4	4	4	5	32
of others	—	—	—	—	—	—	—	—	—	—	—	—	—
Total	49	69	67	58	54	67	36	46	55	143	95	119	861

Source: CO 814/12/1937, Annual Report of the Palestine Administration

TABLE 9

Incidents of Violence, 1938

Nature of incident	Jerusalem	Haifa	Jaffa	Nablus	Nazareth	Gaza	Frontier	Total
Attacks and sniping on military	125	71	141	293	88	70	193	986
Attacks and sniping on Arab public	14	10	16	19	6	3	6	74
Attacks and sniping on Jewish public	23	49	67	8	10	–	19	176
Attacks on transport	80	57	118	21	24	2	33	335
Armed robbery	131	46	103	94	26	39	18	457
Firing on Jewish settlements and Quarters	83	189	170	35	120	2	52	651
Bomb-throwing	66	86	63	28	61	21	7	331
Abductions	62	32	16	64	18	3	20	215
Attacks on Arab villages and houses	29	10	21	56	21	9	16	162
Damage to Arab property	6	10	22	16	3	1	3	62
Damage to Jewish property	44	146	125	46	47	28	59	495
Sabotage of telephones	135	84	165	121	94	67	54	720
Sabotage to railways and roads	51	29	82	62	24	58	35	341
Sabotage to other government property	40	10	40	38	19	28	35	210
Sabotage to IPC pipeline	–	23	–	–	81	–	–	104
Assassinations and attempted assassinations	90	99	84	80	28	10	39	430
	979	950	1,233	981	670	341	594	5,748

Source: CO 814/13/1938, Annual Report of the Palestine Administration

A person is not sure of his life and property. Travel is dangerous, while murder and assassination are rife. The existence of the government is not felt. . . . It has lost its prestige, respect and influence. Everybody is asking 'where is the Government?'[25]

As we have seen, most of the indices of serious crime — the number of murders and assassinations and particularly the incidence of highway robbery, an effective indicator of the condition of internal security — increased markedly in the period prior to and during the take-off stage of the rebellion. They reached a crest in 1938. Similarly, as in Ireland, spontaneous rural crimes declined as political violence, targeted against Jews and the Mandate, superceded it as the prevailing mode of expressive violent discontent (see Table 10).

TABLE 10
Incidence of Serious Crime 1932-38

Type of crime	1932	1933	1934	1935	1936	1937	1938
Murder/manslaughter	119	108	109	115	254	192	594
Attempted murder	118	97	122	115	508	250	569
Highway robbery	57	34	32	32	122	221	600
Theft by breaking into premises	1,040	493	337	858	1,194	935	835
Animal theft	611	312	499	393	463	543	211
Agrarian crime	1,403	829	425	443	688	439	314

Source: CO 814/11/1936 and CO 814/13/1936-38

By 1938, the security position in Palestine was doubly serious because of the conflict between the civil and military authorities on how best to tackle the rebellion. It is upon this schism, the inception of a counter-insurgency, and finally the defeat of the rebellion by that counter-insurgency that the analysis now concentrates.

DEFEATING THE REBELLION

Security operations in Palestine prior to 1938 were, as we have already seen, spasmodic, then restrained, unco-ordinated and hence ineffective. Since the onset of the crisis, the military command had consistently demanded that security operations be centralized under a unitary command. The lesson of Ireland, demonstrating the weakness of multiple security authorities, was lost on the Mandate government. Crucially, the military felt that there was inadequate definition, in statute and practice, of the powers allocated to the civilian and military commands in crisis. Civil-military conflict developed over this issue, and it was the resolution of this debate, giving the military control of internal affairs, that led ultimately to the defeat of the rebellion. At the end of 1938 the military ceased to operate in aid of the civil power. Instead, the civil authority became subject to military jurisdiction. From this point onward the rebels were, for the first time, made to feel the full strength of the Mandate. British security operations assumed an extra dimension. They became aggressive, focused and concerted.

Civil government went temporarily into abeyance in October 1938. MacMichael, the High Commissioner, stressed that he was most anxious to do all in his power to give to the military,

> as free a hand as possible in matters connected with defence and public security with a view to ensuring that there shall be no delay in the conception and execution of immediate and stringent action against the rebels.[26]

However, it was a position on which there was not complete agreement within the civil administration.

CIVIL-MILITARY RELATIONS, 1936-39

Haining, GOC in Palestine during 1938, gave a brilliant summation of the distinction between the civilian and the military mind as he saw it at the time:

> The civil authority has a more complex attitude to the situation than the military, who are concerned chiefly to enforce the principle of the maintenance of the objective, which for them is first and foremost the crushing of the rebellion. The civil side, on the other hand, are concerned with what is going to happen after the rebellion and feel that they will then have to live with the people of the country. There is, therefore, an inevitable tendency . . . for the civil authority to hold back and, directly anybody else is available – in this case the military – to thrust upon them the odium of enforcing unpopular but necessary measures. It is this tendency which makes the present system of dual control so peculiarly difficult. Although the military have increased powers and greater freedom of action, the ultimate responsibility still rests with the civil government and the objects of the two sides are often opposed. The civil government still feels the obligation to provide for the people . . . the ordinary amenities of civilised government such as social and other services, freedom of movement and freedom of action. The military side, if it is to pursue its objective effectively, frequently requires to interfere with these functions of government. The inevitable outcome is that the civil authorities tend not only to invoke their ultimate responsibility in order to water down military measures where they clash with their own principles of action, but also at the same time tend to pass on that same responsibility for measures which may prove unpopular.[27]

It is rather surprising that there should have been civil-military tension over the allocation of powers in Palestine since the statutes of the time were quite clear and explicit on the matter. There was no ambiguity in the 'Notes for Guidance on Imperial Policing', and the King's Regulations of 1935, which delineated the respective spheres of influence, giving overall ascendancy to the civil arm. Paragraph 28 of the latter states:

> The governor of a Colony, protectorate or mandated territory is the single and supreme authority responsible to and representative of His Majesty. He is by virtue of the commission and the letters patent entitled to the obedience and assistance of all military and civil officers, but, although bearing the title of Captain-General or Commander-in-Chief, and although he may be a military officer senior in rank to the Officer Commanding forces, he is not, except on special appointment from His Majesty, invested with the command of His Majesty's Forces in the colony, protectorate or mandated territory. He is not, therefore, entitled to take the immediate direction of any military operation, or, except in cases of urgent necessity, to communicate with subordinate military officers, without the concurrence of O.C. forces, to whom any such exceptional communication must be immediately notified.[28]

General Dill, who had become GOC Palestine on 15 September 1936, was not content with this allocation of powers. He was in favour of total military control, stating in a report:

> my view is that there should be no question of reduction of powers, exercise of prerogative or intervention at all by the civil authorities until order has been restored. Then it would be the duty of the G.O.C. to advise that the civil authorities resumed control. Naturally, it will be the duty of the military commander to seek advice from the High Commissioner on political issues but the responsibility for all action taken must unreservedly be his.[29]

It is perhaps not surprising that this was Dill's attitude since he assumed command in Palestine following a resolution of 7 September 1936 by HMG to restore order in Palestine by 'more drastic measures'.[30]

Dill was undoubtedly under the impression that this meant the imposition of martial law. However, he did see that this was not a practical proposition until adequate military reinforcements were in position and the necessary civil and military preparations completed. He suggested 14 October as a suitable date, since by that time arrangements could have been made. After at first agreeing to this, HMG, as on so many other occasions where both Ireland and Palestine were concerned, began to vacillate. The directive to Dill was changed. In place of the proposed intensive anti-terrorist measures a more formal diplomatic posture of inducing the compliance of the ANC was pursued. It was hoped that, with Mandate pressure and ANC co-operation, the terrorists could be stopped. Even so, on 10 October 1936 the High Commissioner of Palestine was authorized to delegate martial law powers to Dill on 14 October if the General Strike and the campaign of violence had not ceased by 13 October. However, information received indicated that ANC was on the point of calling off the strike and putting an end to terrorism. At the eleventh hour, 10 October, the ANC published orders to cease the strike and violence on 12 October. With sporadic terrorism continuing, the guerrilla bands still fully armed and under no pressure to disperse, the rebellion slowed down almost of its own volition and the strike ended. It proved to be a temporary respite. On 12 October a frustrated Dill, in high dudgeon, issued a Special Order of the Day to the forces under his command stating that the calling off of the strike was 'in great measure due to the resolute and energetic action of the three services in spite of hampering and difficult circumstances'.[31] Publication of the Order in the local press was forbidden by the High Commissioner. Dill regarded the incident as a lost opportunity for enforcing the authority of the Mandate government. In time he was to be vindicated.

It was in the light of the events of 10-14 October 1936 that Dill felt a more adequate and precise formulation of civil-military powers in crisis was necessary. Accordingly, on 28 October he issued a memorandum stressing that, when a situation gets beyond the control of the civil authorities, as it had so clearly done in Palestine by 1936, then the military commander must be given full control and the necessary authority to put down the revolt. Similarly, when such power was delegated to the military commander, he should have power to act under martial law and not statutory law. Finally, when a situation *was* out of hand, the civil authority should act in aid of the military power in the same spirit of co-operation as the military power acted in aid of the civil power in less critical times. He held, above all, that it was most urgent to resolve the following three areas of tension between the civil and military arms of the Mandate: first, the precise stage at which authority was to be delegated to the GOC must be delineated; second, the precise powers the GOC was to have must be made clear; third, the relationship of the High Commissioner and GOC when authority had been delegated to the latter must also be formally set down.[32]

Despite Dill's pressure it became clear, after Wavell had replaced Dill on 12 September 1937 and Lt General Sir Robert Haining, Wavell in April 1938, that martial law was not going to be declared in Palestine. The military would have to restore order under the existing emergency regulations. The British Cabinet had debated the issue fully and advised against the introduction of martial law. A Cabinet paper stressed that the Cabinet felt, it is most desirable to keep the doctrine of Martial Law quite separate from the legislation conferring emergency powers ... to declare Martial Law 'pur et simple' would involve the suspension of all law. I feel that it is unwise on constitutional and practical grounds to mix up with emergency powers legislation of the nature of Martial Law which is the abnegation of law.[33]

However, the reasoning behind the refusal to implement martial law was less principled and ethical. It was that,

in the strict sense of the term, Martial Law in English law implies the replacement, in a part or the whole, of the authority of the civil power in every aspect of government, administrative as well as judicial, by the military not acting under any specific legal provision but upon the fundamental principle giving to military commanders the power and the duty to take charge, when all the means provided for government under the existing laws have broken down. Martial Law applied in this form in Palestine would mean the admission by HMG that all means of governing Palestine in accordance with thelaw at present provided, including the Defence Orders in Council of 1937, had broken down. . . . [34]

In other words, the British government must not lose face in the Middle East, the international community or the League of Nations. Emergency powers would have to suffice. The Cabinet had thus both decided for martial law and then, ultimately, against it.[35]

Wauchope, the High Commissioner, had already told Arab leaders that martial law was to be imposed and imposed harshly. When it was not even enforced it was regarded in Palestine as yet a further demonstration of governmental weakness. The Mandate government had lost another portion of its credibility. Shertok expressed the opinion of many of his contemporaries, British as well as Jewish, when he wrote,

If the determination to put down the disorders had existed right from the beginning then there would have been no need to send out Commission after Commission to enter into the discussion of the political future. What H.G. had to say was that they would not look at the political problem so long as the country was in this state and would concentrate first and foremost on suppression. Only when that end was achieved would consideration be given to future policy.[36]

Eventually it was the military proposals of the High Commissioner, MacMichael, stemming from a Westminster political brief, that broke the administrative deadlock. The civil-military dispute was resolved by granting the military a more or less free hand to restore order. Alongside the military command the fabric of the civil administration remained intact.

THE BRITISH COUNTER-INSURGENCY

The security offensive in Palestine, as in Ireland, was the product of severe crisis, contemplated only when the Mandate's writ has ceased to run in the cities and when the north of Palestine had become what amounted to an independent kingdom of brigands. The internal security situation had deteriorated so much that, to restore order, maximum and not minimum force had to be applied. Formed in September 1938, planned in detail by October and fully implemented in the field by November, MacMichael's proposals, in the main, were directed at replacing the now totally inadequate police and civil security operations with a vigorous military alternative. MacMichael in effect gave power to the GOC to place military commanders in charge of all police districts and to remove from the district and assistant district commissioners all of their powers under the emergency regulations. District commissioners became little more than political advisors to the local military commanders, who had replaced them.[37] Similarly, the GOC of the military was empowered to direct the Inspector General of police. Indeed, the police force was placed under the complete operational command of the GOC from 12 September 1938.[38] MacMichael also saw the need to operate disciplinary courts within the police, restrict all traffic movement in Palestine and curtail trunk telephone calls. From these policy initiatives the British counter-insurgency campaign and the police force situation proper both grew.

The counter-insurgency offensive had in fact begun in May 1938 with the formation of Special Night Squads (SNS) under the command of Orde-Wingate. The Squads spearheaded the attacks on the Arab gangs. They came to be the shock-troop of the British military response — an unconventional force under the leadership of a most unconventional soldier. Conceived by Wingate in early September 1937, the Squads — three in all — did not take the field until May 1938. They were then operational only for the six months until November. Fighting mostly at night, the Squads were officered by British soldiers and made up of British soldiers and Jewish supernumary police, most of the latter also being Haganah members. They had an exceptionally high rate of contact with the Arab gangs owing chiefly to Wingate's own excellent intelligence organization. Again, as in Ireland, intelligence was to prove the key to prosecuting rebellion. In the main Wingate's intelligence agents were drawn from among Arabs of the Emek region and possibly even included gang members.[39] The recruitment of informers for Wingate was accomplished by one Haim Sturmann, a veteran Haganah officer and one of the original settlers in the Emek. Wingate, however, interviewed all informers himself, meeting them in the early hours of the morning before the residents of the village where he had his HQ were awake. Haining, GOC, had stated that one of his objectives had always been that 'we should be "top-dog" by night as well as by day'.[40] Wingate and the Special Night Squads enabled him to achieve this aim. Operating as they did in advance of the main counter-insurgency drive, commencing in November 1938, the Special Night Squads were the first truly offensive, mobile, hard-hitting force the Mandate government had put into the field against the Arab rebels. As such, they symbolized a complete change of emphasis by the British from a policy of concilia-tion to one of coercion. The Squads dealt many salutary lessons to the Arab guerrillas. Not without reason did they become a much feared force. Yet they were not the sole reason for the defeat of the rebellion. Rather, the Special Night Squads were one arm of a systematic policy of surveil-lance and harassment exerted upon the rebels. Haining asserted at the end of 1938 that 'the watchword of the whole period has been pressure'.[41] Shertok, in discussion with the British counter-insurgency expert, felt that,

> the question was whether the military command would at least show the necessary elasticity in adapting itself to the conditions of guer-rilla warfare by splitting the troops into small units which would always be on the move, harassing the bands relentlessly, chasing them from pillar to post, giving them no rest and showing clearly to the Arab population that the initiative had passed into the hands of the military and that the bands were on the run.[42]

Tegart in response observed that this was exactly what he himself was thinking. 'Give me one hundred Wingates' was his slogan.[43] The outcome of the campaign was that the Arab rebels were pursued in a way that the Irish guerrillas had never been.

Yet there were no sudden dramatic successes. Like guerrilla warfare, counter-insurgency is a protracted affair. In Palestine the counter-insurgency took the form of a programme of attrition with few immediately tangible results. Military initiatives straddled the months of May, July, September and November with the new departures in each of those months building on its predecessor. In May, when the Special Night Squads became operational, the policy of village occupation was also begun.[44] Some eighteen or twenty villages were placed under permanent occupation — two-thirds of them in Samaria and another third in Galilee. As a supplement to this action police and military posts were also established or re-established in the main villages. This was the core of the preventive security work. The objectives of this particular exercise were fourfold: first, to prevent the villages and their immediate neighbourhoods from either becoming or continuing as a source of food, shelter and recruitment for the gangs; second, to attempt, ultimately, to re-establish administrative control in those areas where the Mandatory writ had ceased to run; third, to prevent intimidation, protect and then gain the general confidence of the uncommitted and law-abiding Arabs; finally, to effect more strategic control of the disturbed areas by the opening up of previously inaccessible parts of the country for road-making and patrols.[45] It was thus a military, political and administrative exercise seeking to regain territory, re-establish de facto Mandatory control and, above all, to create a secure public.

At the outset, the area of operations of each village garrison was restricted to within five kilometres of the village. But as the counter-insurgency prospered, these areas were expanded in order to overlap and give complete control of certain regions. Where there was no such overlapping and occupied areas did not abut, the intervening corridor of countryside was patrolled regularly by strong columns from battalion and brigade headquarters. This strategy of modified quadrillage soon proved effective. The rebels began to feel the strength of the Mandate government. Acts of terrorist intimidation against Arab moderates and pro-Mandate village notables decreased. Confidence began to be restored in the ability of the Mandate government to maintain a modicum of law and order. Naturally, this had a feedback effect on the number of Arabs willing to express anti-guerrilla sentiments. Pro-Mandate guerrilla bands even began to operate against the rebels. Deprived of support, the gangs were thus flushed out of their previously protective villages into the open and the hills. Military bulletins began to record a noticeable weakening in the resolution of the gangs. The poor condition of their morale was demonstrated by the fact that they showed 'an ever increasing disinclination to face an engagement of any size with the troops' and 'an increasing tendency to leave their casualties behind'[46] — something the guerrillas had previously been most reluctant to do.

With an improvement being effected in the villages, the Tegart Wire began to bring about a change in the disturbed situation on the frontiers. The wire prevented the influx of weapons and the movement of guerrilla gangs across the frontiers. At the same time all the Jordan fords were placed under surveillance. Control of the Trans-Jordan frontier was further improved in July by the second major security initiative which put the whole of the Jordan Valley, from Jericho to the Sea of Galilee, under the command of the officer commanding the Trans-Jordan Frontier Force, Colonel Crystall, with his headquarters at Jisr el Majamie. A cavalry squadron from Roshpinna was also attached to the TJFF having been despatched from Samakh camp.[47]

The effect of this reorganization of security was twofold. First, the rearrangement of the Jordan area command relieved the commanders of the 14th and 16th Infantry Brigades of the burden of controlling the most outlying parts of their respective areas. Hence they were able to concentrate their forces and continue to flush out the guerrillas. Second, the rearrangements enabled a far more efficient policing of the TJFF area. The overall effect was that control of the country by day kept pace with the progress made in controlling the country by night.

Yet, although the rebels were being flushed out of their village enclaves and urban areas, they could not be pursued and tackled in the hills until October 1938, because of the inadequate number of troops. An army bulletin noted that,

> up to the end of October there had not been sufficient troops in the country to hold the main centres and communications and also take effective measures against the rebels outside these areas. Thus, the hinterland — away from the main roads and towns — was a safe refuge from which the rebels could plan, organise and carry out their campaign of sabotage and murder. But with the equivalent of two Divisions in the country [by November 1938] active measures everywhere became possible.[48]

As a result of this influx of troops, the final and most crucial security initiative was taken in November 1938. Haining, the GOC, viewed the new system as the turning point of the revolt, since for him it demonstrated for the first time that the government was both determined and able to take control of the country. The new measures forbade any movement by rail or car without a pass. Passes of different colours were issued giving the bearer greater or lesser privileges of travel. Card-issuing offices were sited in all large towns and traffic-checking posts established at the exits of every town

or village as well as at other random points along the major
roads. A permanent night curfew was also imposed on all
roads outside urban areas. Hence anything non-military that
moved at night, or moved by day without a pass, was fair
game for arrest. This measure crucially allowed the Army to
identify the terrorists — its greatest problem in any internal
security role. Arab terrorists were thus picked up with
increasing ease; the shipment of arms from district to district
ceased; and, above all, the constant surveillance and harassment implicit in the new initiative helped break the spirit of
the rebels. They were no longer operating with impunity. The
rebellion had ceased to be an exciting diversion from the
daily round of peasant life.

By mid-November 1938 the military control scheme was
fully operational and working to great effect. What would
today be designated 'no-go' areas began to be reclaimed. For
example, the Beersheba district was occupied by the Second
Battalion Highland Light Infantry on 21 November 1938.
There had been no Mandate forces in the area since the
burning of the governorate and the seizure of police arms and
ammunition by the rebels some three months earlier.[49] By
December 1938, the whole of the country from Dan to
Beersheba, the Jordan to the Plain of Sharon and the sea-
coast, were in the hands of the British troops and the
TJFF.[50] The gangs were denied security and rest. They were
subjected to constant searches by day and night. Under such
strain the inherent schismatic tendencies of the rebel gangs
were exacerbated. Gangs numbering more than twelve men
became a rarity, whereas one year earlier several gangs had
been composed of one hundred men or more. The collapse of
the rebellion was finally and symbolically registered on 25
March 1939, when, after many months of hunting, Abdul
Rahim el Haj Mohammed, one of the few charismatic figures

to emerge from the guerrilla bands, was killed at the village of Sanur in a raid carried out by the 1st Battalion the Border Regiment.

As the data in Tables 11-13 suggest, the scale of the rebellion had by 1939 been reduced to such a level that there was now a measure of security within the major towns and villages and in most of the intervening rural areas. Preventive

TABLE 11

Rebel Activities, 1939

Month	Murder/attempted murder				Sniping		Sabotage
	Arab	Jew	British	Others	Jewish colonies	Military & police	
January	23	19	—	—	39	43	28
February	93*	23	—	—	78	27	31
March	36	22	—	—	65	42	32
April	23	22	1**	—	65	56	31
May	23	15	—	—	26	26	36
June	68†	8	—	—	18	13	21
July	42	2	—	—	31	28	4
August	24	11	—	2	17	42	14
September	76	14	—	—	57	13	33
October	6	2	—	—	5	1	9
November	9	—	—	—	1	2	7
December	2	1	—	—	1	2	8

* includes 61 Arab bomb casualties — Haifa 27 February 1939
† includes 42 Arab bomb casualties — Haifa 19 June 1939
** attempt on the life of the ADC Acre

Source: WO 201/2/134, 16th Infantry Brigade Intelligence Summaries

TABLE 12

Military Operations, 1939 (16th Infantry Brigade)

Month	Casualties		Captured			Arrests (men)	Villages	
	Military and Police	Enemy	Rifles	Revolvers	Ammunition		Visited	Searched
January	1	29	34	8	1,342	609	21	69
February	3	32	43	5	2,485	567	48	55
March	—	30	38	6	3,200	394	50	85
April	—	8	26	15	2,353	745	44	45
May	—	23	29	18	1,743	295	83	63
June	1	6	26	22	1,610	285	49	76
July	3	4	34	26	1,181	386	88	104
August	6	14	68	33	6,116	284	70	124
September	6	22	32	28	1,103	274	98	59
October	3	—	24	26	2,083	47	121	41
November	—	—	76	26	1,716	128	227	33
December	—	2	364	28	5,681	17	228	4
Total	23	179	737	241	30,364	3,932	1,121	758

Source: WO 201/2/134

TABLE 13

The Escalation of Successful Strikes Against the Arab Guerrillas by the British Military — November 1938-March 1939

Casualties	Captured
a. Ibtah (9 November 1938)	
10 rebels killed and bodies recovered	3 rifles
	3 Mausers
	215 rounds of small arms ammunition (SAA)
b. Beit Faruk (10 November 1938)	
35 Arabs killed	2 rifles
	1 revolver
	89 rounds of SAA
c. Um Ad Darah (28 November 1938)	
43 Arabs killed —	17 rifles
21 bodies recovered	3 pistols
	5 shotguns
	463 rounds of SAA
d. Faqqua (2 December 1938)	
28 Arabs killed	6 rifles
	5 pistols
e. Bani Ma'im (18 December 1938)	
30 Arabs killed	15 Arabs
	11 rifles
	1,977 rounds of SAA
	3 pistols
	71 rounds of pistol ammunition
f. Jerusalem (8 February 1939)	

TABLE 13 (continued)

14 Arabs killed –	5 rebels
12 bodies recovered	24 rifles
	2 shotguns
	1,222 rounds of SAA
	41 shotgun cartridges

g. Nahf (27 February 1939)

19 Arabs killed	12 Mauser rifles
	1 pistol
	730 rounds of SAA

h. Zebal (11 March 1939)

43 Arabs killed –	23 rifles
24 bodies	2,645 rounds of SAA
	1,722 sticks of dynamite
	300 defactors
	3 rolls of fuse

N.B. From November 1938 to March 1939 alone, at the height of the counter-insurgency offensive there were 589 rifles, 204 pistols/revolvers, 105 shotguns and 50,000 rounds of SAA captured. In practical terms this illustrates the degree of success of the offensive.

Source: WO 32/9499

and aggressive action by the military under one command – a command receiving the support of the civil administration and controlling that administration's public security units – had enabled the rebellion to be prosecuted with both method and vigour. The ammunition and armaments of the rebel gangs were also seized in increasing numbers and with greater regularity as the data in the tables indicate. Military opera-

tions became highly effective. In July 1939, after the territory had experienced periods of abnormal tranquility, those
leaders who had survived the counter-insurgency made plans
from the comparative safety of Syria to revive the rebellion.
Under pressure from the military, what was to be their final
incursion into Palestine failed. A revolutionary war with a
developed politico-military component and the cellular
structure of mature underground alternative government may
well have been able to survive such defeats; a peasant war or
rebellion could not. As a result the Arab Rebellion in
Palestine collapsed with the onset of the Second World War
and faded into inconsequence for a decade. Public security,
albeit masking a continuing undercurrent of discontent, had
been restored.

Having thus assessed the events and patterns of the decline
in public security in both Ireland and Palestine, it is necessary
now to turn to a closer analysis of the struggle for
ascendancy between the guardians of the public peace, the
police, and their opponents, the terrorists. It is here, at the
point of impact between the leading edge of the defenders
and that of the attacking forces, that it is possible to
describe, particularly in Ireland, the defeat of a security
apparatus through the systematic application of boycott,
terror and selective assassination.

NOTES

1. P. Marlowe, *Rebellion in Palestine* (London, 1946), 113.
2. Moshe Shertok (Sharett), later prime minister of Israel. See

Shertok's Memorandum from Jewish Agency Palestine to Jewish Agency Executive, London, 7 May 1936 – C2A Z4/10318/I.

3. CO 737/191/77204, Visit of G. T. Garnett to Palestine and Trans-Jordan, containing an extract from Garnett's article in *Political Quarterly* (no date).

4. CZA 325/183, Shertok Memorandum of meeting with High Commissioner, 6 July 1936.

5. CO 733/256, Judicial Reorganisation. Control of Magistrates. Wauchope to Parkinson, 4 May 1934.

6. CO 733/190/77269, Magistrates, non-enforcement of the law.

7. CZA S25/4394, S. Broyde to High Commissioner 8 September 1936.

8. CZA Z4/10318, I Shertok to Weizman 5 July 1936.

9. CO 733/313, Position of Chief Justice 1936.

10. ibid., to W. G. a. Ormsby-Gore, 18 July 1936.

11. ibid., Wauchope to Maffey, 27 May 1936.

12. ibid., Wauchope to Parkinson, 4 May 1934.

13. Air 2/1884, Martial Law Powers to GOC.

14. WO 32/9401, Palestine Disturbances 1936.

15. H. J. Simson, *British Rule and Rebellion* (Edinburgh, 1937), 73.

16. CZA S25/4371., op. cit., 6 June 1936.

17. ibid., B. Joseph – Memorandum of Meeting with Spicer, 19 May 1936.

18. CZA S25/9737, a letter sent from Yehuda Nevi, town clerk, Tel Aviv, reporting a conversation between his brother and Spicer.

19. WO 32/9401, op. cit., letter dated 3 June 1936.

20. WO 32/4178, Respective functions of High Commissioner and GOC Forces. Letter from Colonial Office to Dill, 16 December 1936.

21. Air 2/3312, Palestine Disturbances 1938. An appreciation of the situation by the High Commissioner and observations on the Mufti.

22. WO 32/9498, Despatch of operations by British Forces Palestine and Trans-Jordan, 1 August-31 October 1938.

23. CZA S25/4730, Security 1937. Letter from 'G.A. to Ezekial' on conversation of 'GA' with Watson-Gandy.

24. T129, Public Security in Tiberias – State Archive, Prime Ministers Office, Jerusalem.

25. Translations of Arab newspapers, State Archive, Jerusalem.

26. WO 32/9618, Palestine Disturbances 1936-38 Martial Law Policy.

27. WO 106/1594.C, German Propaganda in Palestine, 1938.

28. WO 32/9401, op. cit., extract from King's Regulations 1935.

29. ibid.

30. ibid.

31. ibid.

32. ibid.

33. Cabinet Paper 86 (37) in WO 32/9618, op. cit.

34. ibid.

35. See 733/315, Martial Law, for full details of the change of policy.

36. CZA A.245/N.171, Shertok — Note of Interview with Sir Charles Tegart, 10 October 1938.

37. Articles 6 and 10 of Palestine (Defence) Orders in Council 1937 in *Palestine Gazette* (827) (18 October 1938), Supplement No. 2.

38. Defence (Control of Police) Regulations 1938. Supplement No. 2. *Palestine Gazette,* Extraordinary No. 826, 17 October 1938.

39. Ephraim Dekel, *Shai: Exploits of Haganah Intelligence* (Tel Aviv & New York, 1959), 328.

40. WO 32/9497.

41. ibid.

42. CZA A245/N171, op. cit.

43. WO 32/9497, 20 May 1938.

44. ibid.

45. ibid.

46. ibid.

47. ibid.

48. WO 32/9499, 1939 Operations in Palestine, 1 November 1938-31 March 1939.

49. Air 5/1248.

50. WO 32/9499.

III

CONCLUSIONS

7

TERRORISM
AND THE POLITICAL POLICE:
The Collapse of the Police Apparatus

> In a contest of violence against violence the superiority of the government has always been absolute; but this superiority lasts only as long as the power structure of the government is intact — that is, as long as commands are obeyed and the army or police forces are prepared to use their weapons. When this is no longer the case, the situation changes abruptly.
>
> *Hannah Arendt,* On Violence *(London, 1970), p. 48*

The revolutionary terrorist and the political police, in both Ireland and Palestine, were the leading edges of their respective governments, incumbent or aspiring. It is their interaction, their contention through political and military combat, that brings us to the core of the breakdown of the condition of security and the police apparatus too. Here it is proposed to examine that interaction, to look into the eye of the whirlwind as it revealed itself particularly in Ireland 1919-21. To achieve this end it is necessary to detail the character of revolutionary terrorism and the application of terror in the internal war situation since this was the means chosen to assault the police and public security. Revolutionary terrorism is conceptualized here by presenting an inventory of its dominant, recurrent traits in Ireland and Palestine with special attention to Ireland where not only was the phenomenon more explicit but its impact was devastating. Similarly a general inventory of the police function is provided. In this way we can see not only the prior assumptions of the police and the terrorist but also their contrasting *modus operandi* which were based on such prior assumptions.

THE POLICE – PERSONNEL AND
BEHAVIOURAL TYPES

The term 'police' of course refers to an administrative function as well as to units of specialist personnel performing a particular controlling and supervisory role in, and over, society. Both individually and collectively, the police operate in many political systems as the initial and most frequent point of contact between the citizen and the paraphernalia of the state – particularly its enforcement machinery. By so regulating, the police personify government. One authority has gone so far as to suggest that,

> a study of the political institutions of any country, desiring of understanding the 'ethos' of any country's government, can hardly do better than make a close study of the police system, which will provide him with a good measuring rod of the actual extent to which government is free or authoritarian.[1]

If this is accepted it remains a puzzle as to why the police continue to be the Cinderellas of political analysis. Indeed, the relationship of the police to the political process is one of the most neglected areas of political research — a state of affairs only now being slightly rectified.[2] It is an especially strange omission when the police are ubiquitous in political life; when the police are dominant or have dominated some political systems and when police-public contacts are such a major zone of interaction between the government and the people.

The individual policeman is as ignored in academic literature as he is damned or romanticized in popular print. What of the individual policeman? Is there a police type? Certainly there is a distinct need to assess individual policeman, politicians, revolutionaries and, indeed, criminals, as individuals in society and not merely as faceless collectivities or stereotyped groups. This is particularly true of the policeman. Though he functions in an authoritarian, disciplined, hierarchically organized and cohesive unit — the force — he is also called upon to act out his public duties individually. Policing is then an atomized as well as a collective activity. It is as well to bear this in mind when assessing the impact of targeted revolutionary terrorism upon the police in both Ireland and Palestine.

Because of his dualism of role the policeman is given a high degree of discretionary power. Similarly, in crisis situations he is often the most isolated man on the street. With reference to the policeman's administrative capabilities it has been observed that the police are potentially the weakest point in the administrative structure precisely because greatest discretion is given to the lowest ranking man.[3] Their natural vulnerability and the possibility of their being, in terms of a cost-benefit analysis, a rewarding target for revolutionaries was one of the principle reasons why they became the focus of revolutionary terrorism in Ireland and Palestine.

Policemen do appear to have certain distinctive cognitive tendencies, both individually and as a collective occupational grouping. Survey data have revealed the contemporary policeman as notably conservative, both emotionally and in his politics.[4] Available evidence strongly favours the opinion that the policeman is the conventional personality. Their professional task is, after all, and in colonial milieux such as Ireland and Palestine in particular, the preservation of the status quo. In Ireland and Palestine the police, militarily trained and organized, represented the punitive and regulatory aspect of the government in society. Perhaps then Colin McInnes was to some extent justified in writing that,

> The true coppers' dominant characteristic, if the truth be known, is neither those daring nor vicious qualities that are sometimes attributed to him by friend or enemy, but an ingrained conservatism, an almost desperate love of the conventional. It is untidiness, disorder, the unusual, that a copper disapproves of most of all; far more even than crime which is merely a professional matter. Hence his profound dislike of people loitering in the streets, dressed extravagantly, speaking with exotic accents, being strange, weak, eccentric or simply any rare minority — of their doing in fact anything that cannot be safely predicted.[5]

It is the interaction of the task or role of policing with the structure of police organization and the behavioural attributes of individual policemen that allows the suggestion of a police type. Indeed, police authorities have themselves consistently stressed the need for conformist, malleable men. A former chief of the London CID wrote that,

The force continues to be recruited mainly from the solid, less sophisticated strata of society and therein lies its strength. If the material is carefully chosen, cultivated, harvested at the peak of condition and is not allowed to run to seed, the service will be well founded.[6]

Such calibre of men formed the backbone of the RIC and the Palestine Police Force. Indeed, as we have seen the RIC preferred to recruit the sons of farmers, primarily because of their size and robust health, but crucially because they tended to be conventional, compliant men. The internal structure of most police forces exacerbates their conventionality and compliance. Certainly initiative was penalized more often than it was rewarded in the RIC and the Palestine Police.

POLICE FORCES – FUNCTIONS AND DUTIES IN IRELAND AND PALESTINE

It is as well to recap here that historically it is possible to detect two broad styles of policing,[7] one based in common law, the other stemming from the Roman law tradition. English policing, where the policeman serves as little more than a professional citizen, best exemplifies the common law mode of law enforcement. In countries adhering to this mode there has tended to be a narrower conception of the functions of government and certainly a less intrusive police apparatus. By way of contrast, the Roman law tradition has historically led to a far more 'positive' or interventionist state apparatus. Government and its agencies are at one and the same time far more pervasive and paternalistic. Policing thus reaches down into the interstices of society. Such police forces exist to monitor the condition of society and the body politic.

The police in Ireland and Palestine resembled the European quasi-military gendarmerie far more than they did the civilian police forces of their parent country. In common with the European police, they had wide-ranging paternalistic functions. Louis Lépine's description of the police of France can in fact be satisfactorily and instructively applied to the police in Ireland. He defined the French police as 'an organised body of officers whose primary duties are the preservation of order, the security of the person and the safety of property'.[8] In Ireland and Palestine, as in France, the police existed primarily to maintain public security, harass subversives and repress anti-regime propaganda. The Irish and Palestine police were control forces. Their duties were typically those of the traditional police state.[9] As such, the style of policing in Ireland differed markedly from policing in England. When assessed in terms of the structure of the national system, the manner of accountability, the definition of police tasks, the role, behaviour and professional image of the police, some most interesting divergencies appear between the police in England and the police in Ireland and Palestine. Table 14 seeks to demonstrate this. Indeed the military nature of the RIC in particular moved Friedrich Engels to write, 'I have never seen so many gendarmes in any country and the drink sodden expression of the Prussian gendarmerie is developed to its highest perfection here among the Irish constabulary who are armed with bayonets and handcuffs.'[10] An anonymous pamphleteer also reported that:

> [the] RIC being free from any local or any Irish control whatsoever, the police have, in the past, habitually conducted themselves — no

doubt in accordance with thy orders of their superiors – not as the servants, but as the masters of the public. A village sergeant and constable is a little king or emperor. Is it any wonder if, under these circumstances, the police have not been popular in the past ...? The extent to which the police make themselves felt in Ireland would, no doubt, astonish most Englishmen. They attend, fully armed, every public meeting of the people.[11]

TABLE 14

The Style and Structure of the Police in Ireland and Palestine Compared with the Parent Country, England

	Palestine	Ireland	England
1. National Structure			
Nature of authority	Central political	Central political	Local civil
Number of distinct forces	Multiple	Dual	Single
2. Dominant mode of force control			
Political	Central	Central	Local
Legal	Unified legal code	Unified legal code	Unified legal code
3. Force duties			
Formal	Extensive	Extensive	Extensive
Informal	Extensive	Extensive	Limited
Litigious	Some	Some	None
4. Internal structure			
Training	Para-military	Para-military	Civil
Distribution	District	Regional-County	Regional
Organizational control	Centralized-national	Centralized-national	Regional-local

5. Perceived character or image

	Authoritarian	Authoritarian	Respected
	Distrusted	Distrusted	Helpful

6. Style of Intervention

	Formal	Formal	Informal
	Punitive	Punitive	Restraining

7. Weapons

	Armed	Armed	Unarmed
	Para-military	Para-military	Civil

Clearly, then, the police in Ireland and in Palestine were concerned primarily with political regulation and control. They were a different creature from the English police. Thus their organization, role and tactics were major reasons for the terrorist attack, when it came, being focused upon them.

It is accepted that most police forces emerged as a response to crisis conditions with the task of supervising either major highways or capital cities. Particularly, they became one of the few organized sources of stability in chaotic urban life. For instance, in 1754 Maria Theresa gave three police officials the task of ensuring order in Vienna; Frederick II established the Royal Police Directorate in Berlin in 1742 with similar duties; Czar Peter likewise created an Imperial Police Administration in St Petersburg in 1768 and Louis XIV his Lieutenance of Police in Paris as early as 1667. England, Ireland and Palestine were no exception to this pattern, with policing first being established in the capital cities and then moving into provincial centres. Similarly, in the European and most colonial environments the police existed not only to control but also to divert opposition to the government of the day on to themselves. Police forces everywhere act as a buffer between governing élites and the masses. One of the prime functions of the police in Ireland and Palestine, as real and symbolic representatives of government, was to divert opposition in this way. The police thus became not only recipients of but also the source of political resentment. Naturally, the police were involved in all manner of societal violence — political and otherwise. Attacks upon the police, both verbal and physical, were, and are, a continuum of social life. The police in Ireland and Palestine were no strangers to violence. In the period 1919-21 in Ireland and 1936-39 in Palestine, what was new to the police was both the systematic and the ruthless nature of the attacks made upon them. Yet, as we have seen, the manner of the attack was dictated by the posture of the police as a political police.

Every society is a policed society. Every society has a political police. Every society *is* a policed society since all societies elect or have imposed upon them some patterned means whereby they are, in varying degrees, protected, censored, guarded and guided by fellow citizens. However, whereas normal day-to-day policing is concerned with objective breaches of the law, the political police seek subjective error revealed in spoken clues, intercepted letters and tapped telephone calls, and they apply 'oriental' methods to detect crimes of thought. The difference is that between the police officer operating as his brother's keeper or his brother's inquisitor. The political police are not so much an instrument for the protection of society as a form of political activity through the medium of the police.[1][2] In Ireland and Palestine the police were a political instrument. A *Manchester Guardian* reporter observed, on 19 April 1920, that,

> There is a double misunderstanding about the Irish Police Force. The average Englishman regards a policeman as an amicable and friendly

person who directs the traffic, whereas at present the RIC is an organ of political repression and is engaged far more on political than on criminal or ordinary social work.

Not only were the police the monitors of subversion and the hammer of rioting and dissent, but they also had extensive social functions after the fashion of the welfare-orientated, paternalistic European traditional police state. In Ireland they supervised Boards of Works and Fisheries, had Coastguard duties, gathered agricultural statistics, carried out the population census, worked for the Congested Districts Boards and supervised Weights and Measures. The RIC had carried out this multiplicity of tasks so efficiently in the nineteenth century that the force was made the model for all British colonial police forces. Sir Neville Chamberlain, Inspector General of the RIC, stressed in 1916 that,

> In recent years several officers of the RIC have been selected for such important Cross-Channel Chief Constableships as Bristol, Glasgow, Liverpool, Birkenhead and the City of London and many county forces in Great Britain. . . . These officers are all trained and brought up in the conditions and arrangements of the RIC. Since I became Inspector General we have had visits from representatives of foreign powers to study the arrangements and distribution of our police force, and the policing of the country. We have had attachments of African police sent here for instruction and we are constantly sending instructors to many of our colonies. For some years past the Colonial Office has arranged for their Colonial officers being trained with us.[13]

This then was the prestige, élite force that the revolutionary terrorists chose to attack, in order to break it in 1919. It was the same force upon which the Palestine police force was consciously modelled.

REVOLUTIONARY TERRORISM –
THE PROBLEMS OF DEFINITION

If there are few treatments of the police in politics, there are fewer of the phenomenon of revolutionary terrorism. There are perhaps only three significant studies, all of them recent, that attempt a rigorous assessment of revolutionary terrorism.[14] Walter's study is not concerned solely with revolutionary terrorism, though both Thornton and Hutchinson attempt to conceptualize the phenomenon. Other authors have made passing reference to revolutionary terrorism while engaged in studies of insurrection and internal war. Thayer saw it as 'the attempt to govern or to oppose government by intimidation'.[15] Crozier, in what was generally a more successful analysis, nevertheless loosely defined it as 'the threat of the use of violence for political ends'.[16] Lucien Pye, in his study of guerrilla communism in Malaya, defined it as a 'peculiar and violent type of political struggle'.[17] Almost two decades earlier, Hardman had sought greater precision when he defined terrorism as,

> a term used to describe the method or theory behind the method whereby an organised group or party seeks to achieve its avowed aims through the systematic use of violence. . . . Terrorism as a method is always characterised by the fact that it seeks to arouse not only the reigning government or nation in control but also the mass of the people to the fact that constituted authority is no longer safely entrenched and unchallenged.[18]

However, Thornton and Hutchinson are more relevant here since they assess revolutionary terrorism, that is terrorism dedicated to challenging the incumbent government, as opposed to that applied by the incumbent government.

Walter makes this dichotomy clear by denoting the terror of the incumbents as a 'regime of terror' and that dedicated to the overthrow of the established system of power as the 'siege of terror'.[19] It is with the 'siege of terror', or as Thornton characterized it 'agitated terror',[20] that this analysis is concerned. However, all terror, depending upon its scale and scope, agitates individuals, society and the body politic. Not wishing to multiply existent terminology unduly, the terms 'insurgent terror' and 'incumbent terror' are used here for greater precision to denote the nature of the terrorism and the source from which it emanates.

There are of course numerous studies of incumbent terror, particularly in the so-called 'totalitarian systems'.[21] Here only passing reference will be made to incumbent terrorism, which was applied in Ireland as a reaction to the tactics of the guerrilla forces. Thus, the emphasis is upon revolutionary terrorism, its effect and the interaction of it with the control forces of the state. With the application of insurgent terrorism the heart of the breakdown of public security is approached. In Ireland and Palestine it was the revolutionary terrorism of the rebels that shattered the more or less stable patterns of expectations required for social and political cohesion. For security, predictability and the expectation of life, revolutionary terrorism substituted insecurity, arbitrariness and a lottery of possible violent death. Terrorism in Ireland and Palestine 'institutionalised anxiety'.[22] It created an aura of real physical and psychic apprehension. This was of course an intended outcome of revolutionary terrorism, which is defined here as the rational, purposive application of systematic political violence, often tactical assassination, against symbolic targets, chosen for their propaganda effect, which aids the reverberation of dread throughout social and political structures. The Narodniks had in fact, at an early stage, observed the multi-functionality of terrorism. They saw it as,

> consisting in destroying the most harmful person in the government, in defending the party against espionage, in punishing the perpetrators of the notable cases of violence and arbitrariness on the part of government and the administration . . . aims to undermine the prestige of the government's power, to demonstrate steadily the possibility of struggle against the government, to arouse in this manner the revolutionary spirit of the people and their confidence in the success of the cause, and finally, to give shape and direction to the forces fit and trained to carry on the fight.[23]

Revolutionary terrorism in Ireland and Palestine fulfilled such multiple functions. It acted as the swift arm of retributive justice against what were regarded as oppressive incumbents; it propagandized the revolutionary cause; it served as an internal sanction, cleansing the underground resistance of spies and informers; it mobilized the movement, its activists and the people generally; it was the leading tactical edge of the plan of campaign operating in tandem with urban and rural guerrilla war. Above all, it helped break the inertia of the residue of support for the incumbent British administration by polarizing public opinion. Neutrality in the face of the terror was virtually impossible.

Given the multiple impacts of revolutionary terror and recent British colonial experiences, all of which verify the effectiveness of revolutionary terror as a politico-military instrument of indigenous peoples against superimposed foreign rule, its neglect in academic literature is a puzzle. Dallin and Breslauer correctly observed that 'we can look on terror as a funnel for multivariate transactions'.[24] Terror and terrorism are not confined to the exotica of political life. It is a *potential* political instrument in most political systems. Walter particularly has stressed that terror is

[a] potential in ordinary situations as well as in unusual situations and reigns of terror are not properly understood if they are conceived as ephemeral states of crisis produced by adventitious events or as alien forms of control.[25]

One final point should be made. Revolutionary terrorism is compounded by two elements. One, terrorism proper, is seen here as the actual tool of political violence — the instrument enforcing the strategy and tactic of violent psychic and physical assault — and as the cadre of committed revolutionaries or rebels. The other aspect is the terror viewed as the psychic state induced by the activities of the terrorists.

TOWARDS A CONCEPT OF REVOLUTIONARY TERRORISM: AN INVENTORY OF SITUATIONAL CONSTANTS IN IRELAND

It is intended here to focus attention upon terrorism in Ireland, where it reached a most sophisticated form. First of all, however, the phenomenon should perhaps be generally characterized in terms of its goals, operation and outcomes. Three crucial points emerge from the Irish situation and from a cross-national survey of its characteristics. First, terrorism was, and is, a means towards securing the political end of mobilizing and disciplining the underground, revolutionary forces. It also sought to achieve the destruction of the incumbent regime, followed by the establishment of an alternative government. Second, terrorism was, and continues to be, a rationally conceived mode of political action, chosen in conditions of extreme frustration as the method which, in the prevailing circumstances, is most likely to achieve the goal of the revolutionaries — independence. Irish political activists felt that, whereas England would concede nothing to the force of argument, it might well yield to the argument of force. Terrorism can thus be viewed as a mode of political agitation distinguished from other modes primarily by its extra-normality.[26] That extra-normality is part of the secret of its impact, since it assaults both physically and normatively the accepted manner of the conduct of civilized political life. Any study of terror or terrorism is thus a study of political power in extremis. As such it is an assault of the frames of reference of society. Hence, terrorism's third characteristic: terror, the induced psychic state composed of deduceable patterns of reactive behaviour and attitudinal responses.

There are then in Ireland, in Palestine and in other colonial internal wars, at the middle-level range of conceptualization, similar clusters of variables, that is, certain constants, which enable one to detect a patterning within revolutionary terrorism leading on to conceptualization. Taking Ireland as our paradigmatic case study, the situational constants can be traced through the following analytical categories:

1. causation;
2. the choice and nature of the target;
3. the organization of revolutionary terrorism;
4. the application of revolutionary terrorism;
5. the effects of revolutionary terrorism.

Causation

A simple factor analysis can be employed here which indicates that, to nurture the situation in which revolutionary terrorism becomes extant, there must be frustration inducing oppression, an organized group or groups, and a leader or leaders capable of exploiting and organizing animosities, both overt and covert, to the full. Above all, there must be an ideology or structured intellectual stimulus, which in Ireland took the curious form of a mix of romantic revolutionary and sacrificial, nationalistic messianism, serving to determine the strategy and tactics of the revolutionary political activists. Such an ideological component in the overall political environment aided the moulding of revolutionary personalities, making them capable of enacting revolutionary terrorism.

The Choice and Nature of the Target

Terror and political assassination had long been employed as a mode of political action in Ireland. Violent direct action was a theme cutting through the continuum of Irish political protest. Members of the Irish Republican Brotherhood, the underground organization at the heart of the 1916 Easter Rising conspiracy and the later War of Independence, all took an assassination oath to the effect that,

> I hereby solemnly swear and make oath before the most high God, before whom I expect to be judged, that I will seek and leave no means untried utterly to exterminate as . . . enemies of Irish liberty, any person who shall be guilty of perfidy, or of giving to our foes the British authorities, any information which shall lead to the arrest or sentence of members of the Irish Republican Brotherhood.[27]

This of course was a purely defensive strategy. Terrorism and assassination became an infinitely more effective weapon when it was used as an *offensive* weapon in the internal war.

Thomas Davis, one of the pantheon of Irish revolutionaries, summed up the goal of the strategy of offensive terror when he wrote,

> The tribunes tongue and poets pen
> May sow the seed in slavish men
> But 'tis the soldiers sword alone
> Can reap the harvest when 'tis grown.[28]

However, it was the guerrilla leader Michael Collins who made what is for our purposes the definitive statement of both the causation and focus of revolutionary terrorism in Ireland in 1919-21 when he wrote,

We organised our army and met the armed patrols and military expeditions which were sent out against us, in the only way. We met them by an organised and bold guerrilla warfare. . . . But this was not enough. If we were to stand up against the powerful military organisation arrayed against us something more was necessary. . . . England could always reinforce her army. She could replace every soldier that she lost. . . . But there were others indispensable for her purposes which were not so easily replaced. To paralyse the British machine it was necessary to strike at individuals. Without her spies England was helpless. It was only by means of their accumulated and accumulating knowledge that the British machine could operate. . . . Without their police throughout the country, how could they find the men they 'wanted'? Without their criminal agents in the capital how could they carry out that 'removal' of the leaders that they considered essential for their victory? Spies are not so ready to step into the shoes of their departed confederates as are soldiers to fill up the front line in honourable battle. And even when the new spy stepped into the shoes of the old one, he could not step into the old one's knowledge. . . . We struck at individuals and by so doing we cut their lines of communication and shook their morale. . . .[29]

This in essence was the plan of campaign for the revolutionary terror mounted by the IRA in 1919 revealing the motives for and the nature of the target chosen. The targets were, as Collins indicated, threefold: first, spies and informers operating within and against the movement; second, any native Irishman working for the Castle government or any colonial government officers; third, as the predominant target, the police in Ireland, and, within the police, Special Branch officers in particular. The motive for directing terrorism against the police is summarized in one sentence from the journal *The Gael* of 26 February 1916, which urged its readers to 'Remember, England holds you in slavery by having a few policemen in every village.'

The actual choice of the police as the target was of course somewhat more involved than this. Nevertheless, it was the nature of the police in Ireland that provided the main stimulus for the attack. The police were, in the eyes of Irish revolutionaries, the barrier preventing any mutation of government. The journal *Bean na L'Eireann,* as early as January 1911, suggested,

> We Irish Nationalists have not devoted enough attention to the police. We want nothing less than a campaign of exterminating the police. I don't mean that we should begin a wholesale massacre of them say tomorrow. But we should lose no time in creating such a public opinion in Ireland that the man who joins the police may be branded a traitor for all time. . . . since the establishment of the RIC in Ireland one point above all else in connection with the police forces [sic] itself to the front. As soon as Irish Nationalists make an active move, eiter by passive resistance or otherwise against England the first body that blocks the way is not the army but the police force. In the police force is a standing army of upwards of 12,000 men. Nationalists of the present as of the past know to their cost that the first blow to be struck at a militant movement in Ireland

nowadays is struck through the police . . . . as matters stand the first line of English occupation to be struck at must be the police. For the police are a garrison force in every town and village, in every parish, almost throughout the country. When we make a move against England the police bar the way. . . . Worse still, Irish Nationalists can be taunted with the cry that the members of the RIC are young men from the people themselves. It is mainly the Nationalist Districts that supply the police forces with spies and baton men to make existence in Ireland impossible for Irish Nationalists. For that is the means adopted by the force for which we pay more than for our primary education — to nip the Nationalist movement in the bud. We, in our turn, must use the same method against them — we must make existence in Ireland impossible for the police.

The article then goes on to suggest some of the means which should be adopted against the police and to outline a scheme indicating the nature of the political work required.

In the first place, there should be a widespread agitation especially in country districts, against the whole police force. The people should be warned against the baneful habit of making friends among the police. The RIC and the DMP should be ostracised, cut off entirely from the social life of the people. The youth of the country must be taught that the police are the enemies of Ireland and of the people of Ireland; the whole people must be taught to hate the police in order that recruitment for the constabulary may stop. A vigorous movement against joining the police should be organised wherever a national club or an individual Nationalist is to be found. By persistant argument — and other means — even a single Nationalist could poison the minds of the people of a whole countryside against the police. That to my mind should be one of the first things a national movement in Ireland should push vigorously.

The plan of campaign against the police in Ireland followed this projected course very closely. By September 1919, the

boycott and ostracism of the police was well established and
the systematic assassination of police officers had begun. The
revolutionary terrorism focused on the police in Ireland was
thus a mix of the threat and application of terrorism. Its
impact was such that it not only influenced behaviour patterns but also achieved significant military results. Widespread assassination neutralized and then broke the police.
The Irish case goes some way towards nullifying Thornton's
assertion that 'the military function of terror is negligible. It
is a small-scale weapon and cannot in itself have any appreciable influence upon the outcome of military action'.[30]
Bloody Sunday alone, as the climax of revolutionary terrorism in Ireland, would refute this.

The police then were the focus of revolutionary terrorism
in Ireland. They were chosen not simply because they were
the symbolic representatives of government, but because in
actuality the police were the leading edge of government
regulation and its control apparatus. Hence any attack on
what we have already characterized as a paternalistic, politicized police would also be a more or less direct assault upon
the governmental apparatus. Thus a terroristic attack upon
the police would have the military utility of immobilizing or
weakening the control apparatus, while at the same time
challenging the authority of the government by assaulting its
representative in society. Attacks upon the police would also
provide arms and ammunition for the terrorists and perhaps
provoke excessive police reaction, which in turn would
escalate the insecurity of the internal political situation by
damaging government prestige. Similarly, since the police
were so visible, being uniformed, and policing being such a
public act, any attack upon the police served to propagandize
the terrorist organization and, if successful, strengthened the
resolve of that organization to struggle with the government

in an effort to accomplish its defeat. Should the attacks upon the police be widespread and intensive, as they were in Ireland, public security again suffers, since with the police force under such great strain it cannot patrol or detect as efficiently as before. Sheer volume of work defeats it. Hence political crime and general lawlessness increase as societal constraints begin to crumble. In such a crisis situation, induced in Ireland by terrorism, the violent revolutionary opposition has already achieved one of its fundamental goals, namely the demonstration of the ineffectiveness of the incumbent government. It is in this way that the inertial relationship between government and the governed is broken down and support for the alternative, underground government's as yet untried political formulae enhanced.

The Organization of Revolutionary Terrorism

In both Ireland and Palestine revolutionary terrorism was carried out by small, dedicated, cohesive groups of well trained gunmen. Killing, when developed as a political method, of necessity produces a class of professional gunmen. Collins created his own élite cadre of gunmen known as the 'Squad' or 'Twelve Apostles'. The Squad not only operated as his bodyguard but were reserved for carrying out the most important assassinations in and around Dublin, such as that of the chief of the Dublin Metropolitan Police, Redmond, and the attempted assassination of the viceroy, Lord French. In Palestine, Aref Abdul Razzik was the leading exponent of terrorism though most of the guerrilla bands possessed terrorist squads operating as their appendages in the towns and cities. Similarly in Palestine and Ireland, terrorism operating mainly in the urban areas worked in tandem with the guerrilla struggles being waged in the rural areas. Both were parts of the continuum of organized, targeted, political violence moving through from individual assassination to conventional warfare.

In time terrorism became institutionalized as the revolutionaries' dominant technique of political action. Gross has suggested that this process of institutionalization procedes along the following lines:

> a professional class of terrorists gains influence in, and control of, the terrorist organisation. Meanwhile, sporadic and transient conspiracies, once the act of terror had been repeated, change slowly into permanent and highly institutionalised associations.[31]

Certainly both the Irish and Palestinian terrorist organizations could be characterized as Blanquist in the Leninist sense that their emphasis was upon the military component. In Palestine, and to a lesser extent in Ireland, the terrorists were politico-military conspirators with a strategy and tactics rather than any developed political philosophy or *Weltanschaung.*[32]

The Application of Revolutionary Terrorism

The application of revolutionary terrorism, particularly in Ireland, was systematic and purposive. It was applied as a mix of actual violence and intimidation, the latter being the attempt to effect, by threat of violence, a change in the patterns of political behaviour. There was of course the embellishment of occasional irrational or accidental killings. Thus terrorism can be seen to include not only a policy of severe or arbitrary violence but also its credible threat. However, the critical element in the application of revolutionary terrorism was discrimination. Indeed, Thornton has stressed that,

> Terror must always have at least some element of indiscrimination, else it becomes predictable, loses its broad character and can no longer be legitimately designated as terror . . . .
>
> However, total indiscrimination is not desirable, for the insurgents will wish to concentrate their attacks on specific targets of intent, social structures and symbols, to achieve economy of effort and ensure the maintenance of those structures that are of potential value to them. They must therefore determine which structures are to be preserved, which structures are the most vulnerable to attack, and which are the most crucial in holding together the fabric of the society they wish to split. . . . the optimum targets are those that show the highest symbolic value and are dominated by symbols that are most vulnerable to attack.[33]

Hence the choice of the ailing police forces in Ireland and Palestine. Thus, 'terror is most effective when it is indiscriminate in appearance but highly discriminate in fact'.[34]

In Ireland terrorism originated with the systematic boycotting of the police and the intimidation of their relatives and friends by Sinn Fein, the Irish Volunteers or IRA activists and sympathizers. The terror was thus high discriminate in fact, focusing particularly upon Special Branch officers. However, it had the appearance of being indiscriminate because informers, spies, officers of the government, magistrates, wavering Republicans et al. were all terrorized. Thus, while being focused, its apparent random nature created a general aura of anxiety. In this way the terror had maximum effect.

The Effects of Revolutionary Terrorism

The visible effects of revolutionary terrorism in Ireland and Palestine were that it destroyed the morale and then effectiveness of the police, neutralized the Special Branch and ended local government and justice as well as, in time, the authority and credibility of the Irish administration. All of this was achieved by means- of disorientation. Terrorism erodes the relatively stable patterns of expectations required by social organisms.[35] More precisely, both incumbent and insurgent terror,

> serves the two functions of eliminating rival authority figures — actual, potential or imagined — as well as their sub-elites, disciples and subordinate bureaucracies; and eliminating incongruent value structures, either by neutralising or removing groups identified *a priori* as carriers of such values, or else by isolating the population from access to them.[36]

Similarly, terror is not a hermetic process, but reverberates, despite its focus, throughout the social and political matrix. Its prime function then is to create insecurity. Terror is at the very nub of the breakdown of public security. Hutchinson indeed suggests that,

> Terrorism affects the social structure as well as the individual, it upsets the framework of precepts and images which members of society depend on and trust. Since no one knows what sort of behaviour to expect from other members of society the system is disorientated. The formerly cohesive community dissolves into a mass of anomic individuals, each concerned only with personal survival.[37]

With the systematic application of revolutionary terrorism

predictability in affairs of state, in day-to-day events and in social relations is ended. The societal catalogue of expectations appears jumbled. Such an effect is critical for the preservation not only of public security but also of governability since, as Chalmers Johnson has observed, 'The *sine qua non* of a society . . . is the possession of mutual expectations by members of society, allowing them to orientate their behaviour to each other'.[38]

The behaviour changes achieved by terrorism are particularly visible in Ireland. Such changes can also be seen to effect the question of allegiance or disaffection to, or from, the regime. Gurr suggests that,

> If people are intensely discontented and are fundamentally sympathetic to rebel objectives, symbolic violence against a hated regime is likely to have a conversion effect. . . . But the most common consequence of terror, especially if it is widespread and random, is mass disorientation and anxiety. Whether a disorientated, terrorised public will withdraw support from the incumbents is problematic; they may give greater support to the regime in hope of protecting themselves. If terrorism is severe and the regime weak they can be coerced into providing support for the dissidents, but support given under coercion is unlikely to develop into a more enduring allegiance unless it can be systematically maintained over a long period.[39]

In Ireland and Palestine there was sufficient spontaneously generated antagonism towards the respective governments to make extensive coercion of the native population unnecessary. What the revolutionary terror did achieve was seriously to disorientate the behaviour patterns of those, especially those native, serving with the colonial government. Terror disorientated, by breaking the ties between the masses and the incumbents and by removing essential structural supports of society – the police and the judiciary. Terror also disorientated by demonstrating that the incumbents could neither govern nor protect. Its prime aim in Ireland and Palestine was as we have seen to break the control apparatus of the colonial government. Exactly how that was achieved can be illustrated by a deeper analysis of the Irish case.

THE IMPACT OF REVOLUTIONARY TERRORISM ON THE ROYAL IRISH CONSTABULARY

The preface of the terror was, as we have seen, the episodic and later the systematic application of a boycott of the police. Implicit in that boycott was the use or threat of violence not only against the initial target but against those who broke the boycott. The boycott was itself legitimized as an act of the revolutionary underground government when it was introduced by De Valera in the Dail Eireann, the Republican Parliament. De Valera stated that,

the people of Ireland ought not to fraternise, as they do, with the forces which are the main instruments in keeping them in subjection. It is not consistent with personal or national dignity. It is certainly not consistent with safety. They are spies in our midst. They are England's janissaries. They are the eyes and ears of the enemy.... Their history is a continuity of brutal treason against their own people. From their very foundation they have been the mainstay of the privileged ascendancy, and the great obstacle to every movement for social as well as national liberty. These men must not be tolerated socially, as if they were clean, healthy members of our organised life. They must be shown and made to feel how base are the functions they perform and how vile is the position they occupy. To shun them, to refuse to talk or have any social intercourse with them or to treat them as equals, will give them vividly to understand how utterly the people of Ireland loathe both themselves and their calling.[40]

Just how complete that ostracism was to be is illustrated by a further statement in the Dail to the effect that,

I am directed by the Home Secretary to state that social ostracisation of the police implies that the police forces must receive no social recognition from the people; that no intercourse with them be permitted . . . that they should not be received into private houses as guests; that they should be debarred from participation in games, sports, dances and all social functions conducted by the people; that intermarriage with them be discouraged; that, in a word, the police should be treated as persons having been adjudged guilty of treason to their country.[41]

In this fashion the police were isolated from the people, and more importantly were systematically defamed both as a collectivity and as individuals. In time such defamation made it far easier both to assassinate and to accept the assassination of policemen for the Republican cause.

Without doubt, the most effective method of relating the impact of revolutionary terrorism on the police in Ireland is to detail the written evidence of those police officers who experienced it. For example, in 1919, after the declaration made by De Valera in the Dail to boycott the police, proclamations were posted throughout Ireland declaring,

The people in this area are warned that for their own safety and in the interests of the country they should avoid absolutely all communications of a friendly nature with the members of the RIC. This force of men is specially organised for the maintenance in our down-trodden country of a tyrannical foreign government by a system of spying and corruption unrivalled in the history of any land. The police (who came from among the people themselves) are traitors to their own flesh and blood, sworn to spare neither parent, brother, sister, wife in the discharge of their degrading duty, the overthrow of the God-given rights of their fellow countrymen. They should therefore be avoided as more dangerous than the plague and more ruinous than any other group of ruffians to the morale of society. Let no Irish man or woman with any sense of principle or honour be seen speaking to or in any way tolerating the existence of a peeler either in public or in private. Beware. This is not an appeal but an order of the Irish Republican Government. To those who ignore it will be meted out the punishment of traitors.[42]

This was not mere rhetoric. Both the boycott and the threat were applied. Catholic priests participated in the boycott denouncing the RIC from the pulpit. The Inspector General of the RIC reported,

This great and loyal force has passed through many difficult and dangerous ordeals with unswerving fidelity unaffected by the taunts and abuse of the politicians; but it is a new experience for it to be assailed through their consciences by members of their Church. The clergy as a body have not only engaged in this conspiracy to corrupt the constabulary but certain priests have addressed very strong appeals to them on spiritual grounds.[43]

As a result of boycott, defamation and vilification, the RIC became virtual pariahs. As has been observed already, such vilification justifies and facilitiates the use of violence. It encourages a climate of violence within which violent acts become part of a normative system — a sub-culture of violence. From the enforcement of boycott and the rhetoric of violence it was thus one short step for the Dail to begin issuing leaflets in May 1920 to the effect that,

We hereby proclaim the South Riding of Tipperary a military area with the following regulations. A policeman found within the said area will be deemed to have forfeited his life, the more notorious police being dealt with as far as possible first. Every person in the pay of England — magistrates, jurors who help England rule this country will be deemed to have forfeited his life. Civilians who give information to the police will be executed, shot or hanged.[44]

The effect of the application of the revolutionary terrorism was soon revealed in the resignations from both police and magistracy. In the period April to September 1920, 1,069 of the 5,000 magistrates in Ireland resigned.[45] Similarly, in the eighty-two weeks from January 1919 to 31 July 1920, seventy-three police officers were assassinated and many more terrorized and threatened.[46] Once the revolutionary apparatus focused the terror on the RIC the Constabulary deteriorated rapidly. The Inspector General of the RIC reported in September 1919 that,

In many parts of the country, indeed throughout almost the whole of Munster and Connaught and to a lesser extent in Leinster, the police lived under conditions so irksome, depressing and hazardous as to impose a strain which very few bodies of men, however highly disciplined, could be expected to bear. How much longer it can be borne is questionable. . . . Resignations from the force are becoming very numerous and no body of men can be expected to support indefinitely the conditions under which the police in many places are forced to live, boycotted, ostracised, forced to commandeer food, crowded in too many instances into cramped quarters without proper light or air; every man's hand is against them, in danger of their lives and subjected to the appeals of their parents and their families to induce them to leave the force and so put an end to the danger and annoyance to which continued service exposes them.[47]

The effect of the revolutionary terrorism on the police was

dramatic. The resignations, coupled with so many assassinations, effectively brought about the end of the old RIC since it proved impossible to recruit native Irishmen into the force. It was an attempt to bolster up the crippled public security apparatus that the Black and Tans and Auxiliary Police were recruited.[48] The full impact of the revolutionary terror upon the police is however captured vividly in one document of the period — a plea from the police in the Ballinasloe District to the Chief Secretary, urging him to disband the force. The document captured the mood within the force more effectively than any theoretical or academic assertions. It emphasized, and is worth quoting at length, that,

> We consider it is almost an impossibility to carry out our function as a civil police force under the present circumstances. The strain on the force is so great, by the daily assassination of our comrades who are ruthlessly murdered and butchered by the roadside without getting a chance to defend themselves and by the boycotting and threats arraigned against us, against our families, our relatives and our homes, that the agony of a long suffering force cannot be much further prolonged. . . . men are resigning in large numbers and the old ranks of the RIC are growing thinner daily. These men are not resigning through cowardice but because there was no adequate protection for their lives. . . . We are now useless as a civil police force. We are simply trying to defend our lives — every day we are being more alienated in platform and press, and even the moderate section of the community are so terrorised or apathetic that not even a voice of sympathy nor ray of hope comes from any side . . . men are separated from their families — their wives and children left behind in hostile localities. There is no provision made for houses or homes for married members of the force. . . . No policeman will get a house or accommodation, and even where a house may be found the possibility is that it is generally blown up or burned to prevent occupation by policemen. . . . The dead bodies of our murdered comrades are even insulted, booed and jeered and

there is the greatest difficulty getting them to their last resting place
— in short there is no such thing as sympathy or charity today for a
policeman dead or alive. . . . Our functions are now being carried out
by others and our jurisdiction is dwindling daily. We as a body are
not able to restore law and order in this country today nor is there
any hope on the horizon for a changed order of things when we
could do so. . . . We consider the best thing to be done is to wind up
the force.[49]

What made this assault on the police all the more effective,
leading ultimately to the collapse of the old RIC, was the fact
that, once anxiety neuroses had been institutionalized in the
force and the police disorientated by the application of
terrorism. Sinn Fein, the political arm of the IRA, began to
operate, in tandem with the terror — a more conciliatory
police offering alternative employment to Irish policemen.
Together the two policies had great effect. Indeed, the problem of how to treat the resigning RIC men took up a good
deal of debating time in Dail Eireann. It would appear from
available evidence that the tactic of offering alternative
employment to the police was triggered by a letter to the
Dail from an RIC officer in which he wrote,

I think I might be pardoned for giving what I consider the true
feelings of the great bulk of the police — I mean the Irishmen. They
are nearly all willing to come out, but, having in their mind's eye
some comrade or acquaintance who has done so, and is yet unemployed, they would point to him as an example of what they
themselves would expect to get from the Sinn Fein. . . . I would
therefore with the best possible intentions for all concerned suggest
that if the Irish people are really serious about breaking up the
present force in Ireland, the first step is to safeguard the interests of
those who have already come out and are now willing to assist us in
our fight against the oppressor.[50]

He went on to suggest that employers in Ireland should offer resigning officers jobs, and then the police would 'resign by the hundreds, the Volunteer ranks would be greatly strengthened with good fighting material, and English rule, if not completely broken, would at least be seriously shaken'.[51]

The outcome was that the alternative government established a Police Employment Bureau to cater for resigning officers. A sum of £350 was voted by the Dail to enable the bureau to become immediately operational under the Republican Department of Labour. Individual firms soon began to offer jobs; but it was each Sinn Fein Club, appointing deputations to pressurize policemen and their families and propagandize the Police Employment Bureau, that guaranteed the success of the scheme. This new attitude of the underground government to the police, a political luxury of the kind that the IRA could allow itself only after the resolve of the police had already been broken by terrorism, was summarized in a communiqué from Sinn Fein headquarters in July 1920, stating,

Now that the English controlled police forces in Ireland are breaking up, the country should take cognizance of the position of individual ex-members of these forces. Every man of Irish birth should get a chance of becoming a loyal citizen of the Irish Republic and of earning an honest living in Ireland. This is true even of those Irishmen engaged in doing the work of the enemy in Ireland as members of the RIC. Many of these men joined without any clear understanding of what they were doing. They were young; they had no knowledge of Irish history. The national tradition may have been weak in their own family and in their native district. It should be made clear that those who resign should get credit for an honest intention. They should be welcome back to their native place.[52]

These then were the essential ingredients of the collapse of
the public security apparatus in Ireland. A similar proces
occurred in Palestine. Both police forces, but the RIC in
particular, had sown resilience under extreme stress. However, as one author has suggested,

> No police force is invincible. The police can only hold out against a
> disunited opponent who scatters his strength. It will never fight to
> the last man because it lacks an ideal. The policeman is doing a job.
> In the face of danger he will not make an ultimate sacrifice. A part
> of the leadership will also change sides if the opponent will give it a
> chance.[53]

The number of RIC men who lost their lives between 1919
and 1921 and those who died in Palestine from 1936 to 1939
does not refute this statement entirely. The police, though
trained as military units, were not prepared to accept military
scales of casualties. Policemen in both countries defected,
failed to carry out duties and deserted in a manner and to a
degree that would have been anathema to any military corps.
Perhaps a valid point to make in conclusion is that no police
force, no matter how large, technically well equipped or
politically committed,

> can act as a substitute for at least a minimal sense of moral com-
> munity . . . . The police may supplement the social consensus, may
> enforce its dictates against those who deviate — provided the
> deviants are only a small proportion of the population. They cannot
> replace the informal controls inherent in community.[54]

Such unity and coherent support for the government was
lacking in Ireland and Palestine. Once systematic revolutionary terrorism was applied to the police, compounding the
agglomerate of difficulties they already faced, duties were
ignored, defections occurred and the forces began to break.

The maintenance of public security in the long term, in any society, is dependent upon shared values and a willingness to live together without massive outbreaks of political violence, if not necessarily in complete peace and harmony. Political conflict *is* ubiquitous. The dilemma is how much political conflict can a system experience before it is thrown into disequilibrium? In the short term, order and public security depend upon efficient or at least adequate security forces able to control insurgent movements while they are germinating – or containing them once they have mobilized. As we have seen in both Ireland and Palestine, these essential ingredients conducive to public peace were lacking. Thus public order evaporated for significant periods of time in Palestine, while in Ireland the government ultimately ceased to exist. The condition and activities of the police as well as the condition of the opposition groups – and their interaction – thus provide the threshold between the preservation of the status quo, with a certain realignment of power, and the onset of a period of anarchy, as in Palestine, or of an irreversible alternative government, as in Ireland. With the police forces in both countries no longer able or indeed willing to protect the government and the people, public security passed into abeyance. In Ireland the restoration of the public peace was to lie with the Republican forces and Dail Eireann, while in Palestine it was achieved by the British military acting in aid of the civil power.

NOTES

1. D. H. Bayley, *The Police and Political Development in India* (Princeton, 1969), 11.

2. By authors such as Bayley and Chapman in the *Police State* (London, 1970) and the *Journal of Contemporary History,* which has begun to devote issues to the problem of policing. See particularly here G. L. Mosse (ed.) *Police Forces in History* (London, 1975).

3. R. Rose, *Governing Without Consensus: An Irish Perspective* (London, 1971), 143.

4. T. Parker, 'From the Other Side of the Fence', *New Society* (29 August 1963).

5. Colin McInnes, *Mr Love and Justice* (London, 1963), 74.

6. William Gay, quoted in C. H. Rolph, *The Police and the Public* (London, 1962), 167.

7. B. Chapman, *The Police State* (London, 1970).

8. From *La Police Extrait du Repertoire du Droit Administratife* (Paris, 1905), 4.

9. Chapman, op. cit.

10. Engels to Marx, Manchester, 23 May 1856 in *Marx and Engels Selected Writings 1846-1875* (Harmondsworth, 1961), 92-93.

11. *Sundry Tracts on Ireland* (Central Reference Library, Manchester), 19.

12. Chapman, op. cit., 137.

13. Cd 8279 Evidence and appendix (1916), 236.

14. T. P. Thornton, 'Terror as a weapon of political agitation' in H. Eckstein (ed.), *Internal War* (New York, 1964); E. V. Walter, *Terror and Resistance* (Oxford, 1969); and M. C. Hutchinson. 'The Concept of Revolutionary Terrorism', *The Journal of Conflict Resolution* XIV (3) (September 1972). Paul Wilkinson's recent study, *Political Terrorism* (London, 1974), can however now be taken as one of the most thorough studies of the phenomenon.

15. C. W. Thayer, *Guerrilla* (New York, 1965), 116.

16. B. Crozier, *The Rebels* (Boston, 1960), 159.

17. Lucien Pye, *Guerrilla Communism in Malaya* (Princeton, 1956), 102.

18. J. B. S. Hardman, 'Terrorism' in *Encyclopaedia of the Social Sciences* (London, 1948), 575.

19. Walter, op. cit., 7.

20. Thornton, op. cit., 71.

21. The most recent being A. Dallin and G. W. Breslauer, *Political Terror in Communist Systems* (Stanford, 1970) along with standard works such as H. Arendt, *The Origins of Totalitarianism* (New York, 1968); Z. Brzezinski, *Th Permanent Purge* (Cambridge, Mass., 1956); R. Conquest, *The Great Terror* (London, 1968); C. J. Friedrich, *Totalitarianism* (Cambridge, Mass., 1954) and, of course, Trotsky's *Terrorism and Communism* (Ann Arbor, Michigan, 1961).

22. See Dallin and Breslauer, op. cit., 104.

23. *Programme Istpolnitelnago Komiteta* 1879 ('Programme of the Executive Committee 1879'), reprinted in *Sbornik Programmi Programmniki statey partii Narodney Voli* (Geneva, 1903) 7-8, in Hardman op. cit., 577.

24. Dallin and Breslauer, op. cit., 103.

25. Walter, op. cit., 3.

26. Thornton, op. cit., 75.

27. *Sundry Tracts,* op. cit.

28. P. Pearse, *Political Writings and Speeches* (Dublin, 1962), 324.

29. M. Collins, *The Path to Freedom* (Dublin, 1922), 69-70.

30. Thornton, op. cit., pp. 75-76.

31. F. Gross op. cit., 450.

32. See here V. I. Lenin *'Letter to Comrades' Collected Works* Vol. 26 (Moscow, 1967) 212-213.

33. Thornton, op. cit., 81.

34. ibid., 82.

35. Dallin and Breslauer, op. cit., 4.

36. ibid., 24-25.

37. Hutchinson, op. cit., 388.

38. Chalmers Johnson, *Revolutionary Change* (Boston, 1966), 8.

39. T. R. Gurr, *Why Men Rebel* (Princeton, 1968), 213.

40. Quoted in P. Beaslai, *Michael Collins and the Making of the New Ireland*, Vol. 2 (London, 1926), 301.

41. Dail Eireann file DE 2/175, 24 April 1919, State Paper Office, Dublin Castle.

42. *Hansard* 122 (4 December 1919), 611.

43. CO 904/105, 1918, Inspector General's Reports.

44. *Hansard* 129 (20 May 1920), 1721.

45. *Hansard* 133 (25 October 1920), 1957.

46. CO 904/188/97, Sir John Anderson's Papers.

47. CO 904/109, 15 September 1919, Inspector General's Report.

48. The Auxiliary Division was inaugurated on 27 July 1920. Its members were contracted to serve for six months with an option on a further six months. They were paid £1 per day, all found, but had no pension rights. Cmd 1618, 'The RIC Auxiliary Division', 6-7. The first Black and Tan recruits for the RIC arrived in Ireland 25 March 1920; see R. Bennett, *The Black and Tans* (Amersham, Bucks., 1959).

49. CO 904/188/97, Sir John Anderson's Papers.

50. DE 2/81, Letter to Constance Markiewicz, Minister of Labour, State Paper Office, Dublin Castle.

51. ibid.

52. ibid.

53. Hsi-Huey Liang, *The Berlin Police Force in the Weimar Republic* (Berkeley, Calif., 1970), 95.

54. Richardson, reviewing Liang's book in the *Journal of Contemporary History* (June 1972), 272.

8

THE BREAKDOWN OF PUBLIC SECURITY:
Some Conclusions

It has been accepted throughout this study that most political systems exist in unstable equilibrium or exhibit varying degrees of deviance away from that condition. Political change and political violence are ubiquitous in political life. We have seen here that the extent of stability and security turns upon the degree of change and violence more than upon any other variables. Similarly, it has been demonstrated that many systems are either a balance or an imbalance of positive, that is system-supporting, elements and negative, that is system-destructive, elements. On the negative side in Ireland and Palestine, operating against public order and inducing a decline in governability, were first, the presence of organized, alienated, frustrated and aggressive citizens prepared to use force of arms to alleviate their perceived frustration; second, the lack of legitimacy of the colonial governments, both of them regarded as super-impositions rather than innate growths, the product of free choice; third, a weak consensus of support for the colonial administrations and, crucially in both areas, the indeterminate nature of the control forces – the police. On the positive side, operating in favour of the respective regimes, was inertia, or the habit of obedience. Both administrations possessed a monopoly of force of arms and a considerable body of experience in processing rebellion, riot and indeed revolution as parts of a wider colonial service using laws such as the Peace Preservation Act, Riot Acts, Defence of the Realm Acts and ultimately màrtial law. Yet in Ireland and Palestine the balance created by these parts of a dynamic situation was a fragile one. All that was required to alter it was the thrust of a new force such as an emergent revolutionary movement unchecked, or the loss of political will, or administrative failure affecting security work, and unstable equilibrium would, and indeed did, take a swift downturn into imbalance. In Ireland and Palestine during the periods examined here the net balance between equilibrating and disequilibrating forces broke down – partly because of the intransigence of the incumbent governments and their inability to accept the validity of the claims of the opposition groups or to move to tackle the sources of serious discontent. In such situations reason becomes exasperated.[1] Man then has recourse to political violence with, as he sees it, just‑cause.

There are of course various scales of disagreement within any one political system. A distinctive feature in Ireland and Palestine was that the disagreement was over fundamental issues such as sovereignty and authority. Other discontents aggregated around these basic issues. In Ireland the challenge to the existing government became a revolutionary one, intent not only upon breaking the administration but also upon terminating the hold of its morés and the associated social structure. The Irish opposition sought a complete redefinition of government and society. The Palestinian Arabs, on the other hand, were making demands upon authority in an attempt to change specific policies rather than to alter the fabric of society. It was only late in the day that the Palestinian Arabs attempted to defeat the incumbent government, and even then without any clear ideological or structural alternative to that government. Hence the dichotomy between people's revolutionary war in Ireland and a mutating rebellion in Palestine.[2]

The referents of this study have been that all political systems are mutant and that political change is ubiquitous, though there are modes of change running, with all manner of variations, from the tardiness of programmed, piecemeal reform to the cataclysm of revolutionary action. Similarly, the view has been taken throughout that the political system is a system of interrelated parts and that it is possible for the interdependence to be so strong that the failure or collapse of one essential part can lead to the collapse of the entire system.[3] In the cases examined in this work, so crucial were the police forces for the continued functioning of the respective systems that their failure seriously undermined governability. The police were in the European mode, that is based upon the Roman law, and accordingly had an extensive involvement in actual government. Since there was almost a symbiotic relationship between the police and government, it is not surprising that the failure of the police apparatus led on to the collapse of public security and governability.

POLICING, INTELLIGENCE, WORK AND
THE LOSS OF POLITICAL CONTROL

Policing and Intelligence Work

In a swiftly moving crisis situation sound information is an essential prerequisite of effective governmental policy. The police and their intelligence units should be capable of providing such information. The history of the RIC demonstrates how effective it had been to 1890 in controlling subversion through intelligence. Intelligence operations can be viewed as a court of first instance. Sir Kenneth Strong, a former head of British intelligence, has observed that,

> The intelligence process is neither complex nor obscure. It is based on two premises; that sensible policies can be developed and sensible decision made only when the facts of the case are known; and that warning concerning decisions that must be made in the nearer or distant future are useful.[4]

Similarly, Sun Tzu master of the martial arts and theorist of warfare declared that,

> the reason the enlightened Prince and the wise general conquer the enemy wherever they move and their achievements surpass those of ordinary men is foreknowledge. . . . What is called 'foreknowledge' cannot be encited from spirits, nor from Gods, nor by analogy with past events, nor from calculations. It must be obtained from men who know the enemy situation.[5]

Intelligence is especially important when one notes that rebel units are particularly vulnerable in their initial organizational phase — a phase through which all units must pass. At this

stage the activists are training and at the same time attempting to mobilize a popular supportive movement on which the
revolutionary vanguard can feed. An alliance between the
activists and the people has not been consolidated at this
stage. Hence the revolutionary vanguard and the wider movement are particularly susceptible to infiltration and attack
during this 'take-off' stage. Brigadier Kitson, one of the
British Army's experts on counter-insurgency, notes that the
time spent by insurgents in preparing the assault on the
government can vary considerably.[6] In Ireland organizational
preparations for the assault were made in the period 1917-19
following upon the trauma of the defeated Easter Rising, but
more important still were the arrangements made after the
release of the internees, who had continued to train, organize
and radicalize themselves in the internment camps. It therefore took two years for the IRA under Collins to create the
structures, evolve the tactics and build up the popular
support necessary to sustain protracted rural and urban guerrilla warfare.

In Palestine the disturbances were a far more spontaneous
acephalous affair. What organization there was grew in the
months following Al Qassam's death in 1935 and continued
to develop under cover of the six-month General Strike. It
was at these initial stages in Ireland and Palestine that the
security forces using necessary force could, if the lessons of
history had any relevance, have cauterized what was then still
a latent threat to internal security. Yet in both Ireland and
Palestine the security forces moved against the rebels only
after they had consolidated their organizations and after the
threat that they posed had become overt. By such time they
were much more difficult to defeat. Few governments it
seems will act against a putative threat, especially governments imbued with the bargaining emphasis of the liberal

democratic style of governance. Governments much prefer to wait and act against an existent threat. Again, Kitson writing from experience suggests that,

> if the government builds up a really effective intelligence organisation quickly, insurgents operating without the insulation provided by a closely linked system of secure cells, will be eliminated before they can become dangerous.[7]

In Ireland and Palestine such action was prevented by the application of financial stringency and political expediency to public security work. The crisis that such a state of affairs induced in Ireland and Palestine was compounded by the fact that, even when political criminals were brought before the judiciary, they were discharged or, in rare cases, given token sentences. In both Ireland and Palestine juries, for a variety of reasons, refused to convict. Accordingly the authority of government laws was destroyed.

The Loss of Political Control

It is possible then to build up the picture of the collapse of political control from the initial failure in the intelligence sphere. Certain critical variables appear, in both Ireland and Palestine, to have induced the collapse of public security. For example, the condition of the political will was a critical factor in both cases. In neither of the internal crises was it made explicit through statements of intent, policy or action that the incumbent British administration or the British people and government at home possessed the necessary resolve to endure a bloody, costly war of attrition. The authority of the Dublin Castle administration had been destroyed as early as 1914 by the Home Rule Act. From that point onwards the Irish administration was a 'lame duck'. The officers of that government, especially the police, were aware that for them there was only a very brief future. Once the revolutionary war had developed, events in Ireland became an acute embarrassment to Britain in the international arena — especially in the somewhat euphoric atmosphere of post-Versailles Europe. Lloyd George's coalition government was subjected to stress by pressures from both at home and abroad. It became clear, certainly to Lloyd George, that the political costs of such a war could not be endured indefinitely. The IRA, through its most efficient propaganda bureau, exploited these pressures to the full. The effect was the breaking of the political will, with the British government eventually coming to the conference table in a mood of compromise.

Palestine, being a Mandated territory, was also an impermanent British holding. The will to govern in protracted crisis was feeble, especially since the government was in the hands of administrators serving short tours of duty. The native government officers, especially Arab personnel, were torn between plural loyalties. In crisis they chose their natural brothers. However, the geographical position of Palestine in the Middle East meant that it was on the periphery of the British people's political concerns. The most cursory examination of the British press at the time reveals a very patchy coverage of the rebellion. Ireland, by comparison, because of its proximity to England, monopolized the front pages and leader columns from 1919 to 1921. British resolve over Palestine was thus in no way as severely tested as it had been over Ireland. Accordingly, in Palestine the military were left virtually undisturbed to prosecute the rebellion as they saw fit. Nevertheless, it remained a possibility in both cases that the will of the British administration would yield to force of arms.

A second critical variable in both areas was the condition of the incumbent administrations. This was of course dependent to a great extent upon the policies of the British government. The application of two policies in particular — financial stringency and political expediency — seriously debilitated the public security forces. The failure of intra-governmental communications, that is the relations between the departments of justice, police, civil administration proper and the army command, exacerbated the problems resulting from the strictures imposed by government policy. It is worth recalling that Sir Mark Sturgis, a senior Dublin Castle administrator, had described the Irish administration as 'a great sprawling hydra-headed monster spending much of its time using one of its head to abuse one or other of the others'.[8] He emphasized this point elsewhere in his diary, noting, 'What we lack is unity of command. It is extraordinary to me that Lloyd George, who saw so clearly the need for it in France, does not see the absolute necessity of it here.'[9] And again that, 'Just so long as the soldiers, the police and the civilians are three distinct bodies jealous of each other, so long we will do no good.'[10]

In Palestine the administration was even more seriously afflicated with schism between the civil administration and its prosecuting agency, the judiciary, and between the former and its punitive arm, the military.

However, it was the policies of financial stringency and political expediency that proved to be the most damaging to public security. In both areas there was a quest for short-term peace rather than for resolution of the conflicts. Disturbances were to be avoided at all cost. If enforcement of the law or punitive action could be construed by the opposition as provocative, then such action would not be taken. The outcome was that violence and political criminality grew. Financial stringency and political expediency led to a very low-profile security stance. Few salutary lessons were handed out to the opposition organizing quietly in the political underground. In both Ireland and Palestine the British drew the erroneous conclusion that, since all was quiet, there was little danger. The result, in Palestine especially, was that cuts were made in security additional to the standard economies made over the years. Because of such economies fewer police were recruited and police strength was actually cut back. Hence in quiet times and even for normal duties the police apparatus was placed under stress. Police reserves were, of necessity, fewer. Thus when disturbances occurred, such as the riots in Jerusalem in 1929, reinforcements were not readily available and the disturbance seriously escalated, requiring an inordinate degree of force, itself often dysfunctional, to restore compliance.

Thus in Ireland and Palestine the rebels were able to accomplish the crucial 'take-off' into self-sustained insurrection. The people had been mobilized to lend support or at least be passively sympathetic, and the cellular structures of the guerrilla undergrounds had been established and disciplined in the vacuum produced by the low profile of the security forces. This can be regarded as the median point in the breakdown of public security, since the opposition has mobilized; the authority of the government is no longer evident; administratively it has lost direction; and crucially its resolve and ability to preserve the status quo is open to serious doubt.

It is at this juncture, in Ireland and Palestine, that alternative sources of authority, alternative values and alternative structures appeared to become the new reference points for increasingly disorientated citizens. The established order of things, the old values and old structures, had begun to crumble. At this point too political violence became increasingly systematic, targeted and goal-oriented. The goal in both areas was to break public security and so end the credibility of the incumbent government. The instrument chosen to achieve this end was revolutionary terrorism operating as the leading edge of urban and rural guerrilla warfare. By attacking the government and its officers through the medium of revolutionary terror, the rebels achieved a disorientation effect with the terror's psychic impact even inducing loyalist police officers to change their allegiance. In this way public security was broken, governability declined and in Ireland the regime ceased to exist.

Two main conclusions emerge then from this study of the breakdown of public security. First, in both cases, once the political systems began to experience severe internal stress, the police and particularly their intelligence sections were the forces standing for system maintenance and against a striking alteration in the conditions of political life. The defeat of the police and the nullification of their intelligence services, achieved dramatically in Ireland with the Bloody Sunday assassinations, led directly to the decline of security and of governability through riot, rebellion and, in Ireland, people's revolutionary war. Second, the nature of the opposition forces out to break security, especially their level of politico-military development, determine both the degree and the duration of the breakdown of control. Upon the interaction of these two elements, the police and the terrorists, the outcome of the struggles in Ireland and Palestine turned. Thus in Ireland, with its sophisticated underground army and alternative political structure represented by Dail Eireann, there emerged between 1916 and 1921 a fully fledged alternative government. In Palestine, however, there developed a peasant rebellion suffering from tribal, anarchic lapses. Nevertheless, even here the violent opposition was developing towards the sophisticated Irish model of people's revolutionary war and seriously threatened the survival of the Mandate government. However, it was only in Ireland that the breakdown of security and collapse of governability was total, leading on to independence. The lesson of both cases is perhaps that 'Institutions are like fortresses. They must be well designed and properly manned.'[1]

NOTES

1. Man has always had recourse to violence; sometimes the recourse was a mere crime. . . . But at other times violence was the means resorted to by him who had previously exhausted all others in defence of the rights of justice which he thought he possessed. It may be regrettable that human nature tends on occasion to this form of violence but it is undeniable that it implies the greatest tribute to reason and justice. For this form of violence is none other than reason exasperated. [Ortega y Gasset, *The Revolt of the Masses* (New York, 1932), 82]

2. 'Conflicts over values and conflicts over interests both may produce insurrections and the distinction between these two kinds of conflict is related to the distinction between rebellions and revolutions.' (Chalmers Johnson, *Revolutionary Change* (Boston, 1966), 14.

3. For a similar point of view see C. J. Friedrich, 'Opposition and Government by Violence', *Government and Opposition* VII (1) (Winter 1972), 5.

4. Major General Sir Kenneth Strong, *Men of Intelligence* (London, 1970), 152.

5. Sun Tzu, *The Act of War* trans. S. Griffiths (Oxford, 1963), 144.

6. Kitson notes:

> In the Phillipines the Communist Party issued its strategic directive in 1946. But it was not until 1950 that the PLA stated their military offensive. . . . The time spent in preparing the ground in Algeria was much shorter, and in fact the insurrection launched suddenly and violently only eight months after the political body which had sponsored it was brought into being. In Cyprus Grivas started preparing as early as 1951 for the insurrection which broke out in 1955. . . . for the first few years his activities were concerned with planning, building up supplies and dealing with Greek and Cypriot national leaders. . . . and in Malaya the Communists had started preparing for the rebellion which broke out in 1948 as soon as the Japanese had been driven out of the country in 1945 if not earlier. Low Intensity Operations (London 1970).

7. Kitson, op. cit., 89.

8. Sir Mark Sturgis's Diary, August 1920, PRO 30/59.

9. ibid., vol. 4, 28 February 1920.

10. ibid., 6 March 1920.

11. Karl Popper, *The Poverty of Historicism* (New York, 1964), 6.

BIBLIOGRAPHY

This bibliography is selective rather than comprehensive. No attempt is made to detail all the primary sources studied since at least some of these appear in the notes in the text. It has also been necessary to compartmentalize material under the following headings:

A. Primary sources, documents and parliamentary papers;
B. (i) Secondary material on the Irish case study;
    (ii) Secondary material on the Palestine case study;
C. Theoretical material on political violence, riot, rebellion, revolution, conflict and the police.

A. PRIMARY SOURCES

Ireland

State papers and documents relating to the period 1910-21 in particular, especially all available police and military reports, were consulted in the following centres.

311

i. The Public Record Office, London, for all the Royal Irish constabulary, Dublin Castle and War Office documents.

ii. The State Paper Office, Dublin Castle, for the Dail Eireann minutes and records and all the Government Letter Books of the period. Similarly some material of the Castle government, especially Colonial Office files not transferred to London in 1921, were consulted.

iii. The National Library, Ireland (Dublin), where the Bryce Papers, the records of the Dublin Brigade, IRA, some papers of Michael Collins, IRA Ministry of Defence Records (microfilm) and many newspapers of the period were consulted.

iv. The Liverpool University Library for a small but most interesting collection of the Birrell Papers.

v. John Rylands Library, Manchester, for original copies of the IRA news bulletin and propaganda paper, *The Irish Bulletin.* Some five or six volumes, including Dublin Castle forgeries, are held in this library.

vi. Parliamentary papers and pamphlets.

   i. The Parliamentary Debates (*Hansard*) for the period 1908-21.
   ii. Police and Crime Reports 1900-21, various Command numbers.

   Other papers

   iii. Documents relating to the Sinn Fein Movement, Cmd 1108, 1921.

   Documents relating to intercourse between Bolehevism and Sinn Fein, Cmd 1326, 1921.

   Commission on National Education in Ireland C 2223, 1877 (particularly for the Christian Brothers schools).

   The Vice-Regal Commission on Reorganization and Pay of the Irish Police Forces, Cmd 603, 1920.

   Dublin Metropolitan Police Statistical Tables (Crime etc.) for the years 1903-19:

   i. 1894-98, Cd 7734, 8255, 8486, 8879, 9302.

ii. 1899-1915, Cd 176, 615, 1166, 1621, 2093, 2549, 2999, 3551, 4094, 4785, 5234, 5759, 6384, 6860, 7587, 8065, 8417.

iii. 1916, Cmd 301; 1917, Cmd 364; 1918, Cmd 624; 1919, Cmd 1318.

The Amount of Force employed in each county and city in Ireland 1 January 1840 H.C. 290, 1840.

The Amount of Force employed in each county and city in Ireland 1 January 1850, H.C. 432, 1850.

English Government Departments (Powers in Ireland), H.C. 191, 1907.

Constabulary Bill. Memorandum on Financial Provisions, Cmd 1649, 1922.

Estimates of Probable Expenditure, Cmd 393, 1919.

Disbandment Terms of the RIC, Cmd 1673, 1922.

The Royal Irish Constabulary Auxiliary Division, Cmd 1618, 1920.

Outrages in Ireland. A report showing the number of serious outrages in Ireland reported by the RIC and DMP during the months of July, August and September 1920, Cmd 1025, 1921.

Reports of the Proceedings of the Irish Convention, Cd 9019, 1918.

Report of the Committee of Inquiry into the RIC, Cd 1087, 1901; Evidence and Appendix, Cd 1094, 1901.

Shooting Outrages on the Police, H.C. 188, 1913.

Report of the County Inspector, RIC, Galway, East Riding, as to the state of the Riding, October 1907, Cd 3949, 1908.

Royal Commission of Inquiry into the Origins of the Easter Rising 1916, Cd 8279, 1917; Evidence and Appendix, Cd 8311, 1917.

Restoration of Order in Ireland Act, Cmd 2278, 1920.

Committee of Inquiry into the RIC and DMP, Cd 7421, 1914; Evidence and Appendix Cd 7637, 1914.

The Case of Mr. Sheehy Skeffington and Others, Cd 8376, 1916.

Howth (the landing of arms), Cd 7631, 1914-16; Evidence, Cd 7649, 1916.

Royal Commission of Inquiry into the Dublin Disturbances 1914, Cd 7269, 1915; Evidence and Appendix, Cmd 7272, 1915.

Irish Police Forces. A Vice-Regal Commission into the Reorganisation and Pay of Police Forces, Cmd 603, 1920.

Judicial Statistics (Ireland) 1900-17, Cd 725, 1208, 1746, 2218, 2632, 3112, 3654, 4200, 4747, 5320, 5866, 6419, 7064, 7600, 8077, 8636, 9066, 8636.

Emigration Statistics (Ireland) 1900-1921, Cd 531, 976, 1489, 2030, 2467, 2868, 3376, 3987, 4550, 5088, 5607, 6727, 7313, 7883, 8230, 8520, 9013; Cmd 77, 721, 1414.

Pamphlets (mostly undated)
iv. 'The Irish Question. A Series of Tracts' (Irish Press Agency, London, 1886).

Colonial Home Rule: would it settle anything?' Anon.

Peace with Ireland Council pamphlets — various.

'The Case of Ireland', Sinn Fein Series No. 12.

'A Plea for Justice', G. W. Russell (AE) published by the Irish Homestead.

Gaelic League pamphlets:
   No. 1 Rev. M. P. O'Hickey, *The true national idea.*
   No. 23. P. P. Kavanagh, *Ireland's Defence — her language.*
   No. 25. W. P. O'Riain *Lessons from Modern Language Movements*
   No. 29. M. P. O'Hickey, *The Irish Language Movement*
   No. 32. S. L. Poole, *The Irish Battle of the Books.*

Palestine

State papers, private papers, memoirs, and original documents were examined in the following centres.

i. *The Public Record Office, London,* particularly the War Office files relating to the Arab Rebellion; Colonial Office, Cabinet and Air Ministry papers for the period 1920-39.

ii. The Central Zionist Archive, Jerusalem, particularly the classes CZA S24 and S25. Political Department of the Executive of the Zionist Organisation and the Jewish Agency for Palestine in Jerusalem, Tel Aviv and Haifa. 1921-48; and class A 245 the Sharett (Shertok), Moshe, papers.

iii. The State Archive, Prime Ministers Office, Jerusalem, for daily press summaries, 1928-39, of both Arabic and Hebrew newspapers in translation and various documents left by the Mandate government in 1948 with particular reference to the Arab guerrillas.

iv. The Hebrew University Library, Jerusalem.

v. The Jewish Library in Central Reference Library, Manchester.

vi. Parliamentary papers and original documents of various Jewish organisations.
High Commissioner's Interim Report, Cmd 1499, 1921.
Haycroft Commission on the Disturbances of 1921, Cmd 1540, 1921.
Churchill White Paper, Cmd 1700, 1922.
The Shaw Report, Cmd 3530, 1930.
The Hope-Simson Report, Cmd 3686, 1930.
The Passfield White Paper, Cmd 3692, 1930.
The Peel Report, Cmd 5479, 1937.
The McMahon Correspondence, Cmd 5974, 1939.
The 1939 White Paper, Cmd 6019, 1939.
The Anglo-American Committee Report, Cmd 6808, 1946.
Acts of Violence in Palestine, Cmd 6873, 1946.

Report of HMG to the Council of the League of Nations on the Administration of Palestine and Trans-Jordan Colonial Number 129, 1936.

Palestine Paper No. 4. *Palestine Arabs under the British Mandate.* (Jewish Agency for Palestine, 1930).

Policy in Palestine 1937, Cmd 5634, 1937.

Memorandum submitted to the Royal Commission on behalf of the Vaad Leumi — the General Council of the Jewish Community in Palestine, CZA 5604 (Jerusalem, 1936).

Report of the Executives of the zionist Organisation and Jewish Agency for Palestine, August 1939, CZA 7448 (d).

Parliamentary Debates *(Hansard)* for the period 1930-39.

B. SECONDARY SOURCES

Ireland

Addis, W. E. and Arnold, T. *A Catholic Dictionary* (London, 1970).

Anon. *Irish Seditions: their Origin and History 1792-1880* (London, 1880).

Anson, Sir William, *Laws and Customs of the Constitution* (1892).

Barry, Tom, *Guerrilla Days in Ireland* (Tralee, 1968).

Beaslai, Piaras, *Michael Collins and the Making of the New Ireland* (London, 1926), 2 vols.

Bennett, R., *The Black and Tans* (Amersham, 1959).

Birrell, Augustine, *Things Past Redress* (London, 1937).

Blanchard, J., *The Church in Contemporary Ireland* (Dublin, 1963).

Blanshard, P., *The Irish and Catholic Power* (London, 1954).

Bowyer Bell, J., *The Secret Army* (St. Albans, 1970).

Broeker, Galen, *Rural Disorder and Police Reform in Ireland 1812-1836* (London, 1970).

Brugsma, R. P. C., *The Beginnings of the Irish Revival* (Netherlands, 1933).

Bryan, D., 'Guerrilla Warfare in Dublin', *An Cosantoir* (1964).

Burton, D., *Edmund Rice – Merchant Adventurer* (Dublin, 1964).

Callwell, C. E., *Field Marshall Sir Henry Wilson. His Life and Diaries* (London, 1927), 2 vols.

Capuchin Annual, several articles on IRA reorganization 1917 (1967).

Childers, Erskine, *Military Rule in Ireland* (Dublin, 1920).

Clarkson, J. Dunsmore, *Labour and Nationalism in Ireland* (New York, 1925).

Collins, M. E., *Conquest and Colonisation* (Dublin, 1969).

Collins, Michael, *The Path to Freedom* (Dublin, 1922).

Connolly, James, *Revolutionary Warfare* (Dublin, 1968).

——, *The Re-Conquest of Ireland* (Dublin, 1968).

——, *Erin's Hope* (Dublin, 1968).

——, *New Evangel* (Dublin, 1968).

——, *Socialism Made Easy* (Dublin, 1971).

Coogan, T. P., *The IRA* (London, 1971).

Corfe, T., *The Phoenix Park Murders* (London, 1968).

Curtis, R., *A History of the R.I.C.* (Dublin, 1871).

Curtis, L. P., *Coercion and Conciliation in Ireland 1880-1892* (Princeton, 1963).

Doob, L. W., *Patriotism and Nationalism* (New Haven, 1964).

Doyle, L., *The Spirit of Ireland* (London, 1935).

O'Dubhghaill, M., *Insurrection Fires at Easter Tide* (Cork, 1966).

Forester, M., *Michael Collins – the Lost Leader* (London, 1971).

Fox, R. M., *The History of the Irish Citizen Army* (Dublin, 1944).

French, G., *The Life of Field Marshall Sir John French* (London, 1931).

Gleeson, James, *Bloody Sunday* (London, 1962).

Greaves, C. Desmond, *The Life and Times of James Connolly* (London, 1961).

Hawthorne, James (ed.), *Two Centuries of Irish History* (London, 1966).

Heckethorn, C. W., *Secret Societies of All Ages and Countries* (London, 1875), 2 vols.

Hobson, Bulmer, *Ireland Yesterday, Today and Tomorrow* (Dublin, 1968).

Lieberson, G., *The Irish Rising 1916-1921* (CBS Legacy Collection Book, Dublin, 1966).

Lockington, W. J., *The Soul of Ireland* (London, 1920).

Lynch-Robinson, Sir Christopher, *The Last of the Irish R.M.'s* (London, 1951).

Lyons, F. S., *The Irish Parliamentary Party* (London, 1950).

Macready, General Sir Neville, *Annals of An Active Life* (London, 1924), 2 vols.

MacGiolla Choille, Breandan (ed.), *Intelligence Notes 1913-1916* (Irish State Paper Office, Dublin, 1972).

Mansergh, N., *The Irish Question 1840-1921* (London, 1965).

Marlowe, N., 'The Irish Bishops, the War and Home Rule', *Contemporary Review* (October 1918).

Martin, F. X., *The Irish Volunteers 1913-1915 Recollections and Documents* (Dublin, 1963).

—— (ed.), *Leaders and Men of the Easter Rising Dublin 1916* (London, 1967).

Martin, H., *Ireland in Insurrection* (London, 1921).

Moody, T. F. (ed.), *The Fenian Movement* (Cork, 1968).

Mankivell, J. M. and Loch, S., *Ireland in Travail* (London, 1922).

Neeson, Koin, *The Life and Death of Michael Collins* (Cork, 1968).

Neligan, D., *Spy in the Castle* (London, 1969).

Norman, E. R., *The Catholic Church and Ireland in the Age of Rebellion 1859-1873* (London, 1965).

——, *A History of Modern Ireland* (London, 1971).

O'Brien, R. Barry, *Dublin Castle and the Irish People* (London, 1912).

O'Broin, Leon, *The Chief Secretary. Augustine Birrell in Ireland* (London, 1969).

——, *Dublin Castle and the 1916 Rising. A Life of Under Secretary Sir Mathew Nathan* (Dublin, 1966).

O'Connor, Frank, *The Big Fellow. A Life of Michael Collins.* (London, 1937).

O'Connor, T. P., *Memoirs of an Old Parliamentarian* (London, 1929), 2 vols.

——, *Sketches in the House* (London, 1893).

O'Conor, W. J., *Changing Ireland. Literary Backgrounds of the Irish Free State 1889-1922* (Cambridge, Mass., 1924).

O'Donoghue, F., 'Guerrilla Warfare in Ireland 1919-1921', *An Cosantoir* (May 1963).

O'Faolain, Sean, *The Irish* (Harmondsworth, 1969).

O'Farrell, Patrick, *Ireland's English Question* (London, 1971).

O'Leary, John, *Recollections of Fenians and Fenianism* (Dublin, 1969), 2 vols.

'One Who Knows', *Promotion in the RIC* (Dublin, 1916).

Pearse, Padraig, *Political Writings and Speeches* (Dublin, 1962).

'Periscope', 'The Last Days of Dublin Castle', *Blackwoods Magazine*, No. 212 (1922).

Philips, W. Alison, *The Revolution in Ireland 1906-1923* (London, 1923).

Pollard, H. B. C., *The Secret Societies of Ireland. Their Rise and Progress* (London, 1922).

Porter, F. I., *Twenty Years Recollections of An Irish Police Magistrate* (London, 1880).

Robinson, Sir Henry A., *Further Memories of Irish Life* (London, 1929).

——, *Memories: Wise and Otherwise* (London, 1923).

Robinson, Lennox (ed.), *Lady Gregory's Journals 1916-1930* (London, 1946).

Rose, P., *The Manchester Martyrs – A Fenian Tragedy* (London, 1970).

Rose, R., *Governing Without Consensus. An Irish Perspective* (London, 1971).

Ryan, Desmond, *Michael Collins and the Invisible Army* (London, 1968).

'Southern Loyalist', 'Ireland Today' *Blackwoods Magazine*, No. 206 (1919).

Street, C. J. C., *The Administration of Ireland 1920* (London, 1921).

Talbot, Hayden, *Michael Collins' Own Story* (London, 1923).

Tynan, P. J. P., *The Irish Nationalist Invincibles and their Times* (London, 1894).

Wheeler-Bennett, J., *John Anderson, Viscount Waverley* (London, 1962).

Williams, T. Desmond, (ed.), *The Irish Struggle 1916-1926* (London, 1966).

Wilson, Trevor, *The Political Diaries of C.P. Scott. 1911-1928* (London, 1970).

——, *The Downfall of the Liberal Party. 1914-1925* (London, 1966).

Winter, Sir Ormonde, *Winter's Tale* (London, 1955).

Younger, Carlton, *Ireland's Civil War* (London, 1968).

Palestine

Abcarius, M. F., *Palestine Through the Fog of Propaganda* (London, no date).

Anon., *Haganah Becomes an Army* (Tel Aviv, 1949).

Anon., *Background of the Struggle for Liberation in Bretz Israel. Facts on the Relations between Irgun Zwai Leumi and the Haganah* (Tel Aviv, 1947).

Antonius, George, *The Arab Awakening. The Story of the Arab National Movement* (London, 1961).

Arab Centre, *Punitive Measures in Palestine* (London, no date); State Archive, Jerusalem.

Arab National Bureau, Damascus, *Atrocities in the Holy Land* (No details): Central Zionist Archive Jerusalem CZA 23. 307.

Assaf, Michael, *The Arab Movement in Palestine* (New York, 1937).

Ayrouth, Habib, *The Fellahin* (Cairo, no date).

Bauer, Y., *From Diplomacy to Resistance. A History of the Jews in Palestine* (no details); CZA 25556a.

——, 'From Co-operation to Resistance', *Middle Eastern Studies* II (3) (April 1966). The story of the Haganah Organisation, 1938-46.

Bein, Alex (ed.), *Arthur Ruppin: Memoirs, Diaries, Letters* (London, 1971).

Ben-Gurion, David, *My Talks with Arab Leaders* (Jerusalem, 1972).

——, 'Our Friend. What Wingate Did For Us', *Jewish Observer and Middle East Review* (27 September 1963).

——, 'Britain's Contribution to Arming the Haganah', *Jewish Observer and Middle East Review* (20 September, 1963).

Bentwich, Norman, 'The Legal System in Palestine Under the Mandate', *Middle East Journal,* II (1) (January 1948), 33-46.

Brenner, Y. S., 'The Stern Gang', *Middle Eastern Studies* II (1) (October 1965).

Burstein, Moshé, *Self-Government of the Jews in Palestine since 1900* (Tel Aviv, 1934).

Canaan, T., *Conflict in the Land of Peace* (Jerusalem, 1936).

——, *The Palestinian Arab Cause:* pamphlet, State Archive, Jerusalem.

Cohen, Aharon, *Israel and the Arab World* (London, 1970).

Courtney, Roger, *Palestine Policeman* (London, 1939).

Curtis, Michael (ed.), *People and Politics in the Middle East* (New York, 1971).

Dekel, Efraim, *Shai. The Exploits of Haganah Intelligence* (Tel Aviv and London, 1959).

Duff, Douglas, *Sword for Hire* (London, 1934).

——, *Palestine Picture* (London, 1936).

Esco Foundation (an acrostic of Ethel S. Cohen), *Palestine. A Study of Jewish Arab and British Policies* (New Haven, 1947), 2 vols.

Ferguson, Bernard, *The Trumpet in the Hall* (London, 1970).

Finn, E. A., *Palestine Peasantry – Notes on their Class, Warfare, Religion and Laws* (no details): CZA 22818.

Gabbay, R., *A Political Study of the Arab-Jew Conflict* (Geneva, 1959).

Golomb, Eliyahu, *The History of Jewish Self Defence in Palestine 1878-1921* (Tel Aviv, no date): Zionist Library No. 4.

Hain, S. G. (ed.), *Arab Nationalism – an Anthology* (Berkeley, 1962).

Hay, A. I., *There was a Man of Genius* (London, 1963).

Hirszowicz, L., 'Nazi Germany and the Palestine Partition Plan', *Middle Eastern Studies* I (1) (October 1964), 40-65.

Joseph, Bernard, *British Rule in Palestine* (London, 1948).

Kedourie, Elie, 'Sir Herbert Samuel and The Government of Palestine', *Middle Eastern Studies* V (1) (January 1969), 44-68.

Kirkbride, Sir Alec, *A Crackle of Thorns. Experiences in the Middle East* (London, 1956).

Kisch, F. H., *Palestine Diary* (London, 1938).

Klieman, A. S., *Foundations of the British Policy in the Arab World. The Cairo Conference of 1921* (Baltimore, 1970).

Koury, Enver M., *The Patterns of Mass Movements in Arab Revolutionary Progressive States* (The Hague, 1970).

Kraines, Oscar, *Government and Politics in Israel* (London, 1961).

Mardor, A., *Strictly Illegal* (London, 1964).

Marlowe, John, *The Seat of Pilate* (London, 1959).

——, *Rebellion in Palestine* (1946).

Meinertzhagen, R., *Middle East Diary 1917-1956* (London, 1959).

Melka, R., 'Nazi Germany and the Palestine Question', *Middle Eastern Studies*, V (3) (October 1969), 221-33.

Military Administration of Palestine and the Jews. (no details): CZA 885.

Morton, G. J., *Just the Job – Some Experiences of a Colonial Policeman* (London, 1957).

Nuseibeh, H. Z., *The Ideas of Arab Nationalism* (Ithaca, N.Y., 1959).

Pearlman, M., (M. P. Waters), *The Mufti Over the Middle East* (London, no date).

——, *Haganah. Jewish Self Defence in Palestine* (London, no date).

——, *The Mufti of Jerusalem* (London, 1947).

Perlmutter, Amon, *Military and Politics in Israel* (London, 1969).

Royal Institute of International Affairs *Great Britain and Palestine 1915-1945,* Information Paper No. 20 (Oxford, 1946).

Samuel, M., *What Happened in Palestine. The Events of 1929* (Massachusetts, 1929).

Shihadeh, Aziz B., *The ABC of the Arab Case in Palestine* (Jaffa, no date).

Simson, H. J., *British Rule and Rebellion* (London, 1937).

Sykes, Christopher, *Orde Wingate* (London, 1959).

——, *Crossroads to Israel* (London, 1965).

Taylor, A. R., 'Zionist Ideology. An Interpretive Analysis', *Middle Eastern Journal,* XVIII (Autumn 1964), 431-442.

Verete, Mayir, 'The Balfour Declaration and its Makers', *Middle Eastern Studies*, VI (1) (January 1970), 48-76.

Weizmann, Chaim, *Trial and Error* (London, 1950).

Williams-Thompson, R., *The Palestine Problem* (Cambridge, no date).

C. THEORETICAL MATERIAL ON POLITICAL VIOLENCE, RIOT, REBELLION, REVOLUTION, CONFLICT AND THE POLICE

The Police

Adam, R. L., *The Police Encyclopaedia*, 8 vols. (London, 1912).

Applegate, R., *Riot Control. Material and Techniques* (New York, 1969).

Aston, G. G., *Secret Service* (London, 1931).

Banton, M., *The Policeman in the Community* (London, 1964).

Bayley, D. H., *Police and Political Development in Europe*, (paper prepared for discussion at the Seminar on State and Nation Building in Western Europe, Centre for Advanced Studies in Behavioural Sciences, Stanford, June-August 1970).

——, *The Police and Political Development in India* (Princeton, 1969).

Bordua, D. J., *The Police: Six Sociological Essays* (Chichester, 1967).

—— and Reiss, A. J., 'Command, Control and Charisma: Reflections on Police Bureaucracy', *American Journal of Sociology*, LXXII (July 1966), 68-76.

Bramstedt, E. K., *Dictatorship and the Political Police* (London, 1945).

Brzezinski, Z. K., *The Permanent Purge* (Cambridge, Mass., 1956).

Chapman, B., *The Police State* (London, 1970).

——, 'Himmler's Apparat', *Government and Opposition* IV (3) (1969), 299-341.

Cobb, R. C., *The Police and the People. French Popular Protest 1789-1820* (Oxford, 1970).

Davies, A. M., 'Police, the Law and the Individual', *The Annals* (January 1954), 143-151.

Delarue, Jacques, *The History of the Gestapo* (London, 1970).

Derbyshire, R. L., 'Children's Perceptions of the Police. A Comparative Study of Attitudes and Attitude Change', *Journal of Criminal Law, Criminology and Police Science*, LIX (2) (June, 1968).

Emerson, D. E., *Metternich and the Political Police – Security and*

Subversion in the Hapsburg Monarchy 1815-1830. (The Hague, 1968).

Epstein, D., 'Police Role in Counter-Insurgency Efforts', *Journal of Criminal Law, Criminology and Police Science,* LIX (1) (March 1968).

Fogelson, R. H., 'From Resentment to Confrontation: The Police, the Negroes and the Outbreak of the 1960's Riots', *Political Science Quarterly,* LXXXIII (June 1968).

Fosdick, B., *European Police Systems* (New Jersey, 1970).

Gourlay, G. D., 'Police-Public Relations', *The Annals* (January 1954), 135-42.

Gwynn, Sir Charles, *Imperial Policing* (London, 1936).

Höhne, Heinz, *The Order of the Death's Head* (London, 1969).

Jeffries, Sir Charles, *The Colonial Police* (London, 1952).

Johnson, D. and Gregory, R., 'Police – Community Relations in the USA; a Review of Recent Literature and Projects', *Journal of Criminal Law, Criminology and Police Science,* LXII (1) (March 1971).

Journal of Contemporary History VII (1, 2) (January-April 1972): A special issue on the police.

Key, V. O., 'Police Graft', *American Journal of Sociology* (January 1934).

Lambert, J. H., *Crime, Police and Race Relations* (Oxford, 1970).

Lane, Roger, *Policing the City. Boston 1822-1885.* (Cambridge, Mass., 1967).

Lévy, Yves, 'Police and Policy', in *Government and Opposition, Volume I: 1965-1966* (London, 1965).

Liang, Hsi-Huey, *The Berlin Police Force in the Weimar Republic* (Berkeley, 1970).

Lipset, S., 'Politics and the Police', *New Society* (6 March 1969).

Martin, J. P. and Wilson, G., *The Police: A Study in Manpower. The Evolution of the Service in England and Wales 1829-1965* (London, 1969).

Okonkwo, Cyprian O., *The Police and Public in Nigeria* (London, 1966).

Payne, H. C., *The Police State of Louis Napoleon Bonaparte 1851-1860* (Washington, 1966).

Radzinowicz, L., *A History of English Criminal Law and its administration from 1750. Vol. 3: Cross-Currents in the Movement for the Reform of the POlice* (London, 1956).

Reynolds, G. W., and Judge, A., *The Night the Police went on Strike* (London, 1968).

Rolph, D. R., 'Police Violence', *New Statesman,* LXVI (102) (1962).

Simpson, H. B., 'The Office of Constable', *English Historical Review,* (October 1895), 625-41.

Skolnick, J. H., *Justice Without Trial* (Chichester, 1966).

Squire, P. S., *The Third Department – the Political Police in the Russia of Nicholas I* (Cambridge, 1968).

Stead, P. J., *The Police of Paris* (St. Albans, 1957).

Volmer, August, *The Police and Modern Society* (New York, 1971).

Westley, William A., 'Violence and the Police', *American Journal of Sociology,* LIX (1953), 34.

——, *The Police. A Sociological Study of Law, Custom and Morality* (Chicago, 1970).

Political Violence, Riot, Rebellion, Revolution and Conflict

Aberbach, J. D., 'Alienation and Political Behaviour', *American Political Defence Review* LXIII (March 1969), 86-99.

Ahmad, Eqbal, 'Revolutionary War and Counter Insurgency', *International Affairs,* XXV (1) (1971), 1-47.

Alastos, Doros, *Cyprus Guerrilla* (London, 1960).

Alavi, Hamza, 'Peasants and Revolution', in *Socialist Register 1965* (London, 1965), 241-77.

Amman, P., 'Revolution: A Redefinition', *Political Science Quarterly* LXXXVII (March 1962), 36-53.

The Annals (September 1970)' special issue on 'Collective Violence'.

'Approaches to the Study of Social Conflict. A Colloquium', *Journal of Conflict Resolution,* I, (2) (1957).

Apter, D. (ed.), *Ideology and Discontent* (New York, 1964).

Arendt, H., *On Revolution* (New York, 1963).

——, *On Violence* (Harmondsworth, 1970).

Ashford, D. E., 'Politics and Violence in Morocco', *Middle East Journal*, XIII (1) (Winter 1959), 11-25.

Baechler, Jean, 'Revolutionary and Counter-Revolutionary War: Some Political and Strategic Lessons from the first Indo China War and Algeria', *International Affairs*, XXV (1) (1971), 79-90.

Baldwin, R. N. (ed.), *Kropotkin's Revolutionary Pamphlets* (London, 1970).

Beloff, M., *Public Order and Popular Disturbances 1660-1714* (London, 1963).

Benewick, R., *A Study of British Fascism* (Harmondsworth, 1969).

Bernard, J., 'Where is the Modern Sociology of Conflict?' *American Journal of Sociology* LVI (1) (July 1950), 11-16.

Bienen, H., *Violence and Social Change – a Review of Current Literature* (Chicago, 1968).

Black, C. E., and Thornton, T. P. (eds.), *Communism and Revolution: the Strategic Uses of Political Violence* (Princeton, 1964).

Bradbury, William C., *Mass Behaviour in Battle and Captivity – the Communist Soldier in the Korean War* (Chicago, 1968).

Bramstedt, E. K., *The Technique of Control by Fear* (London, 1945).

Brinton, Crane, *The Anatomy of Revolution* (New York, 1965).

Budge, I., *Agreement and Stability of Democracy* (Chicago, 1971).

Bushkoff, L., 'Revolution and Nationalism', *World Politics* (3) (April 1963).

Calvert, Peter, *A Study of Revolution* (Oxford, 1970).

——, 'Revolution: the Politics of Violence', *Political Studies,* XV (1) (1967), 1-11.

Cantril, Hadley, *The Psychology of Social Movements* (Chichester, 1941).

Cohn, Norman, *The Pursuit of the Millenium* (New York, 1961).

Cookridge, E. F., *Inside S.O.E.* (London, 1963).

Coser, Lewis, 'Some Social Functions of Violence', *The Annals* (March 1966), 8-18.

——, *The Functions of Social Conflict* (New York, 1956).

Crozier, Brian, *The Rebels – a Study of Post-War Insurrections* (London, 1960).

Dallin, A., and Breslauer, G. W., *Political Terror in Communist Systems* (Stanford, Calif., 1970).

Darvall, F. O., *Popular Disturbances and Public Order in Regency England* (Oxford, 1969).

Davies, J. C. (ed.), *When Men Revolt and Why. A Reader in Political Violence and Revolution* (New York, 1971).

——, 'Political Stability and Instability: Some Manifestations and Causes', *Journal of Conflict Resolution,* XIII (1969), 1-17.

Debray, R., *Revolution in the Revolution?* (Harmondsworth, 1967).

Denton, F. and Phillips, W. 'Some Patterns in the History of Violence', *Journal of Conflict Resolution,* XII (1968).

Deutsch, K., *The Nerves of Government* (New York, 1966).

Dicey, A. V., *Law of the Constitution* (London, 1927).

Easton, David, *A Systems Analysis of Political Life* (Chichester, 1965).

——, *Varieties of Political Theory* (Englewood Cliffs, N.J., 1966).

Eckstein, H. (ed.), *Internal War – Problems and Approaches* (New York, 1964).

——, 'On the Etiology of Internal Wars', *History and Theory,* IV (2) (1965), 133-63.

Edwards, L. P., *The Natural History of Revolution* (New York, 1965).

Endleman, S., *Violence in the Streets* (Chicago, 1968).

Etzioni, A., *Demonstration Democracy* (New York, 1970).

Eysenck, H., *The Psychology of Politics* (London, 1954).

Fanon, F., *The Wretched of the Earth* (Harmondsworth, 1967).

Feierabend, I. K. and R. L., 'Aggressive Behaviours Within POlitics 1948-1962: A Cross National Study', *Journal of Conflict Resolution,* X (September 1966), 249-71.

Finer, S. E., *The Man on Horseback: the Role of the Military in Politics* (Oxford, 1962).

Fishman, W. J., *The Insurrectionists* (London, 1970).

Friedrick, C. J. (ed.), *Revolution* (New York, 1966).

——, 'Political Pathology', *Political Quarterly,* XXXVII (1966).

——, 'Opposition and Government by Violence', *Government and Opposition,* VII (1) (Winter 1972).

Girling, J. S., *People's War* (London, 1969).

Goodspeed, D. J., *The Conspirators: A Study of Coup d'Etat* (London, 1962).

Gottschalk, L., 'Causes of Revolution', *American Journal of Sociology*, (July 1944), 1-8.

Graham, H. D. and Gurr, E. R. (eds.), *Violence in America. Historical and Comparative Perspectives* (London, 1969).

Grinker, R. R. and Spiegel, J. P., *Men Under Stress* (Philadelphia, 1945).

Gurr, T. R., *Why Men Rebel* (Princeton, 1970).

——, and C. Ruttenberg, *The Conditions of Civil Violence First Tests of a Causal Model*, Princeton University Research Monograph No. 28 (Princeton, 1967).

Gurr, T., 'Psychological Factors in Civil Strife', *World Politics*, XX (January 1968), 245-78.

——, 'A Causal model of Civil Strife: A Comparative Analysis Using New Indices', *American Political Science Review*, LVII (December 1968), 1104-24.

Gusfield, J. R., *Protest, Reform, Revolt. A Reader in Social Movements* (Chichester, 1970).

Hamer, W. S., *The British Army. Civil-Military Relations 1885-1905* (Oxford, 1970).

Hobsbawm, E. J., *Primitive Rebels* (Manchester, 1959).

——, *Bandits* (London, 1969).

Hoffa, Eric, *The True Believer. Some Thoughts on the Nature of Mass Movements* (London, 1952).

Huntington, S. P., 'Political Development and Political Decay', *World Politics*, XVII (April 1965), 386-430.

——, *Political Order in Changing Societies* (New Haven, 1968).

Hutchinson, M. C., 'The Concept of Revolutionary Terrorism', *Journal of Conflict Resolution*, VI (3) (1972).

Jessop, Bob, *Social Order, Reform and Revolution* (London, 1972).

Johnson, Chalmers, 'Civilian Loyalties and Guerrilla Conflict', *World Politics*, XIV (July 1962), 646-61.

——, *Revolutionary Change* (Boston, 1966).

——, *Revolution and the Social System* (Stanford, Calif., 1964).

Kedourie, Elie, *Nationalism* (London, 1971).

Komer, R. N., 'The Impact of Pacification on Insurgency in South Vietnam', *International Affairs*, XXV (1) (1971).

Kornhauser, W., *The Politics of Mass Society* (New York, 1959).

Korovessis, Pericles, *The Method* (London, 1970).

Leiden, C. and Schmidt, K., *The Politics of Violence: Revolution in the Modern World* (Englewood Cliffs, N.J., 1968).

Leonard, R. A. (ed.), *A Short Guide to Clausewitz on War* (London, 1967).

Levytsky, Boris, *The Uses of Terror* (London, 1971).

Malinowski, W. R., 'The Pattern of Underground Resistance', *The Annals* CXXXII (March 1944).

Marighella, Carlos, *Minimanual of the Urban Guerrilla* (Harmondsworth, 1971).

Mather, R. C., *Public Order in the Age of the Chartists* (Manchester, 1959).

Moss, R., *Urban Guerrillas* (London, 1972).

Mrazek, James, *The Art of Winning Wars* (London, 1970).

Nasution, Abdul Harris, *Fundamentals of Guerrilla Warfare* (London, 1965).

Nieburg, H. L., 'Violence, Law and the Informed Polity', *Journal of Conflict Resolution*, XIII (1969), 192-209.

Osanka, M. Franklin (ed.), *Modern Guerrilla Warfare* (New York, 1962).

Payne, James, 'Peru: The Politics of Structured Violence', *Journal of Politics*, XXVII (May 1965), 362-74.

Pruitt, D. G., 'Stability and Sudden Change in Interpersonnel and International Affairs', *Journal of Conflict Resolution*, XIII (1969), 18-37.

Pye, L. W., *Guerrilla Communism in Malaya* (Princeton, 1956).

Qualter, T. H., *Propaganda and Psychological Warfare* (New York, 1965).

Rhyne, R., 'Patterns of Subversion by Violence', *The Annals*, CCCXLI (May 1962).

Riezler, K., 'The Social Psychology of Fear', *American Journal of Sociology*, XLIX (May 1944), 489-98.

Rokeach, Milton, *The Open and Closed Mind* (New York, 1960).

Rose, G., 'Anomie and Deviation. A Conceptual Framework for Empirical Studies', *British Journal of Sociology,* XVII (March 1966), 29-45.

Rude, George, *The Crowd in History* (Chichester, 1964).

Seton Watson, H., '20th Century Revolutions', *Political Quarterly,* XXII (July 1951).

Shanin, T. (ed.), *Peasants and Peasant Society* (Harmondsworth, 1971).

Sorel, George, *Reflections on Violence* (London, 1970).

Tanter, R., 'Dimensions of Conflict Behaviour Within and Between Nations', *Journal of Conflict Resolution,* X (1966), 41-64.

— — and Midlarsky, M., 'A Theory of Resolution', *Journal of Conflict Resolution* XI (1967), 264-79.

Thompson, R., *Defeating Communist Insurgency* (London, 1966).

— —, *Revolutionary War in World Strategy 1945-1969* (London, 1970).

Walter, E. V., 'Violence and the Process of Terror', *American Sociological Review,* XXIX (April 1964), 248-57.

— —, *Terror and Resistance* (Oxford, 1969).

Weiner, F. B., *Civilians under Military Justice. The British Practice since 1689* (Chicago, 1967).

Williams, P. M., *Wars, Plots and Scandals in Post War France* (Cambridge, 1970).

Wolf, E. R., *Peasant Wars of the 20th Century* (London, 1971).

Wolfenstein, E. V., *The Revolutionary Personality: Lenin, Trotsky, Saadhi* (Princeton, 1957).

Wolfgang, M. E., 'A Preface to Violence', *The Annals* (March 1966), 1-7.

— — and Ferracuti, F., *The Subculture of Violence* (London, 1967).

Zawodny, J. K., 'Guerrilla and Sabotage: Organisations Operations, Motivations, Escalation', *The Annals,* CCCXLI (May 1962).

INDEX

331